Plenty Gay Bilson Digressions on food

Plenty

Gay Bilson Digressions on food

LANTERN

an imprint of
PENGUIN BOOKS

for Edith and Alf Irwin, with love

Lantern

Published by the Penguin Group
Penguin Group (Australia)
250 Camberwell Road, Camberwell, Victoria 3124, Australia
(a division of Pearson Australia Group Pty Ltd)
Penguin Group (USA) Inc.
375 Hudson Street, New York, New York 10014, USA
Penguin Group (Canada)
10 Alcorn Avenue, Toronto, Ontario, Canada M4V 3B2
(a division of Pearson Penguin Canada Inc.)
Penguin Books Ltd
80 Strand, London WC2R 0RL, England
Penguin Ireland
25 St Stephen's Green, Dublin 2, Ireland
(a division of Penguin Books Ltd)
Penguin Books India Pty Ltd
11 Community Centre, Panchsheel Park, New Delhi – 110 017, India
Penguin Group (NZ)
Cnr Airborne and Rosedale Roads, Albany, Auckland, New Zealand
(a division of Pearson New Zealand Ltd)
Penguin Books (South Africa) (Pty) Ltd
24 Sturdee Avenue, Rosebank, Johannesburg 2196, South Africa

Penguin Books Ltd, Registered Offices: 80 Strand, London, WC2R 0RL, England

First published by Penguin Group (Australia), 2004

10 9 8 7 6 5 4 3 2 1

Cover and text design by Sandy Cull © Penguin Group (Australia)
Photography by Earl Carter
Typeset in Granjon by Post Pre-press Group, Brisbane, Queensland
Printed in China by Midas Printing (Asia) Ltd

National Library of Australia
Cataloguing-in-Publication data:

Bilson, Gay (Gay Morris), 1944– .
Plenty: digressions on food.

Includes index.
ISBN 1 920989 03 X.

1. Restaurateurs – Australia – Anecdotes. 2. Gastronomy.
3. Gourmets. I. Title.

647.95092

www.penguin.com.au

'At meal-times I will rise from my small exquisite portions,
still hungry, just, and mildly restless, forever.'

FROM PETER GOLDSWORTHY'S TEXT FOR GRAEME KOEHNE'S *Mass for the Middle Aged*

Contents

A prologue: Early Watermelon is not fruit

My mother used to say, don't you even think of touching the skin of pine-apples or bananas, Chinamen have touched them; wash your hands.

My grandmother ate fruit by cutting mouthfuls with a small knife. I thought then, and I think now, that this must have been the way that Grandma avoided all the bruises. How could she even think of eating bruised fruit? As a child I found bruised fruit repulsive. An apple, a pear (these were the fruits she nicked with the small knife, carrying the piece of flesh to her mouth on the blade) with even one bruise should be thrown on the compost or at least wrapped in the torn sheets of old newspapers that awaited the rubbish bin in those days before plastic bags. I was desperate to escape the frugality on one side of the house and the maternal discontent on the other.

Younger, I would eat porridge sitting on the floor of Grandma's kitchen. This kitchen was connected to ours by the shared bathroom. The porridge had raisins and linseeds in it; linseed is a laxative. Grandma sipped hot tea by tipping some from the cup into the saucer; nicks of fruit and sips of tea. I braided her hair and she told stories of the goldfields at Ballarat and of Chinamen with conical hats and a stick across their backs holding two baskets of fruit. Don't touch them, my mother, my grandmother's daughter, said.

My father wrote in elegant copperplate. His 's's and 'c's were lines of twirl-ing beauty. He sharpened pencils while we sat around the radio and listened to Gladys Moncrieff and Peter Dawson sing. He peeled pears for us with the same attention to detail and neatness that he gave to the pencils and to the copperplate script. He was the foreman in a factory that made gears. We played cricket in the back yard. I loved throwing and catching a ball, as round as a plum. He was gentle and loving and hardly said a word throughout all of my childhood. My mother was the hard talker, wanting attention.

I climbed onto the lowest branch of the fig tree in the back yard to escape the talk. The branch broke. I left home for two hours in preference to owning up. The fruit on the fig tree seemed always to be hard and green, uneaten except by birds. It seemed to never become flesh, probably by order from my mother who was frightened by the idea of it in children, especially her daughter. In the front garden among my grandmother's roses, love-in-the-mist, may and orange blossom, was a locquat tree whose fruit I ate: yellow skin, yellow flesh, slippery chocolate seeds like twins or sometimes triplets in a womb.

Auntie Irene next door, not really an aunt, a single woman with a lemon tree, offered lemons and chat while I rode a bicycle around and around the house in a furious, completely private challenge to not touch a bush or part of the paling fence. My mother took the lemons, but what did she do with them? Fish was never on the menu. Lemon Delicious was not in her repertoire. The only cake my mother made was one she called The Jewish Cake. The recipe came from *The Women's Weekly* (once a week I'd skip, with ninepence, up Clive Road to the corner of Riversdale where the trams lumbered towards the city) and had spices – cinnamon, ginger powder, cloves – in it. Now I know something about the Sephardic and Arabic influences in much of Spanish cooking, of which this teacake was not an authentic example. I'd crook one leg behind the other, raise one arm above and in front, stretch the other behind and tap to the hum and words of 'If I knew you were coming I'd have baked a cake' in lime-green tap shoes with lime-green bows.

Uncle Harry was the only exotic guest. He cooked, played the piano and the clarinet, wove silk and linen, read the hundreds of books in his library, drank too much alcohol; he tied me to the rotary clothesline and taunted me, played me *Peter and the Wolf*. He lived with a man. He scared me, but was my hero and confidante. I said to him, I'm going to cook and weave and read and live in a house like yours with piles of books and a piano and the smell of exotic curries.

My mother used a cream with almond essence in it to cleanse her face, read *The Women's Weekly* and made 'Early Watermelon'. Relations came for an annual gathering. It must have been at Christmas; this was the only time the house seemed hospitable. Songs around the pianola, and Pimms. To make Early Watermelon you must have a clear glass bowl that is wider at the top. Dissolve strawberry jelly crystals and whisk to turn them into a cloud of pink flummery. Fold through it some passionfruit seeds, and set in the glass bowl. Make a thick custard, from custard powder or real, and spoon a layer on top of the whipped pink jelly. Dissolve lime jelly crystals and cover the custard with a green layer. To appreciate Early Watermelon, observe the whole from the side of the bowl. A bowl with a stem is an advantage. Early Watermelon is not fruit.

I climbed the apricot tree very early in the morning on balmy summer days, no one else out of bed. The edge of the hot Melbourne days was still to come. The tree was so far down the back yard that I seemed to have left the house, the suburb, the city, the country, the world, the universe. Just me, a diary and a pen in the apricot tree. I ate too many apricots. Apricot was one of the pastel colours of the decade. My grandmother's house, in which we lived, was painted cherry-red and foam-green. There was a tall plum tree near the gully-trap, which I climbed too. The other plum tree produced purple ovals, each with a deep crease down the middle. Angelinas, Grandma called them, but when I say angelina now no one knows the plum I mean. The flesh inside was an opaque dull yellow, not juicy like the red plums of the tree I climbed – what South Australians call prune plums. I was the mistress of the climb. The plum tree was Everest, the rotary clothesline my Big Tent. I was the trapeze artist climbing elegantly to the highest point, crowds below with their hearts in their mouths. I timed the climbs, faster and faster to the best branch, gymnast above the laundry and the outdoor loo. I ate too many plums and read books up there. Up in the apricot and even further up in the plum were the vertical ways to flee the suburb.

There was an uncle who was not an uncle. Aunts and uncles who were not really aunts and uncles thrived in the fifties. This uncle sent boxes of oranges from Merbein. A friend came to the house and we ate so many oranges that my bottom especially was covered in hives and intolerably itchy. Calamine lotion soothed the itch. We had thrown the orange peel onto the garden. There was a lot of peel; we had eaten far too many oranges. I got the strap from my mother, who kept a riding whip in the broom cupboard. She also kept a part of her flirtatious heart for this uncle in its own cupboard. One day my cousin and I watched the uncle arrive to take my mother to lunch. He had the largest car I had ever seen. My family did not own a house, or a telephone or a car. My mother dressed up, she was all almond milk and lipstick. In secret, we dressed up too and presented ourselves at the front gate. We're coming, we cried! The uncle was amused and took us all to lunch in his big car, gave my cousin and me charm bracelets, buying our complicity with easy charm. I think we were in St Kilda, the St Kilda of the 1950s. This was the first restaurant I had ever been to. My mother barely coped; she was kept alive by fantasies of romance.

I thrived on dreams and fruit. The fruit on the trees planted by my grandmother were my only chance to taste plenty in the suburb. It never seemed to reach our table. Sometimes in the summer my mother would place on the table sugared segments of an oval cantaloupe I had been sent to buy. I adored its perfume, exaggerated by the sugar. My father was paid on a Friday; every Friday he brought home 'Friday Nights', chocolate bars from the corner store, sugar but not fruit. I loved him, would skip to meet him, especially on a Friday. My father never missed a day's work. He was never, ever, angry with me. I wanted to eat half the cantaloupe, even all the cantaloupe, but our portion was only two slices each.

My father's family lived in Eldorado, not far from Wangaratta in northern Victoria. Every year, school out for the Christmas holidays, we went to Wangaratta by train, dressed in our best. I was not allowed to lean out of the window because the soot from the steam engine would dirty the frills on the pale, foam-green, spotted voile dress with matching petticoat. As if she were a woman from Toorak, my mother had spent money on a dressmaker. Now I know why there was no money for more cantaloupes. My father was one of thirteen children who grew up in Eldorado in the twenties. Once Eldorado had had nineteen pubs, but they were long gone. My uncles grew hazelnuts and almonds, shooting the possums who took the nuts and sending in the tails to collect the bounty; two shillings a tail, I think it was. All that seemed to be left in Eldorado were Cheesmans, and this little Miss Cheesman would arrive every Christmas, best dress all sooty. We'd be met by Uncle Tom, who had married Aunty Marj – one of the thirteen, and my favourite. They'd be there on the station near the Bruck Textile Mills with my cousins and we'd be driven to the house with its verandah all the way around. Fifty years later I live in a house with a verandah all the way around.

And my Uncle Ray and our grandpa, with his pipe always upside-down between his teeth, would pick peaches from the orchard near the house. They'd take them to Aunty Marj and she'd peel and sugar them and put them in the ice chest until tea time. Sometimes she would add slices of banana too. That's my Christmas madeleine: sugared white peaches and the sugared smell of them. Yellow peaches don't have that kind of perfume: they might peel more easily and blush on a plate, but they don't have the scent to trigger memory. I see that orchard now, and the kitchen of the Eldorado house, the back gate with its country chain and loop, the cow that might wander off if the city kid didn't close the gate properly, and me swinging on the gate with my cousins.

We swam in the stagnant pond in the dry, eroded country behind the house until our parents ordered us never to use it again because it was the septic fill for the town. We played on the wooden swing-bridge too, while it swayed dangerously, the planks rotting and loose. Hardy and sunburnt, we'd walk home in the afternoon to be told, I remember once, that Uncle Ray had shot a snake in the dairy at the back of the house. Then, all over again, parents in the lounge-room, children on the verandah plotting growing up, we'd smell the sugared white peaches.

God, I imagined, was a man dressed in my father's dressing-gown, and my aunt was at his side handing out fruit and extra sugar. This Eldorado aunt was the maternal goddess of peaches, the Athena of Eldorado, plump and loving. I wanted to fold myself in her lap and apron for ever. Rationing was the only way my mother knew how to make ends meet. It's scary how you can ration love.

Back in the city, in the suburb, the trees kept bearing the fruit that never reached the table. I would climb up into the apricot tree again with a book, whiling away the time until the sixties arrived with the first raspberry.

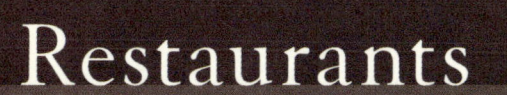

Restaurants

The pieces that follow centre on the three Sydney restaurants in which I was involved from 1973 to the late nineties: Tony's Bon Goût, Berowra Waters Inn, and Bennelong. When I was asked, on putting Berowra Waters Inn up for sale in 1994, how I felt about leaving, and responded with 'It's only a restaurant, for god's sake', the phrase was splashed into ironic headline. It wasn't just a restaurant for me, yet I meant what I said without irony.

This section offers a personal glimpse of one small group of players from those crucial seventies when a different set of culinary principles was adopted by a handful of chefs and restaurateurs. The inchoate notion of an Australian cuisine began to take shape, not from the soil up but from the commercial kitchen down, heralding a new era of public dining. I am not a subscriber to the idea that a new cuisine, in the old sense, is what develops in modern times. Nevertheless, the development of different and airier expectations in restaurant dining-rooms, what Stephen Downes has called 'a miracle', did foster a more discriminating collective palate and issue a call to growers for better produce. In Sydney, for instance, Serge Dansereau nurtured particular suppliers and shared them generously, and David Thompson shopped with confidence for Thai ingredients in Chinatown. In Melbourne, Stephanie Alexander encouraged children to collect snails; in Adelaide, Cheong Liew used Chinese techniques on little known deep-sea fish. It all seemed slightly un-Australian!

Twenty-five years down the track, with a far greater and surely more geographically logical interest in Southeast Asia and China, and with gratitude to the cuisines of our immigrants and neighbours, we might even call the transformation of our palates a version of regionalism.

'Café society in the Antipodes' (Tony's Bon Goût)

Restaurants are usually remembered in writing, if at all, by a collection of recipes between the covers of a book that dates fast and ossifies into a curious glimpse of a past aesthetic. But remembering a restaurant only by its dishes is to leave out everything that was vital and social in this, the second most theatrical of professions.

It has always seemed fitting to me that newspapers and the flightiest magazines are repositories of the little histories of restaurants. What we read today and this month is replaced the next by the shape of different news. Restaurants come and restaurants go. The paper is pulped, restaurateurs and cooks move on. The conversations and litres of wine have become, irretrievably, the compost of living. The review or article makes comment only on the digestions of food and suggestions of service, the comfort of the critic's derrière, and the cost to his, or rather, the newspaper's, purse.

In 1973 I opened, with my then-partner, Tony Bilson, a restaurant that he named, in a serious lapse of taste and respect for language, Tony's Bon Goût. I was straight out of a marriage that had taken me to New York State and one and a half years of passionate domestic cookery, which took the place of employment and taught me very little about food. Tony had been cooking professionally in a different town for some years and was, even then, extraordinarily confident in his cooking. His bible was Auguste Escoffier's *Guide to Modern Cookery* and it probably still is. He had never been out of Australia, let alone to France. We employed a charming and memorable Frenchman, Alain Chagny, who ran the dining-room while we cooked; we became a working *ménage à trois*.

In the years before this, Ken and Lillian Horler, with John Bell and Anna Volska, with Larry Eastwood and the sheer willpower and enthusiasm of a group of actors, opened a theatre called the Nimrod in Kings Cross. By May 1974 the Nimrod had moved to Belvoir Street in Surry Hills, to a building that had once been the Cerebos salt factory and headquarters. John Bell has said of the original Nimrod that 'people were hungry for something primarily Australian and new'. Ken Horler says they put on plays and reviews that were different, subversive, and included new Australian writing. Playwright Ron Blair remembers the adrenalin; Larry, the lighting station that was directly over the lavatory; Ken and Lillian, their baby Sasha in a basket stashed under the stairs. The ticket price was $2.50 and they all got by on tuppence. Even when they moved to Surry Hills, there was an excitement that only skidding by on tuppence generates – it keeps one honest, I reckon, though it's not to be celebrated if it gets in the way of a good production and fine performance. Ken Horler, the original force behind the theatre, a barrister by one profession, director of plays by another, persuaded the licensing court that people wanted not only to go to the theatre on Sundays but to drink a glass of wine as well. Some time after we opened the restaurant, the actor Chris Hayward, a member of the Nimrod crowd, who spent much of his spare time at the Bon Goût, gave me a very large and heavy 'paddle' (it was the size of a hefty long-handled shovel) from the Belvoir Street site, which was said to have stirred wholesale quantities of salt. I kept this paddle right up until I came to South Australia in 1999; I used to say it was part of my wooden-spoon collection, which it was.

What I see, in hindsight, about the Bon Goût was that it shared the excitement that lit up different 'institutions' at the end of the sixties and beginning of the seventies: politics, theatre, and – lagging a little behind, because cuisines are by their very nature conservative – restaurants. At its best and most confident, that sense of excitement was a symptom of a new order; we weren't so much bravely going against the grain as producing something everyone wanted.

The Bon Goût was a couple of rooms on the ground floor of the squalid Mansion House Private Hotel on Elizabeth Street, near Central Station, the unsavoury end of town. I still remember the address, 174 Elizabeth Street, and I can still 'see' the street as it was then. Up the road, across Goulburn and Liverpool Streets, was the

New Hellas, a Greek restaurant where we often lunched and where I learned to love braised sheep's head and rice pudding, and where the other regulars were political journalists and staffers, academics, writers, actors and artists, many of whom became our friends. Rag-traders leased some floors of Mansion House and the rest comprised the 'private hotel', which was exactly as you might imagine – rooms rented by itinerants, regulars and poor families who'd scraped together enough money to visit the Big Smoke but not enough for more than the very cheapest hotel. The rear kitchen door opened into a squalid loading dock where, even in 1973, though not for much longer, the pig man came to collect the pig-edible garbage. (The building was transformed from dank private hotel to spruced-up public hotel in the eighties, but never really looked at ease in its new underwear and jacket.)

The first lunch menu was a fixed price of $1.95 but soon rose to $2.50. I still have the oldest menus: a three-course lunch might be watercress soup, braised oxtail, and pears poached in red wine. My first serious kitchen lesson had been learned from an explosion of boiling watercress soup from a blender on which I had clamped the lid with no space for steam to escape. We had not yet opened the restaurant – the soup was for a private meal – and I was still sewing cheap cotton covers for the banquette cushions as well as teaching myself to cook. The chef-to-be was in the pub up the road with the friend who had suggested we might turn this dump into a restaurant. The only other person around was a man painting the kitchen ceiling. He went to the pub with news of the blotched face and all three returned in time. Now I throw away the part of any blender lid that completely seals the jug.

The restaurant began to fill with articulate, intelligent, hard-living people who took lunch seriously, especially on a Friday when, as writer and Whitlam staffer Richard Hall remembered, it could easily turn into dinner too. These were the heady, early days of Gough Whitlam's years in government. In *One Continuous Picnic: a History of Food in Australia,* Michael Symons called us 'chefs to the court of Whitlam', but George Negus (who reckons he introduced the place to the Labor crowd and he probably did) has said that it wasn't only Labor staff and supporters who filled the tables: 'The Liberals were going through an intellectual transition, too. People got drunk, discussed issues and yelled opinions.

It was almost Parisian, insofar as anything in Australia can truly be called Parisian.' We'd never been to Paris and I suspect George Negus's sophisticated statement was more notional than experiential. The closest we came to café society in those days was the pub; you could talk and drink with libertarian bonhomie, but not talk and drink wine and eat well with the same sense of camaraderie. Our licensing laws never allowed the equivalent of La Coupole or Les Deux Magots. What might mistakenly be thought of as café society today is, in general, a youthful cluster of urban apartment-dwellers spilling onto the street, drinking coffee and signifying nothing much at all, certainly not hatching revolution.

While some may have felt that the shopfront on Elizabeth Street fulfilled a certain parochial idea of Parisian life, Germaine Greer, back in Oz for a moment and proudly brought by film producer Margaret Fink to some of journalist Lenore Nicklin's infamous Friday lunches, scoffed at the notion. Elizabeth Wynhausen quoted Greer in an article on the restaurant in *The National Times* in January 1976:

> Café society! The only thing extraordinary about Tony's is that you can sit there getting drunk on booze you run up the street to get. [It's] too small, too hot, the cooking's good so you spend too much time eating. You can't compare it with the great cafés of the world.

Novelist Frank Moorhouse related close-to-factual scenes at the Bon Goût in one of the stories (first published in *Nation Review* in April 1976) that made up his collection *Conference-ville*. The first part of the table talk is about the book. Frank is reading the twelfth volume and conclusion to Anthony Powell's Dance to the Music of Time, *Hearing Secret Harmonies*, which happened to be the novel I was reading in the small hours after service. One of the women at Moorhouse's table looks around the dining-room and sums it up: 'Café society in the antipodes.' Dick comes in and she repeats this to him: ' "Richard . . . I was just saying," she gestured about, "café society – just like the old Vadim's – except that no one has new ideas any more . . ." ' Dick tells her that the precise meaning of café society is high society: 'whatever that is. God help us. But maybe it's proper for us to get things ironically twisted.' (Vadim's restaurant was a memory by the time we opened. In Challis Avenue in the Cross, it had been the place for 'serious eaters, drinkers and talkers', with a space upstairs filled with 'artists and unruly patrons'. Vadim was a white Russian with, according to Bob Raymond in his introduction to a book of tributes to Rudy Komon, 'a streak of Chekhovian gloom'.)

There's a jug of water in Frank's story and it's emptied over the head of a man at another table. Alain Chagny had been asked to provide the jug and it was Alain who returned to Moorhouse's table: 'You are finished with the jug, Monsieur Friedman, yes?' The Jug of Water Incident confirms both Greer's dismissal of the restaurant and Dick Hall's suggestion of the ironic antipodean twist. This was Sydney, not Paris. We were Labor supporters who just happened to cook food that owed everything to French culinary tradition (though it was more personal, more individual, than 'French cooking'). We had opened the restaurant without a prescription except for Tony's obsession with those French traditions; with hardly enough money to pay for the butter, and with, for myself learning on the site, a giddy naivety. We found an audience, or the audience found us, and the audience settled in. A symbiosis of promise and expectation is at the centre of change. A conversation began and bloomed, and idealism, which has no common place in Australian culture, seemed to hold sway for a while. The unspoken pact between the restaurant and the diner, the little shared glories of place and palate, the genuine and easy conviviality between kitchen, waiting and dining-room personalities in that otherwise depressing, cheap room felt splendid. It was splendid. It was only later, towards the end of the seventies, that the media began to play its irritating part in driving restaurateurs to meet standards that the media itself seemed to prescribe even when supposedly only playing commentator.

Tony Bilson once said to a journalist that I was more serious about cooking than he was. This was long after we had gone our separate ways and was a comment more on temperament than on practice. Tony's casual ease with food belied his unshakeable knowledge that cooking was what he wanted to be doing. In most ways I didn't choose to cook; oh, I was interested in food and cooking, but I took that sweaty place between the stove and the service bench at Tony's Bon Goût because there was no one else and because I vainly fancied myself as a domestic cook. I'd gone to bed with a cook and ended up with a restaurant and a baby. It was our restaurant, despite the silly name, and that joint responsibility, in my head at least, would only be valid if I cooked too. I've never understood people who want to own a restaurant but have no involvement in the kitchen. Tony did the main courses and prepared entrées, which were beyond my knowledge and skills, while I pushed the entrées out during service, made the desserts and served them, cooked very simple vegetables for the main courses, washed a lot of dishes, and had the baby. This sounds an unequal share of the work and it was. Conversely, the main course is just that and it takes a chef to cook it.

The answer, I see now, would have been to employ a third cook, but even though cooks didn't cost much in those days we could hardly have afforded one. Besides, it was all so personal an extra cook might have taken the edge off the grubby charm of the place. We did at least, when things got busier, employ a young recently immigrated French woman, married and even more recently a homeowner in a suburb I had never heard of – its name, St Marys, sounded like paradise when said with a French accent (*Saint Marie:* roll it around your tongue) but it turned out to be somewhere far to the west of Sydney. I remember how, after each day of *mise-en-place* – the preparation of food for service – and washing dishes, she always rubbed a cut lemon over her hands before making the long train journey home. I remember, as well, a young married pair who cleaned and washed dishes for some months and who one night took a carton of milk home without asking. Alain, who was a counter, must have noticed that it was missing. It sounds absurd (after all, it was only a carton of milk) but I felt betrayed; there was an apology. I also remember with affection the young women who waited on a casual basis and always seemed to be studying law.

—

The micro-environment into which the Bon Goût dropped its seed might be illustrated by looking at one of the food magazines of the period. For sixty-three cents in 1973 you could purchase an issue of *Epicurean*, the official magazine of the Wine and Food Society of Australia, whose enduring art director was Les Mason. One

1973 cover has a surrealist *pièce montée* which includes four porcelain-like hands breaking through the paper walls of a room; the 'floor' is a completed jigsaw of T-bone steaks on which sit a pear and an improbably upright egg. The whole seems to be encased, like one of American artist Joseph Cornell's boxes. A 1967 issue included a black-and-white photograph of a hanging light globe filled with wine; a black-and-white cover in the same year featured a model, head and bare shoulders only, whose neckpiece of pasta supported a can-opener pendant and whose hat was a hand of bananas. A 1971 cover included a brilliant assemblage of milk bottle, red-wine bottle, meat pie, tomato, egg and can of Heinz baked beans, each connected to a power point (the six switches are on).

Inside *Epicurean* the advertisements were, with one or two exceptions (a gourmet tour of South Africa in 1973, Bertoli olive oil in 1975, for instance), all for wine and liqueurs. The articles in No. 43 – and it is representative of many years – are distributed fairly equitably between wine and food, and are often witty and learned (loyal contributors included Oscar Mendelsohn, Keith Dunstan, Ronald Miller, Len Evans). All but one of the pieces about food, including recipes, are by women. All the food is, also with hardly an exception, French. All the wine journalism is by men. A consistent and confident writer was the novelist Marion Halligan: in this issue she wrote about French meals, referring on the one hand to the 'French housewife' and on the other to herself as a 'Francophile housewife' with no irony at all. In another issue, she explored *la choucroûte garnie*. Her articles show that she practised what she preached, that the kitchen bench was her writing desk and her continuing preference was French food. She was devoted to Elizabeth David's cookbooks.

The cumulative credentials of the people writing for *Epicurean* from, say, 1967 to 1977 were remarkable. In many cases these had nothing to do with the professional world of food and wine, which was refreshing and expanded the horizon considerably. Cyril Pearl, Max Lake and Walter James cropped up; and even Mary Burchett, Stephanie Alexander's mother, writing about the little black book of recipes she inherited and would later leave to her daughter. It was, without doubt, and despite the presence of capable women who wrote about food, a man's world, and it addressed men of a certain age and means for whom a cellar full of

'Café society in the Antipodes' (Tony's Bon Goût)

wine dictated the menu and not the other way about. What didn't crop up much were restaurants and what didn't crop up at all was the celebration of produce – a drop of wine was worth more than a bucketful of fresh local mussels. *Epicurean* reported on dining as an amateur's delight; the food journalist as newshound and commodity-maker seemed not yet to have been invented.

The interesting thing about the magazine over this period is that while the art-design policy (the artist, the designer and the policy-maker in fact seemed to be a one-man band) supported a creative, witty and sometimes irreverent approach, the articles reverently celebrated *la cuisine ancienne* and the status quo of looking up to the French. By 1979, however, the cover was wine-red, a fork was stuck into a cork, Les Mason had disappeared from the credits, and his quirky and often brilliant games to a theme had ceded to a new era in which food and wine would be good editorial business: those who read food and wine magazines could be sold an idea that promoted careers and sold brands.

I've dwelt on *Epicurean* because it presents us with the stage on which the new players of the early seventies arrived and began to strut. The new stage, the new sets and the new direction included profoundly different relationships, especially the sense of complicity alluded to earlier. The chef, once part of the kitchen's professional machinery, began a dialogue with his diners. The old formality took a battering and a different generation treated the restaurant kitchen as a platform for a different form of expression. In France, nouvelle cuisine became a manifesto in Henri Gault's hands. In Australian cities, particularly Melbourne and Sydney, the ideas of the new French cooking acted as a catalyst and gave us the freedom to see that we were cooking Australian food, not French food, because it was our fresh produce and we were doing it here – we were not developing a cuisine but rather were making our own dishes even when the recipe might have come to us via a French cookbook.

The surreal photographs of assemblages that made *Epicurean* unique in its time also spoke to a different and less complex attitude to food than the one we live with now. There was less and less room for fun and games as food, its presentation and the accoutrements of the table became one of the central indicators of status. Although the magazine is dated and its photographs of food dull

by the standards of food photography now (all dewdrop and drizzle and a light as exclamatory as the Annunciation) I still feel something akin to relief when looking through those old issues, even though the Bon Goût played its part in changing public expectations of food magazines. Wine and food societies like the one that published *Epicurean* still exist, I'm told, but they are conservative comfort zones. A member of a Beefsteak and Burgundy Club in Queensland gave a paper at a recent Symposium of Australian Gastronomy. He was howled down with good humour by young and older women (also men) in the audience. The hero of these men's clubs was André Simon, the great French arbiter of taste in food and wine; but André Simon is long dead.

—

The early seventies was also a time when the exhilaration of a fresh, different and confident informality was allowed to get into its stride without too much attention being paid to the accoutrements of the dining-room. At its best, the Bon Goût produced marvellous food on the cheapest plates one could buy. The cutlery was nasty, the glasses even cheaper than the plates. The chairs, if I remember correctly, were those that came with the place: vinyl and aluminium of no design ('chairs that fall into the category headed Regular rather than chic or comfortable or stylish', Leo Schofield wrote). There wasn't any money to choose and buy anything better, but then no one tried jostling us to make improvements anyway. This is the very opposite of restaurant dining-rooms now, where appearance is everything.

So *Epicurean* spoke, and Les Mason designed, to a different time, and this was when the Bon Goût opened. Tony must have been aware of some of this world, the man's world anyway, because he had worked for Johnny Walker at the eponymous bistro in Sydney in the sixties. I had been reading novels, raising kids and flipping crêpes for late-night poker games at the turn of the sixties into the seventies. With thousands of others in that iconic rally against the Vietnam war, organised by Jim Cairns in Melbourne in 1970, I'd marched with a baby on my back and holding a young child by one hand. Their father and I left for the States not long after: I was to be a 'housewife', like Marion Halligan, and still with the child on my back, the other in hand. Returning to Australia a mere one and a half years later, it seemed a different country.

Something had changed and it had done so in accordance with the premise of evolutionary systems. One act in isolation would have been like a eucalypt falling in remote bush, but there was the coincidence of a shift in government, which in turn seems to me to have been dependent on a particular generation coming of age, increasing travel by the middle class outside Australia (although still looking to Europe), a kind of thirst for places to feel comfortable in while eating as well as drinking, and a new interest in the quality of food (even when most of us needed still to find out what quality was exactly), the gradual death of old boys' clubs, the rise of feminism. There was the energy of theatres like the Nimrod, and in Melbourne, the Pram Factory, and right there in the middle of this, the convivial vitality of the Bon Goût on the wrong side of town, with its depressing little kitchen and its domestic sink, and the old Kookaburra range that served well until the beef stock simmered down to a burned crust one night and caused a fire to blow out the shop-front window. The sprinkler system drenched the kitchen and dining-room, an enforced holiday was taken with gratitude to adversity, and we had to buy a more professional range.

The old fridge; the hand-cranked icecream churn tucked in a corner (the ice bought from the local pub); the laundry bags visible in the connecting space between the kitchen and the dining-room; the menus written in Alain Chagny's sloping Gallic hand on torn-off pieces of sketch paper, dated and changed when things ran out, a messy mixture of sometimes misspelt French and English (16.8.75: 'Fresh Artichaut', 'Duck Livers with Grappes', 'Eel Escoveitch' [sic, Alain]) – how I blush when I read them now but I still feel pride in Tony doing an *escabèche*, a method of sousing fish to which I have returned in recent years, using local Tommy Ruffs; the incongruence of the fine art on the walls (sometimes Fred Williams, Peter Powditch, Brett Whitely, Frank Hodgkinson, borrowed or begged from Rudy Komon) and the increasing incongruity of the affluence in the dining-room, for word had got around and bourgeois society increasingly came to dine. Ah, the bravura bohemian performance of the whole thing, which edged, despite itself, towards middle-class acceptance later in 1973 after Leo Schofield,

'Café society in the Antipodes' (Tony's Bon Goût)

who at that time reviewed restaurants for the *Daily Telegraph*, came one night to see what all the fuss was about.

The one trait the Bon Goût shared with *Epicurean* was the culture of cuisine, even though we practised an apparently irreverent version compared to Wine and Food Society fare. I suppose Tony was doing the kind of food Marion Halligan was promoting in *Epicurean*, but doing it with professional flare, with a fine grasp of classical techniques. He read Escoffier and Pellaprat (two of the three cookbooks he owned; the other was something to do with Viennese cookery) and it was Pelleprat's desserts I turned to for instruction. I was struggling through a difficult friendship with puff pastry, a friendship that has survived and strengthened; enjoying a short love affair with soufflés that left us out of sorts for ever, except for a fine chocolate variation that is more pudding than soufflé and so more body than air; and teaching myself, by elimination, to lessen the bounce in the bavarois.

In returning to this time, and recalling images of the restaurant – the look and feel of it all, the people who worked with us and the people who came to dine – I am surprised by the intensity of the memory and trust this recollection, even though we remember only in the context of the present. Distance lends a complex, selective objectivity: the spaces materialise in three-dimensional colour, and if I took imaginary steps towards a crumbling corner of the kitchen it would have texture. It must be like the kind of video game I have never played, an eerie sense of the physical that can't be touched, including the rat which ran the length of the dining-room using the old picture rail for footing, and the cockroaches which adored the old building. The real surprise, though, is the food suggested when I sort through the menus, which I have stored for all these years in obsessive chronological order. They speak of many more dishes than memory gave the kitchen credit for. How good they were in total is only to be guessed at, but some must have been very good indeed and this speaks of Tony's effortless talent, a talent which I used sometimes to dismiss because it surrounded itself with so much work left for someone else to do. He wasn't one for orderly *mise-en-place* nor for cleaning the bench, both of which are the sacramental duties of the profession.

Not that *mise-en-place* played much of a part in the kind of cooking practised in this kitchen. There was hardly a main course that needed more than *à la minute* cooking; no fish was boned (better for the fish, less work for the cook, more for the diner); sauces were always finished in the pan – the sweetbreads or shellfish, for instance, were sautéed and then it was all splash, sizzle and swirl, and therefore often inconsistent. Reading at random through menus from 1975, as well as the dishes mentioned earlier I find first courses such as 'Stuffed Duck's Neck in Brioche with Truffles', 'Pig's Trotters in Vinaigrette Sauce', 'Galantine of Duck' and 'Hare Terrine'; simple dishes, both hot and cold, using yabbies, prawns, pipis, mussels and Balmain bugs (invariably including the last-minute addition of wine, butter, garlic and parsley to make a sauce); a variety of savoury tarts with ingredients such as fresh tomato and sweated leeks, or onions; soups such as walnut, watercress, and a *soupe au pistou* (a fine dice of vegetables in a lamb stock into which a basil sauce is added).

Main courses offered far greater variety than entrées over the years. Again at random, from 1976 menus, one finds 'Steamed Whole Whiting with Flathead Mousse and Champagne Butter', 'Maigret de Canard (Breast of Duck) with Green Peppercorns and Peach', 'Mud Crab with White Wine and Garlic Butter' (for 2 or, courtesy Alain, 'for 2 *personnes*'), 'Sauté de Poulet au Vinaigre', 'Roasted Filet of Beef with Sauce Bordelaise (bone marrow, red wine and demi-glace)', 'Gâteau de Foie Blanc with Coulis d'Ecrevisse (Duck Livers with Yabby Sauce)' – clearly we had been to France for the first time and equally clearly we had become familiar with Michel Guérard's *cuisine gourmande*. In the same year, desserts included sorbets, crepes baked with a soufflé filling, Bavarian creams, fruit tarts, poached pears and prunes, 'Crème au Calvados' and an alternative, 'French Brie cheese'. (This last is possibly one of the only triple tautologies in menu-writing history.) Alain having advised in writing that the brie was 'just ready to experience', a customer, bless her, boldly crossed out 'experience' and substituted 'enjoy'. By this time, and the restaurant soon to be closed before our move to Berowra Waters, the fixed price was $12.50 for three courses and coffee.

Richard Beckett, writing for *Nation Review* in 1974 under his non-de-plume 'Sam Orr', made much of the seedy end of town, the pub on the corner at which he bought wine for the table and to which his party returned for port after dinner;

he fell for the terrine, the celery soup, the duck with apples, the sweetbreads with truffles, the vanilla soufflé and the charlotte soaked in kirsch. 'French with the usual Australian modifications' is how he described the menu. Sam Orr was a comedy act, a cynic and a drunk, but Beckett was serious about food. Len Evans, writing in the same year, noted that the cost to his table of four was $42 and he deemed it reasonable: 'Highly recommended for those people who love fine food and do not want decor and "atmosphere" instead.' In 1975 Leo Schofield, who the year before had put together the first *Good Food Guide* in Australia, told the magazine *Pol* that the Bon Goût was the best restaurant because 'the price is right, there's lots of variety, and the preparation of the food is done with love'. Reading these articles in 2004, while not completely seduced by the praise, I am astonished by the apparent quality of the food, also by the kind assessment of the dining-room. I had, in memory, relegated the Bon Goût's food to an outmoded cuisine (the mousseline in the fish, the green peppercorns, and especially the sorbet before the main course) prepared in a sometimes slapdash and often amateurish manner.

One of the Friday lunch crowd mentioned in Moorhouse's *Conference-ville* instalment was Don Anderson, who taught English and American literature at Sydney University. When Don completed his Ph.D., he asked for a celebratory dinner at the restaurant. I do remember parts of this meal: a very fine duck sausage accompanied by far too many puréed vegetables. The food processor had come to Australia and we puréed excessively while the blade was sharp with novelty. Anderson presented us with a copy of Brillat-Savarin's *La Physiologie du goût*; many years later this book, first published in 1825, would play its part in my gastronomic education. (Anderson later compiled an erudite and witty collection of excerpts from literature in which meals are central, entitled *Banquet of the Mind*.)

For its time in Australia, a plate of stuffed duck's neck baked in brioche set down on a cheap tablecloth in a nondescript dining -room must have seemed like a tour de force. It would have helped that the usual tricksy garnishes were absent as well, although it didn't occur to us to banish Alain's parsley sprigs. We had taken the kind of food cooked at much more formal and expensive restaurants, to which our lively crowd wouldn't have thought of going, and served it where they felt comfortable – a fact central to the changes that soon took place. In 1976, the year we closed the Bon Goût, Stephanie Alexander opened a small and casual restaurant in Melbourne. I remember her talking about the excitement of serving radishes with a pat of butter and sea salt. This would overturn the expectations of formal dining in Australia – the garden, undisguised, was coming to the table.

—

I've a theory about that restaurant at the wrong end of town, a theory that presents itself in retrospect because in its time the Bon Goût seemed to be, for the press anyway, exciting and successful simply for its food. We took for granted our friends and extras – the last of the Sydney Push, and a fabulous mix of strong, glamorous, sometimes damaged, vocal souls who dined well and long, and whose meeting place was for a time the Bon Goût.

The restaurant wasn't born on cue like Truman Burbank, but it did dance its part to the music of that time. Its culinary success was the sum of specific parts: food that was different from most restaurant fare (Patric and Chrissy Juillet's food and ambience an exception); a kind of breezy, easy French cooking with none of the pretension of haute cuisine yet depending more and more, as we realised we had diners who admired the food and wanted us to be good cooks, on classic stocks and sauces; a kind of doggedness on my part in keeping the cogs oiled, the pastry made, doing service more or less successfully when I'd never cooked professionally before – getting the orders through on time, paying the staff, the bills – a kind of proud, relentless and sometimes deeply resented diligence that gave Tony a viable space to keep on cooking; Tony's great talent for apparently beginning from scratch every time he cooked and without reference to recipes, and transforming, at the last minute, the elements into good, sometimes very fine, food; Alain Chagny's marvellously plump, high-camp delight in his dining-room, his exaggeratedly blue, red and white presence and his warm, yet servile, professional relationship with the growing number of regulars; the price of dining – it was a bargain in terms of the quality of the food and service, but about right if you took the location, accoutrements and lavatories into account.

Take into account also the lack of a liquor licence, the toilet being next to our flat on the first floor (collect the key from Alain, Mauricette, Sue, Marina, Roland, Régis). No wine list, combined with good food, made of Rudy Komon – a man with an extraordinary wine cellar, patriarch of and patron to the Sydney art world, and a bon vivant – a regular diner. Rudy was a Czech and had extraordinarily soft skin, like silk. I liked to greet him with a kiss just to touch that skin. I remember being told that he imported a particular product from Europe to pamper his skin, a surprising vanity. We, in turn, regularly visited him above his art gallery in Paddington and it was in this room that I learned about painters I had never heard of: Jon Molvig, David Aspden, Peter Powditch, George Baldessin, for instance – and to look at canvases with a better eye. I loved the small rug on his table and he sold it to me, a Middle European trader to the end. We borrowed paintings from the warehouse. These included a Fred Williams, a great painting that still haunts me. It went back to Rudy when we left Elizabeth Street, a small canvas, a dark hill, painted differently to, and long before, the works that began to make a particular Australian landscape Fred's.

Rudy brought great wines, marvellous artists and some powerful, famous and creative people to the restaurant. Alain adored him. I remember the pianist Alfred Brendl, the conductor Sir Bernard Heinz, the then-head of the ABC Sir Charles Moses. Alain, inimitably, looked after them and Tony, inevitably, chatted to them at the close of their meal and would be given a glass of something extraordinary by Rudy. I'd finish plating desserts and baking soufflés in the Kookaburra, with Jordan in a papoose on my back, then clean up and sit on the laundry bags. In retrospect I see this connecting space as the one I never left, mentally or emotionally, in twenty-five years of running restaurants and cooking. It is the space still connected to the work and the working staff but edging towards the audience, towards a need for recognition. I didn't always sit there in contentment in those days, but there was that marvellously satisfying sense of fatigue and completion that all professional cooks, brilliant, middling or bad, understand and which seems sometimes to be what one works for.

What I learned on my naive feet was that the reward given to people who cook well and who do so with spirit and generosity and, in the best way, intelligence, is an enormous affection and gratitude. The cook in turn feels the same towards her diners, for she cannot cook without someone to cook for. Michael Symons, in *The Pudding That Took a Thousand Cooks,* posits the (to some people, outrageous) theory that 'cooks made us'; Brillat-Savarin, nearly two centuries earlier, suggested something in the same vein. Symons' historical evidence and argument, combined with a personal sense of what the relationship between cook and table is, convince me that he is making a profound point. In bringing people to the table to dine, the cook turned produce into dishes, promoted conviviality and conversation, and so promoted the development of language and culture.

The charm of the Bon Goût was the pairing of good food and gregarious lives. People who searched for good restaurant food and became regulars did so as a private celebration of gourmandism and conviviality. Of course, media judgement and its persuasion existed: the night after Leo Schofield's first review, Alain managed to fit ninety into a dining-room more used to forty. Vladimir Ashkenazy gave a concert at the Sydney Town Hall that night and I had gone alone, my first night off, returning to a dining-room and kitchen out of control. It was better not to have been there.

None of the above is to romanticise the early seventies, nor is it to make too much of a restaurant. It is to write about how it felt from the inside, but also to observe it from the distance of some thirty years. A rather gaudy butterfly was being made out of the compote of new interests, new money and increased travel, and by the early eighties 'good living' (it was in 1982 that the section under that title first appeared in the *Sydney Morning Herald*) had become an aspiration on parade. The Bon Goût nourished a portion of that generation which saw the beginning of social change in Australian cities. Perhaps it *was* a kind of 'café society' in the convivial and intellectual European sense: the people who ate and talked there were as essential to its reputation as the food. In this regard it was a far more significant restaurant than Berowra Waters Inn, which might be seen to have been far more successful and was certainly far more fêted. That's my theory, anyway.

'Café society in the Antipodes' (Tony's Bon Goût)

Fonds de cuisine (Berowra Waters Inn)

From the dark end of Elizabeth Street to an estuary of the Hawkesbury River an hour's drive north of Sydney, with no land access to its few houses and one restaurant, was not a journey based on weighty decision-making and the balancing of books. It was a romantic, instinctual rush to an opposite; a flight from cheap, cheerful and successful to a utopian landscape of water and cliff, a building that appeared at first flush to be all one would want, and a boat with a sloppy canopy that seemed to work. This was January 1977. The Bon Goût sold for enough to pay a deposit for the building on the river and the banks (not the riparian ones) had the kind of faith common at that time. Interest rates were to soar as we borrowed.

The enjoyment of talking about cooking is best shared if there is a shorthand of references, a shared language, a set of tacit understandings. Simon Hopkinson knew I didn't like honey; I knew he thought tuna irrelevant in a salade niçoise. I loved to talk about food with him above all other cooks. He once said, when he was about to open Bibendum restaurant in London with Terence Conran and Paul Hamlyn in 1987, that he stood by the belief that a truly great restaurant should be open for lunch and dinner seven days a week, all year. I knew what he was referring to: a professionalism in the kitchen that existed because of, but beyond the presence of, a key figure, and the customers' comfortable knowledge that they might always eat there.

Berowra Waters Inn was closed for four days of the week. We opened for lunch and dinner on Fridays and Saturdays, and for lunch on Sundays. This was not to gainsay Simon's theory but rather to address the problems of distance from the city and a need for privacy; after all, it was a home as well.

At Berowra Waters, the buildings along one bank of the gorge (the other is classed as recreational reserve and will never be disfigured by houses) were hardly separated from the cliff, which meant that creatures living in its scrubby undergrowth sometimes strayed into our domain. I saw lyrebirds and echidnas in that first year, and less shy and benign animals too – funnelweb spiders washed out of nesting webs by storms, goannas that ambled into the kitchen and dining-room for handouts of raw meat and eggs – and a territorial couple of diamond-backed pythons sometimes surprised waiters fetching wine from the cellar. The odd poisonous snake made a wrong turning into the dining-room. Not too much should be made of all this. As Colm Tóibín has remarked, one of the problems of biography is that 'it seeks out the colourful and the dramatic at the expense of the ordinary and true'. Melodramatic encounters with wildlife make good stories and place Berowra Waters Inn apart from most other restaurants, but they played no dominant role in the working life of the place, except for the water rats. The goannas gave tourists stories and photographs to take home, even when we suggested that they were better observed outside the dining-room and preferably from a horizontal position as goannas in fright, I'd been warned, climb the nearest vertical. We coexisted, although I sometimes think the second major renovation and extension to the old building (the sandstone area behind the dining-room, which also included the toilets) served more to defy no-legged and eight-legged strays than to make elegant spaces. The entire building, even after its never-quite-finished renovation, had as its most obvious structural element a network of spiders' webs strung always between landing and boat, landing and house, boat and house – threads so long and apparently indestructible that they seemed to act as suspender belts of great tensile strength.

Think of a friend who goes to live in a different place a long way from her last home. Friends vow to visit and few do, which is not to condemn them but speaks of the inevitable separation because of distance and also of other shifts, the imperatives of different ambitions and perspectives. The Bon Goût diners didn't shift their Friday table to Berowra Waters Inn, not only because it wasn't practical in the light of their gregarious needs (you can't pretend to be returning to work if it takes two hours of travelling time to and from your desk, on top of four hours at the table) but also because to travel to this new place was somehow to take food too seriously.

It certainly wasn't the price that stopped the old crowd coming to the new place – we opened with a *prix fixe* of $15, hardly more than the fixed price at the Bon Goût, and it included a glass of champagne, which in those days really was champagne. Even allowing for inflation this was not a viable charge, and so it was raised to $18.50 within four months after a kindly paternal lecture on business acumen from Leo Schofield, who held ever-increasing sway over public culinary taste. When I closed Berowra Waters Inn eighteen years later, the price was $90, still including an appetiser, a glass of sparkling wine, three courses and coffee, but not allowing champagne from Champagne and inadequate to sustain the upkeep of the restaurant. The point is that things were changing, as they are wont to do, and within a year Berowra Waters Inn had begun to find its new crowd and was blessed with having that time to become something approaching professional. The grace of such a rehearsal period would not be allowed by diners or media today.

We arrived with a friend and carpenter who stayed with us until the place seemed reasonably tidied and tables made. We cleaned an old but professional range of years of stale, rancid oil. In crazed repetition of the opening of the Bon Goût, when I had made the banquette covers to save money, I spent far too long sewing bedcovers from old curtains. We opened less than three months after moving in and one diner complained about the food, writing to Leo Schofield that 'poor Gay is so pregnant I think the smell of food is too much for her' (the obsessed archivist, I still have that letter). There is no dialogue to be had between critic and restaurateur, even when the complaint is near the truth. Even if criticism is relevant, one should simply respond with 'Thank you for your letter of . . .'. If it is pointless and spiteful, then one hopes the writer has told his/her friends not to patronise the restaurant and so no response is needed. There is a necessary pact between cook and diner, and if it cannot be arrived at then there are other restaurants, other relationships which are only in part commercial. In this instance, overtired, I cried and answered the letter; the writer apologised for her tone, the food got better and we found more help – although it was often from schoolboys who lived on the river. They were better than us at handling boats but were rotten dishwashers.

The first month was a befuddled attempt to cope with the river and a shambles of amateur service. The first menus are best forgotten, an embarrassment of divided energies: one weekend I realised that all the first courses were edging towards soup, that I should wash fewer dishes and practise more thoughtful cookery. The little things needed to become the big things: the gas for the stoves (trying not to run out during service); the rubbish removal (trucks don't cross waterways); the maintenance of the boat (transforming it over and over again from rubbish 'truck' to passenger ferry, until years later a real and separate passenger boat was commissioned – neither the Venetian taxi I dreamed of, nor the elegant wooden boat designed by architect Richard Le Plaistrier, which never progressed beyond an initial sketch, but a practical oyster barge dressed up just enough); finding the diners who couldn't find the public wharf (no one ever stumbled upon a restaurant that had no land access: the telephone was our lifeline and often the lines were down and damaged by storms); persuading suppliers to deliver to a launching ramp instead of a loading dock (this we resolved in the long run by going to the suppliers instead).

The restaurant's saving grace in those ridiculous and fraught days was the reason we went there in the first place. It is extraordinary country, not a landscape because it has in most part never been manicured into one, and because so much of it is water, a gorge remarkably close to urban centres yet so isolated and separate from them. The artist John Olsen, who lived quite close to the river, told me that the Aboriginal people of the area called the *Angophora costata* that graced the cliffs 'the tree that grows in the night' because of its spreading branches, which seem not to know what they are reaching out towards; they twist sensuously, for no apparent reason. This apparently illogical growth habit makes sense if you perceive the branches as doing some sort of balancing act to counteract the meagre hold of the shallow root system on this eastern, coastal sandstone. Magnificent trees, whose smooth phallic trunks bleed once a year and glow blood and orange in late afternoon light. In the morning there is no sun on the river and in winter the frost stays long on the pontoons: the cliff we faced would grow sombre, with an increasing dark line across it, as the sun set; at that time of day I understood why European painters sometimes mistook it for something un-Australian; it became an amorphous, different green.

Fonds de cuisine (Berowra Waters Inn)

John Brack, another Australian painter, sat staring at the cliff with his friend Fred Williams one day in 1977. Williams, of all Australian painters, might have been able to make sense of that cliff on canvas but never did, although we talked about it. But I would never have hung paintings on the wall of the dining-room that faced the cliff: it wasn't asking for competition. Brack, looking across the water to the cliff, turned and asked ingenuously if I didn't get sick of the view. Even if he had asked this eighteen years on, I would have answered the same: no, I do not tire of it. The fact that the environment was an exhausting one to work in was a different thing altogether – and now a stand of mature South Australian red gums plays the same contemplative role in my life, but this is private. Brack responded by explaining that he had moved into an ugly street in an ugly suburb in Melbourne a while back and now he didn't even notice it. Both Brack and Williams are dead now. You need to look at John Brack's paintings to make partial sense of his contrariness.

These cliffs were buffer and barrier for eighteen years. Their inhospitality caused, I think, the hospitality of the restaurant to appear larger than life. It is the cliffs that make impossible any road access for those who live on the river. The residents wouldn't have it any other way, and the complaints are proudly made, but the cliffs have an inescapable effect on everyday life. They are always observed, yet remain aloof; all connection is with the river, which always has to be crossed. In the best of all possible worlds Berowra Waters Inn would have employed, until it closed, a full-time builder, plumber, marine mechanic, handyman, engineer, electrician, disposer of kitchen and human waste, fire-fighter, water carrier, nanny, priest and counsellor. It got by on cooks, waiters, one extraordinary dishwasher (Gonzalo), a boat driver, a cleaner and a lot of help from tradespeople and friends. This involvement, forced on us by the nature of the land, is the key to that exaggerated sense of kinship that developed among all of those who worked there for any length of time. I've heard people who own restaurants talk of their staff as family, even of the idea of love, but this is mostly, I think, to convince themselves and their workers of binding loyalty. Differently, at Berowra Waters we worked and lived together for half the week, all year, and there was a genuine camaraderie.

Storms caused most of the problems: often enough to be a threat to normal service, a tree would fall on the power lines that brought electricity to houses along the river. The particular sound that a dying cold-room motor would make, a dishwasher silent in the middle of a cycle, a mixer not beating, the fan of the convection oven stopped, and an eerie darkness in the kitchen except for the flames on the stove-tops, always took us by surprise, though we grew adept at coping. Cooking with gas was indeed the culinary imperative at the base of a cliff with unstable power lines. Difficulties such as these continued to dog us for the entire life of the restaurant, with the response increasingly refined, especially under Janni Kyritsis' rule: a Greek chef is good for his cultural heritage as well as his food, food which for most of our years working together, was a reaction against his Greek self rather than an ingredient. Janni made extra lamps from champagne corks bobbing in olive oil; they gave the dining-room an accidental and Orthodox air.

The telephone lines went down with some regularity as well. No telephone, no bookings, no notice of cancellations and no notice of deliveries (although we went to most of the produce, most of the wine came to us). A neighbour might motor past and yell that a truck was at the loading dock: it might have taken around five years to be accepted on the river, but the exigencies of rescue, like those in arid areas, were never in question. When a new telecommunications line was being laid along the centre and bottom of the river bed, the technicians worked from a pontoon anchored across from the restaurant. At morning-tea time, when you would expect a cuppa and biscuit break, the diver practised t'ai chi. In this context – the deep water, the cliff, the silence – his slow formal rhythmic movements on that mundane little pontoon were like a ritual dance to the river gods. A young man who worked at the restaurant for most of its early years, when asked what he remembered about the river, replied with a poem about that dance.

In the first years we also had problems with water supply: commercial kitchens use excessive, immoral amounts of water. When our supply sometimes turned to a dribble (the row of houses was connected to the mains supply, but this was stored in tanks so that pressure was not lessened as the line followed the houses), a neighbour allowed the tap from her tank to supply good water for coffee and the river sometimes supplied water for dishwashing, hauled up in bins and boiled. Berowra Waters, an inlet not all that far from the sea at Brooklyn, has a fairly high salt content and, although every year growing cleaner through management and environmental controls, does not provide water that I would choose for blanching tripe or making stock. The irony of sometimes having no water in such an environment was not lost on us, and was rivalled only by the supreme irony of the attention we needed to pay to both kitchen ('grey') and human ('black') waste.

Eating in a restaurant is essentially about being served, paying other people to do the cooking and not having to do the dishes; one pays to have the effort disguised. The body is a grease-trap and its waste, if not to be directly returned to soil, needs to be treated. Tom Jaine, erudite past editor of the *Good Food Guide* in the UK and publisher of *Petits Propos Culinaires* – which is read only by a few, yet was created in part to allow Elizabeth David (who anyone my age and interested in food at least pretends to view as a seminal influence) to publish research – reckons he judges a restaurant on its toilets. If he had applied this rule to Berowra Waters Inn after the second part of the renovations, they would have earned his highest accolade. In the first two years he would have fled back to Devon.

Dealing with the 'black' waste was the restaurant's major problem, again caused by the magnificent inhospitality of the cliffs and the need for far too much water. In the beginning, we were pushing excessive quantities through an inadequate and probably illegal system that did not separately handle kitchen and human waste, a legacy of the last occupants. The solution turned out to be a treatment plant resembling a small industrial city, at least painted green, built on council land next to the property. It churned, rested, gurgled, churned and barely coped with the flow because so much water was being pushed through. People sometimes asked if this enormous plant treated all the waste produced by the row of houses along the bank, but mostly they showed no interest – it wasn't their problem, except intermittently in the first years when an ill wind reminded them that all was not well in paradise.

When Tony and I first arrived in 1977 there was no grease-trap at all and the tiny one we naively had plumbed in was a useless fibro-cement box into which a large Alsatian dog once fell. His owner was so disgusted by his grease-smattered coat that he was made to swim home. This trap was once cleaned by a dishwasher named Dudley ('Just call me Dud') who was my one pathetic attempt at using the local government employment office to find staff. Dud stated with affable honesty that he had a 'record' and I, equally affably, accepted his little foibles and used to chat to him on a Thursday (the day before we opened for the week and therefore the grease-trap's last day of weekly rest) as he helped with loading provisions. Dud was found removing a lot of wine from the cellar a month or two into his employment, and was taken to the boat without it.

All along the settlement, water from domestic kitchens and laundries had simply run off into the river for decades. By the mid-eighties the council had made some gesture towards proper policing of the environment and, at the restaurant, the number and strength and size of the grease-traps increased. By the end of the eighties, having earlier partly left the kitchen for the dining-room and a different set of clothes, I partly left the dining-room for the grease-traps, developing another working wardrobe whose smell made it particular and kept it separate. While the stocks and demi-glaces of the kitchen were the legitimate, primary, classical *fonds de cuisine*, those dark separating chambers were the ultimate one. The tools used to complete both equally necessary tasks were the same – trays, stockpots, ladles, strainers. Skimming the surface of three grease-traps from the inside out, even while it was done at least once a month, was not a solution to the serious problems of waste and environmental damage, but it helped my conscience to live with them. It was delusory, filthy work, self-flagellation in the face of an apparently unsolvable problem and a last crazed gesture of effort in recognition of the 'real' work the staff were doing and in which I was losing interest. The job description for cooks, waiters, boatman and dishwasher had never included periodic grease-trap cleaning. In some cranky way I rather liked the irony of those last years when I became obsessed with the grease-traps while the culinary accolades were for the food that caused the problem. When I fretted to architect Glenn Murcutt about the grease-traps and the kitchen waste washed into them, he responded with the suggestion that we might stop cooking with oils and fats. At the time I grinned and dismissed his lateral thinking – after all, I knew about cooking, he knew about designing buildings – but he was right. One answer to the problems caused by cooking for, on average, somewhere between one hundred and two hundred diners three days a week, increasing to way over three hundred in the

Fonds de cuisine (Berowra Waters Inn)

summer, was to cook differently, to create less unfriendly waste. This would have been to truly create a *cuisine de la région*! The only other and more responsible answer was to stop altogether. It is now obvious that the local council should never have allowed a restaurant to be operated in that environment in the first place. In the fifties the property had included a small shop and a fuel bowser (the holding tank for boat fuel was still there, closed off, under a platform built over the water's edge). Halvorsens, launches beautifully suited to leisurely river trips, could pull up and holiday-makers stay, I have been told, for roasted turkey dinners or cold turkey lunches. There were six buoys in front of the property, reduced to three not long after we arrived because I wanted the vista to the cliff to be as uncluttered as possible. It would have been much better for business to have left all six. It was so easy to celebrate paradise, not so easy to keep it clean and healthy.

In comparison to the plumbing, rubbish removal was simple: a boat-run at the close of each weekend. Bottles we recycled separately, although even this was refined only after different and messy solutions involving contractors meeting us at the ramp, extra skips, more spending, and finally persuading the council that they needed to become part of the process. Comic relief, as usual involving ridiculous amounts of extra work, came in the nineties only when, workboat so full of a summer's garbage run that it barely sat above the surface of the water, a wash was set in motion by a speeding launch that caused the workboat to make a slow dive into Berowra Waters, drowning its engine and leaving the bagged garbage, flattened boxes and bottles to float and bob. Simon Bowley, a potter who was the boat's driver for some months and stayed to wash dishes, swam back to the restaurant to report the spillage. We (a group of about twelve tired workers ready to go back to the city after three days of labour) took the passenger boat, grabbed a foam surfboard from one of the cellars, borrowed next-door's neat little runabout and spent a couple of wet hours pulling the garbage from the water, which at least was warm. It was also still light. Janni fell from the runabout and seemed not to be able to swim very well – he, who could fix anything mechanical and make silk purses from sows' ears, had never driven the boats and did not seem at home in water.

Every one of these stories of the continuing struggle to make Berowra

Waters Inn run smoothly enough to be lauded as the quintessentially Australian restaurant adds up to a constant battle with the very elements that caused it to be so admired. I have not yet mentioned the scares from bushfires, even the one that caused horrendous damage to the cliff behind the line of houses, discourteously disrupted Sunday lunch and saw diners divided into two different kinds: those who climbed towards the fire and fought it off with the local bushfire brigade, and those who sat and basked in a little drama, stupidly confident that things would be resolved in favour of humans and their property. With most of the waiters and cooks in the bush, and the boat driver manning the pump, we only managed to feed a few guests on time; and later thanked the brave with their meals.

—

This was, then, a place of *restauration* in a ridiculously unwelcoming environment. Signs to the public wharf defied many customers and losing them to the car ferry meant that they turned up on the other side of the river hungry. In the days before mobile phones this meant that they were stranded with no help unless they took the car ferry back, and even when these devices did appear the magnificent cliffs frustrated communication. Even if the building had had a commercial sign (something I would never have countenanced) it would not have been visible from the shore access point, again one of the restaurant's exasperating attributes.

Friday nights were often slow, so slow that it was common in winter to feed only two to six people. On one such day some time in the eighties (certainly Janni Kyritsis was chef and he came to the kitchen in 1981), we greeted a disgruntled couple from Melbourne. They had crossed on the car ferry to the wrong side of the water and had to be found. I felt sorry for them, wanted to cheer them up, coddle them and make them see the extra journey as part of an adventure and not a nuisance, and asked the kitchen to send out a little extra bite to appease their fury. I even remember what it was we gave them: croutons of saffron brioche with warm *brandade* (salt cod pounded with garlic, olive oil, milk) and lemon, this in addition to the appetiser served to everyone on arrival. Of course, this raises the question of how much a person can comfortably eat; most restaurants err in giving too much of what is at hand, food, when they want to express generosity. Be that as it may, we made our gesture, and back in Melbourne the woman, a restaurant critic, opened her severe review by suggesting that I had given her free food because I knew she was going to be writing about us. I did know she reviewed restaurants, I even knew her name. I took her this little extra dish out of a separate kindness. She had misunderstood the motive.

I have always remembered the hurt caused by this wilful assumption, that I gave something only to win one of the little skirmishes between critic and restaurateur. There may have been multiple and legitimate aspects of food and service to criticise that night (and it was not easy to feel comfortable in that dark landscape in an almost empty dining-room unless you brought with you your own vitality and a sure sense of why you wanted to be there), but that extra mouthful of food should not have been one of them. To tell this apparently trivial story is to make a larger observation about the hospitality of strangers. When motive is mistaken or, worse, mistrusted, things go awry and the centre doesn't hold.

⁓

This picture of the constant vicissitudes that attended our blithely taking on the gorge, its water and cliffs, expecting to cook for a dining-room that sat eighty in a restaurant that was hidden from view, had no sign and no door to the street, and was an hour's drive from the city, might cause the reader to disbelieve the extent of the problems we faced. Certainly I have pooled them in order to underline the 'invisible', but I have not exaggerated. Yet to write about the restaurant from inside out – like showing the tacking, frayed gussets, the seams and backstitching of a homemade garment – years after I closed it (unsold), and to do so honestly, is to be reminded, and also to have revisionist memory of the constant battering the environment gave us and the constant battering we rudely and sometimes destructively gave it in return.

When diners marvelled at the place and the sum of its parts, usually by concentrating on the food (which was pivotal, but not the only and absolute centre of the gestalt, which included their own journey), we thanked them for making that journey and thanked the kitchen gods that expectations were mostly fulfilled.

A part of me always wanted to crack up and spoil it all with an hysterical tirade detailing the trouble their eating put us to, in spite of the fact that we had asked them to come in the first place. Perhaps that's why some people have said I looked stern and formidable waiting to greet them at the top of the stairs – the effort to contain the real story (that wine you're drinking: I'll tell you about the time that forty boxes fell into the river from the pontoon when a lout caused an unholy wash that set the pontoon swaying and every box tipped in and floated; that I was there alone and jumped in, pulling the boxes back onto the pontoon before they split – Rothbury Estate Semillon, a good wine in a stout box, I hope you enjoy it).

In the best of all possible worlds a restaurateur would have lived there for two years before opening, taking stock rather than making stocks. Instead we fumbled through, hardly addressing what needed fixing, pulling our audience along through thick and thin. Tony was there long enough to refine his menu and cook some wonderful dishes; he bothered less about the details in which, Mies van der Rohe famously said, God presides. When Janni Kyritsis arrived in 1981 (after Tony and I split up and he went to the city to open Kinsela's with Leon Fink), attention was at last paid, beginning with the installation of floodlights over the stove. How could we ever have cooked in so little light? And with the arrival of the gentle and modest Murray Smith, sommelier and manager of the dining-room for many years until the closing, a second practical person came into the family. The longest-serving boat driver, Doug Hawkins, who managed to build a house on the river from Monday to Thursday over a few years, was another who knew how to fix things. Between them, and with the support of other staff, the details of water and waste were addressed. The costs were horrendous. Just as grease-trap cleaning had never been written into a cook's job description, or cleaning the underside of boats into a waiter's, so the running costs of a restaurant had never included building a major waste-treatment plant.

'To feast upon the view'

As a child in a working-class Melbourne suburb in the fifties I gave points out of ten to the houses in my street. This served to give the walking a repetitive, obsessive interest. It wasn't much different to counting stairs as one climbs, but it did point to aspirations to live in something more pleasing than the house owned by my grandmother and which we shared with her. I judged the houses by space and line and signs of family life, and played with changing this triage of criteria. I believed I had imprinted the image of that street for ever, but was shocked to find, on returning forty years later, that it was entirely different and shrunken. Even my own house was much, much smaller. How did I ride a bicycle around and around that house with so little space to manoeuvre? How perform those audacious lone feats of poetry, song and dance on such unprepossessing low pedestals at the foot of the steps to the front verandah and door?

When I escaped Clive Road for a room in Drummond Street in Carlton (leaning out of the window with my partner, who was pretending to study electrical engineering in the same way that I was pretending to study arts, to chat, when the landlady called down that John Kennedy had been assassinated) and the giddy life of an inattentive student, I fell in with a group of architecture undergraduates. While I wept for Macbeth tied like a bear to a stake, and recited Gerard Manley Hopkins by heart, they were obsessive in their push for simplicity, minimalism and clean design. They had lost their heads to modernism: they scraped the lids of Vegemite jars so that the only colours were silver and vegemite (which is a colour); they scraped their toothpaste tubes to rid them of advertisement; they limed their shelves; they drove Citroën 2CVs. One of them lived with one of Robin Boyd's daughters and we went to her home, of Boyd's design, in South Yarra. I remember a central courtyard, privacy being addressed in a way totally at odds with the Australian front and back yards. Another friend's father was an engineer who worked with Roy Grounds. The girl from Clive Road, where her eventual bedroom, after years of sleeping in the passage, was a sleepout attached to the kitchen, whose only way of ordering things and taking aesthetic charge was to arrange over and over again her writing desk, had fallen in with a seductive crowd. They had all, except for the one I shared the room with, been to private schools. He and I read Scott Fitzgerald, Ring Lardner, Nathaniel West and Aldous Huxley. We lived on three pounds a week, his mother's care packages, and crumpets with ground pepper.

Rubbing against that different milieu at Melbourne University, I found a pile of glossy magazines (my mother subscribed only to *The Australian Women's Weekly*) in someone's house and tore out photographs of the home of Luis Barragán in Mexico City. This would have been in the early sixties, myself twenty years old, and forty years later I still have the pages filed under Architecture. Barragán had designed the house of my naive dreams: one entire wall was glass, although divided into four huge panes, and it looked over a wild yet private garden. Best of all, the glass met the wooden floor as though it continued beneath the boards so that the pavement outside was a virtually uninterrupted extension of the inside space and vice versa. This took my breath away. I had never heard of Georgian architecture, never imagined that the end of the eighteenth century fostered similar Arcadian ideals. When much later I came to Bennelong Restaurant at the Sydney Opera House, one of the marvels of that space included a similar conceit: the outside granite steps carry on through the restaurant space. The staircase to the second floor of Barragán's house is grey volcanic rock and stands against a rough plaster wall, but it has no balustrade and so calls to mind one side of a Mayan pyramid. It is a bold and sculptural extension of the wall but does not dominate the room; it is bravely useful. The minimalism of the space and the strength of the materials are softened by furniture that makes reference to simple, comfortable folk styles. I fell in love.

In 1976, the last year of Tony's Bon Goût, *The National Times* ran a piece by Elizabeth Wynhausen (coincidentally, one of the central regular diners at the Bon Goût) in which she interviewed a few of the few exceptional architects in Australia, including, and especially, Glenn Murcutt. The year before, two of his houses had won merit awards in the annual Royal Australian Institute of Architects appraisals. I tore out the article and it went into the architecture file alongside the photographs of the Barragán house.

Many books have now been written about Glenn's buildings and he has made many published statements about architecture and location, courtesy to the land and response to climate, but nearly thirty years ago what he said in that interview was fresh, revelatory. He spoke about his admiration for Spanish architect José Coderch, who had said to him 'I have done nothing but add one very thin layer to the centuries of architecture before me. But you in Australia . . . are expected to invent something new every Monday morning'. Murcutt saw Australian architecture as 'desperately interesting', unrelaxed, not seeking simplicity. In almost exact parallel to the development of public and domestic architecture in Australia has been the dramatic increase of interest in eating well and in the idea of an Australian cuisine. The expectation of 'invent[ing] something new every Monday morning' is as much the enemy of good food as it is of good architecture.

One of the houses for which Murcutt won an award in 1975 was built on two hectares in Terrey Hills, a still-leafy Sydney suburb, inland but edging coastal bush. The living areas have glass walls that can be rolled back so the inside and outside merge. This was the different but connected seduction of that Barragán house in Mexico City. This was the work of the architect who should renovate Berowra Waters Inn. Not long after we opened in 1977, I spoke to Glenn Murcutt. I did not know that he had dined at the restaurant for the first time only one week earlier, and that his friends had said he should redesign this building whose only crumbling charm was its location. And so he did – although it occurred in four stages and took over five years, from 1978 to 1983.

For the first conversion in 1978, we closed for three months and gave priority to the cooks as well as the public; a real kitchen (with a curved Lexan window at the rear so that work might be more pleasant) and a dining-room from which

'To feast upon the view'

to see the wide waterway and glorious cliff and into which we introduced a second fireplace. Not long after this, sandstone slabs were laid to make a terrace to the south-east of the dining-room. Later the laundry and toilets were built; and next, the small apartment that later also completed the wall of louvres along the facade of the building. I found that Luis Barragán was also one of Glenn Murcutt's heroes. Glenn knew and understood far more about him than I did, of course. The wall I asked for, and which gave definition to the rear of the sandstone terrace close to the cliff behind the restaurant, was to hide the kitchen bins and kitchen workers who sat on upturned milk crates in between services. This wall became our homage to Barragán, who died in 1988. He had won the world's most prestigious prize for architecture, the Pritzker Prize, in 1980. Glenn Murcutt won the Pritzker Prize in 2002.

The grammar of architecture is one of proportion and separation. Our wall was thick and its height pleasing; it stands separately as a linear sculpture. I had asked Glenn to consider that the cooks, dishwasher and waiters should be able to share with diners the view of the cliff when they ate meals outside but away from the public. He cut into the solid mass and angled the cut, which was open at the top, so that the eye had maximum breadth of view. At the end of the terrace a jacaranda flowered late every year. We painted the wall a deep jacaranda mauve, which incidentally increased the reference to Barragán, who designed lovely, lonely walls of bright colours in his Mexican landscape. The only other major work (not including the unmentionable city of holding tanks and pumps for effluent) was the replacement of a sinking wooden pontoon with a much larger one of aluminium, and a serious, lovely ramp designed by Glenn to connect the pontoon to the land. Both these elements came to Berowra Waters via a long, slow, processional tow along the Hawkesbury from Brooklyn.

These periods of deconstruction and construction were intense, but felt slow and endless – as does all building, but epecially building with a wide stretch of river between materials and site. Everything that would be unloaded at a normal building site directly from the truck had to be brought in across the water – the steel load-bearing and structural parts from Wollongong, the sandstone from Gosford (carried on the backs of the Lebanese stonemasons, who only accepted cash), the glass bricks, the heavy working parts of the commercial kitchen, and much more – and boatloads of rubble taken back across the water to become fill for the marina. All building along the river bank is beholden to this repetitive and time-consuming transport system, but most houses at Berowra Waters had been built from conventional materials. The appearance of the pontoon and its ramp, already complete except for installation, was a marvellous relief and cause for celebration. Perhaps this is, in part, the attraction of fast food.

While the wide sandstone pathway, staff bunkrooms and the apartment were still being completed, the bank decided we should open again. At the close of evening service I would take five cooks with me to a house halfway between Berowra Waters and Sydney, rented because of its proximity to my daughters' school. The waiters slept in the dining-room, which was also where Janni Kyritsis and I had our first excited and long conversations about produce and dishes and developed a personal jargon of cooking. After years of these often creative exchanges, our different culinary attitudes might be precis-ed as follows: Janni was always telling cooks to 'shubble it in' (he always said he kept his Greek accent and slip-ups because he wanted to, it gave him character) and I was always, in opposition, ordering them to 'chuck it out'. 'Shubbling it in' certainly kept the restaurant viable.

This was 1982. A couple who dined regularly at the restaurant had a very public falling-out one night with much mutually flatulent ill-will whirling about their table. He left (I have never forgiven him this cruelty) and she in feminine stoicism sat on, much to her own and our embarrassment, as she continued to drink in order to cope with being centre stage, while everyone pretended this one-woman show did not exist. She managed to board the restaurant boat and we presumed she had called a taxi. When we were about to drive away from the river to our makeshift beds in Pennant Hills, one young cook yelled that I should stop or I would run into a large boulder on the riverbank near the public wharf (the public wharf was hardly more inviting than the one we replaced at the restaurant). The boulder turned out to be the wife-left-behind: we bundled her in and put her in a taxi at the closest large town. Part of me felt I should offer her a bed, but the other part felt her mortification, her need to pretend this wasn't happening. Both people became good patrons of the restaurant again years later, each with a different partner, and none of us ever spoke of that night. Why do couples choose to eat publicly when it is inevitable that mutual furies will not be tamed by civilised service and good food? And why choose a restaurant so hard to get to and especially so hard to leave without being watched? How perverse and blindly hopeful mankind is.

The first consort of builders were old friends from Melbourne, virtuosi of the mud-brick building trade, led by Ray who looked like a gypsy but worked like a Protestant and who, having stayed with us before, knew the site. All were new to the exacting relationship of glass to steel, ready for anything, perhaps with the exception of the rigidly proper supplier of kitchen equipment when he was accidentally witness to Peter plaiting Eddy's hair one night. They slept rough and managed to build us a dining-room and leave in good humour. The second group were Finnish master builders who had become Glenn Murcutt's constant team. When the foreman arrived to survey the site, I expected the usual introductory period of small talk and confusion over the impossibilities of water and materials. Instead they simply got to work. They brought their plumber to the site when the time came to figure out how to cope with water and waste, and he continued as plumber for years, overseeing the accrual of grease-traps and holding tanks.

To recount the full story of the building's transformation, and to truthfully recount the trials and tribulations of the waste-treatment plant, one would have to write a black comedy in the manner of Jaroslav Hasek's *Good Soldier Schweik* (the weekend in the early nineties when the plant broke down and we ladled the untreated waste into triple-lined garbage bins and formed a line to the work boat that took it away) and combine it with something like William Golding's *The Spire* (the Greek swimming-pool excavators, called in an emergency in 1981 when we realised that although a large section of the cliff needed to go, what was left also needed serious reinforcement so that it would not collapse onto what was to be the remarkable new toilet block – it was, luckily, their off-season).

The compilers of *Hobson-Jobson: A glossary of colloquial Anglo-Indian words and phrases, and of kindred terms, etymological, historical, geographical and discursive* – which is best known simply as *Hobson-Jobson* (not the names of the authors, but 'an Anglo-Saxon version of the wailings of Mahommedans as they beat their breasts in the procession of the Moharram – "Ya Hasan! Ya Hosain!"') defined a verandah as 'an open pillared gallery round a house'. A very perplexing word etymologically, according to the compilers, Henry Yule and A.C. Burnell, in the first (1886) edition. Every home should have a *Hobson-Jobson*, and every home should have a version of a verandah.

When I consider the dining-room at Berowra Waters Inn, I think of it as a verandah for eating in. Herman Melville, in 1856, wrote that for a house 'to have no piazza [i.e. verandah] for the convenience of those who might desire to feast upon the view, and take their time and ease about it, seemed as much an omission as if a picture-gallery should have no bench'. To feast on the view at Berowra Waters was also to feast at the table, so I see that dining-room as the ultimate verandah, although it does not meet Glenn Murcutt's ultimate verandah philosophy, which he spoke of to Philip Drew in the late nineties (and which was included in the collection of interviews, *Touch This Earth Lightly)*. He spoke of wanting to build a house that is a verandah and no more, so that the traditional transitional space of shade and shelter becomes the house itself, adjusted by shutters and blinds to cope with different weather patterns. This kind of approach has been achieved by another remarkable Australian architect, Richard Le Plaistrier. Both ask their clients to be, along with the building and its relationship to the landscape, strong, principled and vigorously committed; Richard does so even more rigorously than Glenn.

Elizabeth Farrelly, architect and astute critic, has written that 'truly vigorous architecture results neither from meek genuflection nor from the client's insistence on her druthers'. Although I agree with this, I am more seduced by the idea of choosing an architect as a commitment to artistic patronage, which is to say that by becoming the client the owner never allows him (in this case) less than complete creative freedom. There is no question of the client quibbling over parts of the parcel; this would be to meddle, to undo the very basis of patronage. The

'To feast upon the view'

only real decision on the client's part is that very first one, and there was never any question that this site was Glenn Murcutt's. As a result, unusually boldly, I rang an architect to whom Tony Bilson had talked at a party and who had shown interest in converting the building, and cancelled his arranged visit. Once, when I knew I should ask a cook to leave because he was not committed, I could not do it because I liked this young man so much. Years later he told me that even he knew he should have been banished from the kitchen, that he was just not serious about the craft (he is older, reformed and successful now). But with the building at stake, sterner stuff surfaced.

After Rayner Banham, the doyen of British architectural criticism, came to Australia in 1988, he wrote of Berowra Waters Inn in the Californian journal *Design Book Review*:

> Murcutt's contribution to its design (it is a conversion job, and not quite finished when I was there) is almost invisible – the long wall of louvred glass overlooking the Waters, the stone stairwell that brings you up from the dockside, reveal at first sight nothing that the proprietors and an intelligent local builder could not have thought up for themselves. Murcutt's restraint here seems almost pathological, and one can only thank him for it, because it is absolutely right, and no other architect in the world could have done it.

It seems possible that Banham's hosts, including ourselves, gave him much too good a time at the table. His effusive praise of the restaurant in the hierarchy of world restaurants and his perception that this was Glenn's most famous building when it was, although a major conversion, not more than that, sound like the result of the triumvirate of good food, good wine and good company, which never fails to make people mellow and good-spirited. He did see that the building had not been finished, something only I, Glenn and the odd architect recognised. Still, the line of louvres that marked the point at which the inside and outside touched is so strong, so right for that location, that the building continued (despite its faltering restoration) to feel particular to Glenn Murcutt. Using louvres to form the entire facade of the building was an inspired response to the water and cliff. Glenn talked to Philip Drew about this decision:

> a louvre is a sort of texture on the wall; it delivers a different quality of light; different reflections on each pane of glass from where you sit. It gives you for the first time (which was so important there) the opportunity to be able to feel you're getting a slice of the landscape.

In fact the louvres did more than this. Each, angled differently, provided miniature reflected landscapes; a boat might pass in a single pane. And because several might be opened at once at varying angles in groups of five, they became private and particular to those diners who played with them for breeze and translucent paintings.

The second aspect of the conversion to which Banham referred was the staircase. Glenn, in conversation, had quoted a rule of the modernist Le Corbusier: that one should take the eye away from the view on arrival to a building and then return the eye to it; this is to make a second gift, to renew the sense of, at best, wonder. The one-storey staircase Glenn created at the restaurant began in a sandstone entrance hall that was an open, refined cave. It was as if we were taking diners into the earth rather than to a platform for viewing.

In one of his memoirs, Ved Mehta writes about his family in India moving to a house with a very large verandah. This gave the family great status, not because the house was grand, but because the larger the verandah the greater the number of relatives who could turn up and stay, sleeping on charpoys, sheltered. I like this image of hospitality, even if Mehta's Mamaji might have seen it as a curse. The Berowra Waters Inn dining-room was also a hospitable verandah, which somehow vindicated the craziness of the costs of building on the river: it wasn't for one family but for as many as possible.

I have admired other restaurant dining-rooms over the past thirty years, but the number is small and, unlike Tolstoy's happy families, they are all exceptional in different ways. A restaurant in Port Douglas, on the far north coast of Queensland, for instance, has a dining-room that is not a room at all. It has no walls and no ceiling; it is simply an oval area marked out by palms with orchids growing on their long trunks. This I count as pure enchantment: it is particular to the latitude and to the climate. So, too, a restaurant in a French-owned hotel in Siem Riep in Cambodia, which has a roof but no walls, and its kitchen 'walls' are simply the perimeter of its preparation benches. The dining-room of a small restaurant south of Milan is a simple room with a communal table and in one corner a compact cooking range. It undoes the notion of separation of kitchen from eating, but without the self-importance of purposely semi-public kitchens that demand notice: the dining-room here *is* the kitchen and still unselfconscious, a particularly winning trait peculiar to the Italians (and, differently, to the Third World). They have retained a centuries-old sense of conviviality, never exclusive of young and old, which suffuses the very action of spooning a sauce for pasta, stirring rice, mixing a salad, honouring the past.

The main and splendidly confident dining-room of The Four Seasons in New York, and the more casual dining area on either side of the entrance foyer, are a stunning celebration of warm modernism (the two words are not necessarily contrary). The sense of horizontal space, the beautiful veneers of dark woods, the sheer comfort of the rooms, is marvellous. At the opposite extreme, Harry's Bar in Venice is the sum of miniature parts in a miniature room with nothing out of proportion: 'infinite riches in a small room'. The dining-room of the Aristologist restaurant in the Adelaide Hills, which closed in 1998, was also small but small in a domestic sense (unlike Harry's Bar's stylishness and virtuosic professionalism): it epitomised, for me, a form of sincerity that asked of the paying diner a sense of complicity.

Set Portes in Barcelona is, by contrast, the epitome of stylish bustle on a grand scale. It opened in 1836 and its proud energy is the sum of all those past years. When I first ate there, with a young child, a waiter passed our table holding aloft a very large tray loaded with plates, glasses and flatware. Just at that moment I swept out one arm to make a point: the waiter showed no shock when the tray crashed to the floor; other waiters came to clean the rubble away. Nothing was made of this, it hardly disturbed the momentum of the restaurant – things were got on with, we went back to eating. La Coupole in Paris has much in common with Set Portes, but not the latter's lived-in sense of grandeur and polish.

Magill Estate Restaurant in Adelaide, designed by Keith Cottier (and with its own debt to Barragán, a spare courtyard owing everything to him), is a beautifully proportioned room with God in the details and a view across something only Adelaide offers, a suburban vineyard. Its dining-room is quite small, although not intimate; the serenity of the room pulls the eye through to the outside.

Wakabe, a Japanese restaurant in London, which two chefs introduced to me over a decade ago for its food, turned out to have been designed by John Pawson, a minimalist who had worked in Japan and whose minimalism is often life-threatening (he once designed a kitchen that pretended not to be one). It includes an internal solid 'fence' which divides the entrance from the dining area and which is an unusual and supremely elegant height, from memory somewhere around one and a third metres. The floorboards are also unusually wide and the width is beautiful. The white, curving, glass street facade is usually the most praised feature of Pawson's design for this restaurant, but it is the internal details that I found remarkable.

So, what do we want a restaurant dining-room to be, what relationship do we, as diners, want with it? I spent years learning about French food as a tourist in much-touted French restaurants of one to three stars. I was sometimes seduced, sometimes appalled, but mostly just had to accept the 'nouvelle' decoration that went hand in hand with nouvelle cuisine, for there is surely a connection between the French proclivity for flounce and chintz and the extremes of plating to which nouvelle cuisine sometimes descended. Language plays its part here too: a menu proclaiming that its pigeon is in a lettuce-leaf dress (*dans sa robe de laitue*) goes hand in hand with the plating of a dish in an overdressed room. 'A taste for simplicity cannot endure for long', wrote the French painter Eugène Delacroix.

On a different rung sits the restaurant – a bistro, for instance – that offers comfort and familiarity and is all the more confident for this with no less professionalism. Even when we say we feel 'at home' in a restaurant, the experience is still everything to do with not being at home. In a weekend newspaper review of a Melbourne restaurant in 2002, in which the writer stated that the food was the most important element, nine-tenths of the review discussed the design and the clientele. This was either mistaking restaurant reviewing for the social column, which it is to some extent, or succumbing to the kind of malaise into which restaurants with inchoate pretensions to inchoate standards are always going to be in danger of falling along with the commentators.

What I liked about my own louvred dining-room was that it was purpose-built for something that had nothing to do with dining. Dining was an almost accidental pastime and this made the food easily, modestly, legitimate and reasonable. We cooked very good food and sometimes food better than very good, and we sent it out into a dining-room that was a verandah to a view, even at night when the view was a black space. It was as if everything was there as a passage to something else. While you contemplated the cliff, glimpsed serendipitously that sea eagle catching that fish, listened to the wash lapping the sea wall, watched the rain pour from the edge of the unguttered roof and so make a translucent curtain for the duration of the storm, we would bring you plates of food. This is just about right in terms of proportion. It also spoke to a form of worldliness, the opposite of the cloister, the sum of parts.

Marrow spoon and salamander

In 1976, towards the close of the Bon Goût in Sydney and the shift to Berowra Waters Inn, Tony Bilson and I spent a winter's month in Italy and France. I find a list made at the back of a diary:

The Filipo Lippi fresco in Spoleto
A stainless-steel tool for shaving white truffles
A 'Luna Park' sign in front of the Colosseum
The chocolate cake at Ranieri's in Rome
Italian elegance
Snipe and woodcock on skewers with polenta
The poverty of medieval Tivoli
Trays of *marrons glacés* in the shop near the Ufizzi
The operatic facility of Italian museum guides
The cleansing but flatulent nature of tourism
Fresh anchovies in dark-green olive oil
The lack of humour in Pirsig's *Zen and the Art of Motorcycle Maintenance*
Marquez writing that a train is a kitchen pulling a village behind it
Handing three bottles of Australian wine to the Chagnys in France, and
      when one slips from my grasp he graciously says 'Quel bouquet!'
Foie gras, ortolans, truffles, fresh goat's cheese, pear sorbet, lost waistline
The Sunday Times: a cricketing writer uses such phrases as 'the stench
      of imminent mortality' (this is to describe a batsman facing a fast
      bowler)

The stench of Gauloise tobacco surrounding the chef Alain Chapel

The bags under the lascivious eyes of the chef Paul Bocuse in Lyon

The resemblance of the chef Louis Outhier, and of his costume, to the
        faces and figures of the characters in Marcel Carné's 1945 film
        Les Enfants du Paradis

The egotism and vanity of the three-star restaurant proprietors

The pittance paid to kitchen apprentices

In Mâcon, a *boudin noir* (blood pudding)

Pineapple and bananas are, in France, *exotique*

The stone-cold in the cathedral at Brou

Horizon after horizon of deciduous tree branches hung with mistletoe
        and shrouded in fog (*le brouillard*)

⟶

At Tours, in the Loire, we ate at the restaurant of Charles Barrier. One first course was *Brioche de Moëlle au Beurre Rouge*, brioche with poached bone marrow and red-wine butter. The bone marrow is from beef shins and should not be confused with spinal marrow, which the French affectionately call *amourette*, 'a love affair'. As a child I loved to pick out the *amourette* from the mid-loin lamb chops that formed the centre of my mother's severely restricted menu; it is extremely sweet. We made this dish our own at Berowra Waters Inn, somehow a more legitimate, less culpable form of plagiarism when taken from one continent to another, and from its first appearance on the menu in the seventies it remained frozen in the only way food can, by being made again and again and again, right up until the final meal in 1995.

The recipe was refined, of course – ours I mean, not the original, which was perfect. Refinement in restaurant cookery is to take a dish to the point where it cannot be improved and getting this right every time, leaving as little as possible to human error. The only addition we ever made was to include braised shallots, which cut the richness of the melting fat of the bone marrow. One of the discordances of restaurant cooking is that you lose the sense of the legitimacy of a dish by making it so many times without sitting down to the whole. *Mise-en-place* is the sum of the separate parts of dishes and the stove is an assembly line: getting to drive the dish away is the prerogative of the diners. For the cook, this is rather like staring at a written word for so long that the combination of characters begins to seem strangely dissociated from the word we have learned it represents. When you get to the disastrous point of wondering if a dish has any worth at all, you should sit down when hungry and have someone bring the dish to you away from the kitchen.

Bone marrow played its part in the 1993 'body' banquet we created (leaving the river to become Berowra Waters Out) for the Seventh Symposium of Australian Gastronomy at the National Gallery in Canberra. For the third course, 'Bone', we wrapped some of the poached bones with gold leaf and served fat slices of brioche loaves separately. Eliza Acton, in her 1845 *Modern Cookery for Private Families*, includes advice on boiling marrow bones and suggests serving them 'placed upright on a napkin, with slices of dry toasted bread apart'. The gold leaf we included was a private reference to the line 'A bracelet of bright haire about the bone' in John Donne's poem 'The Relique', but the flash of gold also raised the status of the dish. Fergus Henderson, who sensibly left architecture for cooking, serves bone marrow at his restaurant St John, in London. In his collection of recipes, *Nose to Tail Eating: A Kind of British Cooking*, he astonished me by writing that roast bone marrow and parsley salad 'is the one dish that does not change on the menu'. While ours was as refined as it gets and his is like tumbling in hay, we both have family feelings towards it. I ate his once: the marrow came from a calf and was three hunking pieces of bone roasted in a hot oven until the marrow was 'loose and giving, but not melted away'. You had to handle it, and handling it was a pleasure.

One of the more abstruse implements for the table that I treasure is a 1777 English silver marrow spoon that looks rather like a medical instrument for scooping around a vagina. I don't carry it in my handbag, as some do a pepper grinder, but wish I had on that occasion so it could have been produced at St John just for fun. The spoon itself is nearly seven centimetres long, two wide, and as deep as those practical, pointed, old-fashioned soup spoons; the handle is long

Marrow spoon and salamander

and thin. One imagines Mrs Thrale serving roasts and braises to Dr Johnson, and Dr Johnson, who was famously all thumbs, managing with the assistance of this tool. It is interesting to think that a piece of cutlery so sophisticated, and indeed so attractive, was used in a century when serving marrow in its bone was common. If the idea to make an exquisitely crafted silver spoon of such pleasing and practical shape were around in Georgian times, then why wasn't there a similar attitude to refinement where cooking was concerned?

Brioche with poached bone marrow, braised shallots and red-wine butter

This will serve eight to ten, based on the amount of red-wine butter. The parts of the recipe for the dish are all separately useful, so the recommended large amount of brioche dough is worth making. (It is also one of those foods better made in large amounts, for brioche freezes well.) The red-wine butter especially is a fine sauce for salmon or trout. The braised shallots make a fine accompaniment for beef.

Now, instead of those cute little traditional brioches with the fluted sides and huge cupola balanced on top, I'd just make a loaf of brioche dough and cut thick slices from it, brown them in a hot oven or under a slow grill, make sure the plates were hot, dump the slices of bone marrow on top of each slice with the shallots, splash some red-wine butter over the lot, put a sauce boat on the table for seconds, and only serve a green salad to complete the meal, which might be better suited to brunch or supper than part of a series of courses.

THE BRIOCHE

Because brioche dough includes so much butter, you will need to make sure that the butter does not become greasy, in which case it would resist incorporation into the flour mixture. Dissolve 30 g fresh yeast and ¼ cup sugar in 300 ml tepid milk. Combine 1 kg white flour with 2 teaspoons salt in a large bowl, make a well in the centre and add the milk mixture plus 8 egg yolks and 4 whole eggs. Stir to combine, then scrape the dough onto a floured surface and knead until smooth. Add 300 g softened butter in pieces, and knead again until completely mixed through the dough (alternatively, use an electric mixer with a dough hook).

Allow dough to rise until doubled in bulk – this will take a couple of hours, depending on the temperature of the room – and then punch down. Weigh dough into 30-g and 15-g pieces and roll these into smooth balls, using the palm of your hands like a practised baker; hands that are too warm tend to make the balls greasy. Place the larger balls in buttered brioche moulds and push a deep hollow into the centre of each with your thumbs. Add the smaller ball, then leave to rise.

Glaze the brioches with a sieved mixture of egg yolk and milk (1 yolk to 1 teaspoon milk) and bake at 180°C for 12–15 minutes. They should not crisp but be soft and golden, only just cooked through, so that when reheated for the complete dish they do not overcook and become biscuity.

THE BRAISED SHALLOTS

Take 1 kg whole shallots; 125 g butter; 125 ml red-wine vinegar; 500 ml red wine; 5 cloves garlic, sliced; 4 bay leaves; 2 teaspoons chopped fresh thyme leaves; 2 teaspoons salt; and 1 teaspoon pepper. Brown the shallots in the butter, add all other ingredients and simmer gently or braise in the oven until the shallots are soft and the liquids reduced to a sauce.

THE BONE MARROW

You will need many kilos of beef shin bones in order to have enough bone marrow: the best shin might provide enough marrow for three portions at most. Ask the butcher to saw through the bones at about 5-cm intervals; do not take the bone ends. Soak the bones in cold salted water to release the blood, changing the water a few times over at least 36 hours. Push out the marrow carefully with your thumbs – this is best done at room temperature, or the marrow will crumble. Slice it quite thickly (approximately 1 centimetre) and store in cold salted water. The marrow pieces should be poached at the last minute – add to just-simmering water and leave until the fat has melted but still holds together, which should take only about 2–3 minutes. Watch carefully as there is a point at which the marrow is cooked but still whole, and another, not much further on, when it has melted into the water. Drain on paper so that any released fats will be soaked up.

Marrow spoon and salamander

THE RED-WINE BUTTER

This sauce should be timed so that it is used as soon as it is ready, but you can prepare the reduction earlier. Chop 1 onion and brown it in a knob of butter. Add 500 ml each red wine and red-wine vinegar, about 10 stalks of fresh thyme, 4 bay leaves and 5 whole peppercorns, and reduce to one-quarter of the volume. Add a splash of cream and reduce a little more, then add 600 g softened butter, knob by knob, whisking continuously over a medium–low heat. When all the butter is incorporated, strain the sauce. The finished sauce should be quite thick, and acid enough to cause a catch in the throat when sniffed. Season it with salt and pepper to taste.

TO ASSEMBLE THE DISH

Cut the smaller knob from each brioche, taking some of the base as well (make your cut wider than the knob, to make a generous hollow) and then trimming this away. Replace the lid and wrap the whole in foil. Place in a hot oven for about 10 minutes, just to heat the brioches through without making them crisp.

Warm the serving plates before assembling the dish, as the marrow and the red-wine butter would set on contact with a cold surface. Place a couple of shallots and some slices of bone marrow in the hollow of each brioche, and more of each around the brioche. Spoon the red-wine butter over, and gently replace the lid.

The man who ate the first Tripe Lyonnaise at Berowra Waters Inn downed it with a bottle of '53 Richebourg, and he cried. The cook was Tony Bilson; the tears were shed by Anders Ousback, who was running the dining-room at the time and was our first serious maître d'. The restaurant wasn't open, we were just fooling about.

Tripe Lyonnaise (the descriptor alludes to the onions in the dish) appeared on the menu after that – it must have been in 1978 – and it stayed there for ever, along with the brioche and bone marrow and the crème brûlée. In Tony Bilson's days, it was always a splash of this, a ladle of that and a final flourish of parsley, which more often than not resulted in a fine dish; recipe cards didn't exist, but probably should have. The recipe and its preparation were perfected by Janni

Kyritsis in the early eighties and that's when a recipe card was made, after which the dish was always consistent. There are two kinds of cooks, the ones who splash and the ones who measure. I'd gone from one extreme to the other.

This dish freezes well and large quantities were made and frozen in exact portions, twenty portions at a time, then finished with the addition of a little stock and the parsley, which is essential. But it was also a dish that sold very little: if, say, we fed two hundred over the five services that comprised our three-day week, we would rarely sell more than ten portions, sometimes only two or three. Thus the dish we were most proud of, the dish we saw as a one-third metonym for our culinary world, was in fact eaten by very few people. This either makes an affectation of our affection for it or simply illustrates the shift away from offal, especially tripe, made by middle-class Australians. Janni's veal kidneys wrapped in pancetta and caul were chosen frequently, but then veal kidneys, with all that attention paid to microsurgery and the snipping away of connecting tissues and membrane, have always been seen as classy.

Most Australians don't want to eat tripe, remembering white sauce coating something texturally disgusting. (Elizabeth David memorably described it, when overcooked as it too often was by English cooks, as a 'slithery repellent mess'.) But I enjoy it and even enjoyed as a child that humble dish also calling for lots of chopped parsley. Perhaps those who shy away from tripe have been affected by the word also denoting a load of codswallop. Sometimes I'd persuade people to try a small portion as a first course, and win half of them over. The combination of the reduced red-wine vinegar and the veal stock, the inclusion of so very many onions, makes a dish that is rich in flavour. It might legitimately be called *Tripe au vinaigre*, like *Poulet au vinaigre*, and has everything in common with that dish except that it is beef stomach and not chicken. When the restaurant closed, there were still a few bags of Tripe Lyonnaise in the freezer and they were distributed to the deserving; the man of tears, for instance, still loved it. I wouldn't change one part of that recipe now, but a good demi-glace is hard to find in a domestic kitchen.

Tripe, as well as bone marrow, made its appearance at the 1993 Symposium of Australian Gastronomy dinner, when Janni Kyritsis made a tripe tablecloth over forty metres long and one metre wide. (The first part of the word 'gastronomy'

Marrow spoon and salamander

is derived from the Greek for stomach.) It took two months of work to clean the innumerable stomachs we ordered progressively from the slaughterhouse. The bleached white honeycomb tripe commonly seen in butcher shops comes from the wall of the second stomach compartment. The whole and untreated four-part stomachs we were dealing with are another thing altogether: first, they are not white but many shades of dirty brown to black; second, they smell of animal instead of bleach, far preferable for those of us who eat meat and want flavour. So, every Sunday night for weeks, we washed and scrubbed, soaked and salted. So that the banquet would be as meaty as possible, we used sausage casing to sew the tripe together into sections that could be transported more easily to Canberra from Berowra Waters. These were frozen and stored by the butcher as they were sewn.

Delivering the tablecloth to the gallery was a late-night affair and was, I imagine, rather like the stealing of bodies for dissection in centuries past would have felt. Some hours before the banquet Janni and I decided to lay the cloth and make a final decision about whether or not we would use it. It was the sensibilities of the symposiasts that worried us, even though a group of people dedicated to talking about food and food history and culture should have been the perfect, open-minded audience. We placed a couple of the three-metre-long pieces in place and stepped back to view them. In complete agreement we knew it should stay. Once the whole cloth was laid, the table surface ressembled some extra-terrestrial landscape of terrible beauty.

The dinner guests entered the long, narrow room via stairs down from one of the gallery spaces. We had pulled the chairs away from the table. The dinner was offered without explanation until the last course, served when my bandaged daughter Sido rose from under a pile of red figs and grapes and handed out the 'menus'.

Tripe Lyonnaise

For ten portions you will need 2.5 kg 'green' (i.e. unbleached) honeycomb tripe; a couple of handfuls of mirepoix (carrot, celery and onion, finely chopped); 2.5 kg peeled onions, halved and sliced finely; 250 g butter; 250 ml red-wine vinegar; 50 g garlic, finely chopped; a tablespoon of chopped fresh thyme; 125 g tomato paste; 750 ml heavily reduced veal stock; about 1 tablespoon each salt and black pepper; leaves from a whole bunch of parsley, chopped.

Cook the tripe in enough water to cover, with the mirepoix, for 4–6 hours, until tender. Drain, and slice it into thick strips, about 1 cm wide. Next, sauté the sliced onions in the butter until soft, add the cooked tripe and the red-wine vinegar and reduce until the vinegar has almost disappeared. Add the garlic, thyme, tomato paste, veal stock, salt and pepper. Taste, adjust seasoning if needed, and simmer to combine the flavours; reduce more if the consistency is too thin. There should be no sauce left to run away from the portion; rather, the tripe should be one sticky mass of combined flavours. Add the chopped parsley at the last minute and sprinkle more on each portion. Serve with no other accompaniment than a green salad.

Crème brûlée is a dish with as many accents as it has essential ingredients. Some say that, despite its name, crème brûlée isn't French but English. The Catalan version, sometimes called *crema cremada* (which means the same sort of thing, despite burning and cremation not being literally correct), is claimed by Catalans to be the original. Whatever the case, this dish found its way onto just about every upmarket restaurant's menu by the mid-eighties, although it was often bastardised by the addition of buried fruit or jumped-up spices, because one way to make something one's own is to add another ingredient. 'Bits of fruit in a crème brûlée are like finding foreign objects in a handkerchief', a restaurant reviewer wrote in *New York* magazine in 1980.

That velvet-textured, vanilla-scented synthesis of yolks and cream, hidden under a sheet of caramel awaiting destruction by a sharp crack from the back of a spoon, was one of the first dishes that I felt I knew so well that I had control of it and not the other way around, which is often the case with tentative, occasional, domestic cooking. It isn't in the puff-pastry league, or even that of Bavarian creams, but it went into the main catalogue. I loved it for its simplicity, more Shaker than high church, for cream and eggs are simple farm produce. We eschewed garnish except for a very crisp biscuit: *tuiles* or *cigarettes Russes*, thin

Marrow spoon and salamander

crisp *palmiers,* perhaps, biscuits that are all surface and not too sweet, a foil for the custard. A friend once said of a dish that it had a taste 'impossible to un-assemble', which is a very good way indeed to describe all the best dishes: even when it is the pairing of two separate elements, and not a combination that effects a chemical change, the dish cannot be imagined any other way. Another friend saw a retrospective of a great painter and came away vowing never to use adjectives again.

Once I told a food writer about my mother's 1950s pièce de résistance, Early Watermelon. He was indiscreet. My mother read the description and rang only to refute my memory of one layer of the suggested rind: 'It was *not* powdered custard!' Crème anglaise is custard and so too is crème brûlée, except that it sets; crème pâtissière (flour is added) is a thickened custard. Sabayon (and so zabaglione) are not – wine replaces the cream or milk – while syllabub and posset have no eggs. The base for most icecreams is custard; even hollandaise sauce is custard (using butter instead of cream or milk). It is only the flat English word that undoes the idea of it (an English woman to the philosopher Diderot, in Malcolm Bradbury's relentlessly clever *To the Hermitage*: 'I like English for my mouth, French for my ears'). Understanding the effect of heat on eggs and the emulsive properties of the egg, surely the most remarkable food of all and closest to the bone, is to be able to make all custards and emulsion sauces. The trick is not to be scared but to run scared. Before I understood the instructions for making puff pastry (and there's the rub: you have to stumble through and stumble through again and again and only understand afterwards), it seemed ridiculous that the *détrempe* (paste of flour and water) should be required to have the same consistency as a large square of butter, but it does. This is so that one doesn't fight the other when you begin to transform the two elements into the miracle it becomes, by managing to keep them separate until the pastry is cooked.

Stirring or beating eggs or egg yolks over heat with milk or cream or wine, one must confidently wait for a real change in thickness, not a suggestion of change. It is a mistake to think this cannot be done over direct heat. There is a point when, instead of thickening, the custard seems to thin. Continue! When it is truly thickened, the wooden spoon will be 'pushing' its way through the custard. The action of pushing seems as silly as expecting a flour-and-water paste to be able to have the same consistency as butter, but pushing best describes the point at which the actions tells the cook that the custard is nearly at the point of curdling: perfection just before ruination. Continue! Continue past the point at which you think it sensible to remove the pan from the heat. If now you tilt the pan, the custard might show a little curdling on the base. Ah! Catch it now and pour immediately through a fine sieve into a cold bowl, and whisk it to dissipate the heat even more. If you've made a large amount and so the urgency is greater (because greater volume retains more heat), a second person is useful: hold that sieve, whisk that custard, while I tip. It's worth going too far with a custard at least once so that you know what ruin and waste look and feel like, for the texture will now be grainy and distressing. The opposite extreme is simply not custard but a thin, untransformed combination of ingredients on the way to completion. Soups thickened with egg yolks are often not creamy at all because the yolks have not been allowed to cook and truly thicken.

Of course, all this points to the obvious: you need to learn to cook by work-ing with someone else, not by reading books; reading books is a kind of addendum, you recognise what you know and make changes if you know more. You might teach yourself, knife, whisk and ladle in one hand, book in the other, but something will be missing. The point of a recipe is the final product and you need to know what the final product should be like. All recipes should include what many of them don't: a guide to what you are aiming for – texture, taste, consistency. As an apprentice, you'll learn not to add the sugar to the yolks too early lest the two 'cook'. You'll notice the cook place on a kitchen cloth the bowl into which the custard will be poured, so it doesn't skid about during the whisking. You'll notice that this bowl will be the one the original mixture was whisked in, because why use a second bowl when the first is now cold? You'll also pour less of the mixture down the sink this way: more dessert and less waste. And you will have learned all the little *trucs* which stand you in good stead for every kind of emulsion using eggs – a generic skill, practical knowledge.

As for the caramel on the surface of a crème brûlée, it has in modern kitchens been delegated to a blowtorch, but surely there's a limit to how many kitchen appliances one wants which are hardly ever used. It seems best to

Marrow spoon and salamander

stick to history and use a very hot grill if you do not have a salamander – and having a salamander is only useful if you have a stove with burners that have the power to make it red-hot, which most domestic stoves don't. The novelist Alice Thomas Ellis, who years ago had a column called 'Home Life' in the English magazine *The Spectator*, once reckoned the only kitchen tool she'd miss would be her potato peeler and she seemed to understand about cooking. I used to like to make apple pie in other people's houses as a gesture towards dinner, and have made do with all kinds of bottles as the rolling pin, even though I own a whole basketful of different and real ones: a huge and heavy model with handles on ball-bearings for making puff pastry; a tapered Huon pine pin that is more for feeling up than rolling flat; a Chinese rolling pin for the tiny pieces of wonton dough and buns, and crushing sea salt for sourdough; a modern chapati pin which is used for just that, and antique chapati pins that are painted and look like miniature dumbbells and are artefacts rather than useful tools; a standard but long pin for rolling biscuit and pasta dough.

The salamander we used at Berowra Waters Inn was made by the father of one of the cooks (his mother did the books, his brother and sister filled in when things got desperate in the dishwashing and waiting areas) somewhere around 1979. It did the job so well that I made a once-and-only television advertisement for a gas company, as part of a series featuring emancipated women from different professions cooking with gas, and managed to say, without lying, 'It works!', for the sake of commerce and with utter sincerity; it was gas I was referring to as well. A few days before the filming, a gas oven blew up in my face when I opened the door, singeing my hairline and taking some eyebrow too. Although we later replaced this oven with one that had a fail-safe pilot light, I have never since opened an oven without standing to one side and averting my face.

If everything goes according to perfect plan, which is generally not to be expected in life, *all* the sugar will have caramelised and *none* of the custard will have thinned because of the heat. I have ordered crème brûlée in many restaurants over my custard-making years, in the interests of comparison, and have found caramel made separately as a clear, thick, cut circle and plonked on top; caramel made so far in advance that it is already melting into the custard and has lost its brittleness; sugar so thick on the custard that only the top layer has been transformed into caramel. Sometimes it has been near-perfect, which is no less than we managed at Berowra Waters.

Caramel makes good, edible cement. When the cook whose father made the salamander turned twenty-one, we gave him a party. I made a curved wall of choux puffs mortared with caramel. It was large enough to hide my daughter who, dressed in a pink tutu, crouched behind the wall while we carried the 'cake' and the table into the dining-room. She sprang up to say happy birthday when the table had been lowered. The same cook, helping to make a more conventional *croquembouche* one day, knocked the saucepan of caramel onto the floor via my foot which, stupidly, was in a clog but without a sock. Caramel sticks and cooks onto surfaces. Most cooks have the odd horrendous story to tell, but our kitchen was almost accident-free; we were generally a sober, hardworking lot.

In the best of all possible worlds, the portion size of a dessert like crème brûlée would be somewhere around a thimbleful. This doesn't do in a restaurant where size is equated with value, but does do in a meal of numerous small portions which the French call a *dégustation*, a tasting, and which only the most serious and expensive restaurants manage to persuade us to enjoy. This approach to the palate goes against the grain of the wholesome bowl in the middle of the table for everyone to share, and needs many servants or waiters to make the effort to impress successful.

Crème brûlée

This amount of custard fills eight 125-ml ramekins. Bring 1 litre thick cream (around 45% fat) slowly to the boil with the peel of 2 lemons; 1 vanilla bean, split lengthwise; and 1 cinnamon stick, crushed. When the cream is near boiling point, whisk 7 egg yolks with 45 g caster sugar. Add the still-near-boiling cream to the yolks and sugar through a fine sieve and discard the flavourings. Whisk remorselessly to stop the heat curdling the eggs, and quickly tip the custard back into the saucepan. Stir until thickened and you are 'pushing' the spoon through the custard, which will not take long if you have worked fast to get it back on the stove. When thick (and remember you must run scared), pour into a cold bowl, again through a sieve, and continue to whisk for a moment to release more heat.

Fill the ramekins so that the surface of the custard is slightly convex, something you will only be able to do if the mixture has thickened sufficiently. Refrigerate until cold and set: the surface will have sunk to flat.

Sieve extra caster sugar over the top, thickly enough so that it will form a hard crust when cooked and also to protect the custard from the heat. Caramelise under a very hot griller, no earlier than, say, an hour or two before serving.

—

Lack of garnish is the characteristic, in absence, which is common to the three dishes we never took off the menu, and by extension to the kind of food that defined Berowra Waters Inn: the guinea fowl baked in clay; the saddle of hare or fillet of kangaroo with a purée of beetroot and tomato, a Michel Guérard recipe so perfect in flavour and matching depth of colour for those rare, dark meats that nothing else was ever considered; the spatchcock baked in a salt crust and served with a parsley sauce that was as close to a green vegetable as a cream sauce could be; rare tuna with our version of Phillip Searle's complex roasted-tomato chutney, different only because Searle, like all great artists, takes things to extremes, and we took a less formidable road.

Roasted-tomato chutney

This is Phillip Searle's recipe. The ingredients are 2 tablespoons black mustard seeds; 400 ml malt vinegar; 5 kg ripe tomatoes; 300 ml olive oil; 400 ml malt vinegar; 2 tablespoons black mustard seeds; 200 g peeled and chopped fresh ginger; 20 cloves garlic, peeled; 10 bird's-eye chillies (depending on your palate); 2 tablespoons ground turmeric; 4 tablespoons roasted cumin seeds; 2 tablespoons sambal oelek; 250 g palm sugar; and 100 ml fish sauce

Soak the mustard seeds overnight in the malt vinegar. Peel the tomatoes and then roast them in the olive oil for up to 3 hours at 200°C. Do not try to roast too many tomatoes at once, for they lose so much water that the oven fills with steam and stops the roasting process; if you have a small oven, do them in batches. They must be dark and almost dry. Blend all the ingredients except the tomatoes

Marrow spoon and salamander

and simmer the resulting paste slowly for up to an hour. Add the tomatoes and their roasting oil, and cook for 1–2 hours more, adding more oil if necessary. The chutney will be thick, dark, staining and hot – it would be against its nature to be mild, so add more chillies if you want.

The very purpose of chutneys, of course, is for the keeping and there's not much this one doesn't go with and enliven. I like it with scrambled eggs, late morning. Making a large amount will only persuade you to make an even larger amount next time.

—

Beetroot and tomato purée

Our version of Michel Guérard's recipe, producing far less (about six serves) than the huge potfuls we made at the restaurant. Sometimes a recipe does not work as well when shrunk – you might like to try doubling the ingredients.

Take 150 g spring onions, trimmed and chopped; 1 clove garlic, peeled and chopped; 1 tablespoon olive oil; ¼ cup balsamic vinegar; ¼ cup puréed roasted tomatoes; 350 g cooked beetroot; 100 ml game stock (reduced beef stock is okay); 1 teaspoon salt; ½ teaspoon pepper; 1 tablespoon cream. Soften the spring onions and garlic in the oil. Add the balsamic vinegar and cook hard, stirring to deglaze the pan. Add the tomatoes and beetroot, stock and seasonings, and cook gently for about 30 minutes. Add cream towards the end of the cooking time.

Purée in a blender until extremely smooth – the smoothness is one of the essential qualities of this dish, and a food processor will not produce a truly smooth purée. It should be thick enough to keep a slightly sloppy shape when plated.

—

Parsley and cream sauce

This quantity will serve eight. Blanch 150 g flat-leaf parsley (leaves only) in boiling water, i.e. throw the leaves into water at a rolling boil, bring back to the boil, leave for about 30 seconds then drain through a sieve and rinse under cold water.

Squeeze the blanched leaves well so that no water remains. Bring 600 ml thin cream to the boil, and reduce by half. If using a thicker cream, use less and reduce less. Add the parsley and boil for a moment longer.

Purée the mixture in a blender, and season to taste (as before, a blender will provide the smooth texture you want, not a food processor). If the sauce is too thin (it should nap the meat thickly and not run), reduce it further.

Why, when I vowed never to write a cookbook, does it seem necessary to include these recipes? Partly because they act as illustration; they are evidence. Partly because they are among the ones I unreservedly still believe in and still cook. Partly because I went to the recipe cards I have kept and then fell into that muffled, time-suspending experience known to all of us from looking through photograph albums.

In one of the essays in American novelist Nicholson Baker's *The Size of Thoughts*, he writes about the glee, the sense of celebration, with which libraries discard their old card catalogues when computerisation has been completed: 'Why would you want to shred or burn or dump these splendid shabby memorials, full of notes and adjustments, and datable by their faded color and their foxed corners . . . They hold the irreplaceable intelligence of the librarians who worked on them.' This reminds me first of sitting once a week at the public catalogue drawers of the Baillieu Library at Melbourne University in the sixties, refiling cards that had been removed by the cataloguing department. I worked there as a descriptive cataloguer, much lower down the hierarchy than the person who gave the book its Dewey number (and where I observed with a certain wry resignation that the smaller and more abstruse a publication, the more work and the more words were needed to describe it; which often applies to recipes as well). A metal rod slipped through the cards in each drawer: the filer sat on a high stool and moved along the groups of drawers. I like putting things in order and enjoyed this self-contained, easy work on the ground floor where students milled, yet from whom I was separate. This comfortable feeling seems to me to reflect one of the rules of restaurant life: you have to enjoy working in a situation where most others are playing.

Because of reading the Nicholson Baker essay I remembered the Berowra Waters Inn recipe cards, all tattered and torn, which fill two grimy wooden boxes. These are the closest thing to a working record of eighteen years of preparing and serving food on the river. The boxes are not large. There are some three hundred 15x10-cm cards, the A to Z tabs thumbed and bent – 'foxed', a cataloguer would say of a book – the cardboard thickened and dirty. One box is for first and main courses, the other for desserts, not because there was more of one than the others but because the physical preparation areas were partly physically separate. Some of the cards are hardly readable because of grease and liquids dispersed over and fading the handwriting. Sometimes there is a relatively new card for a recipe that I know to be old, so either it might not have been used for years or at some stage the original must have become so grubby and unreadable that one of the cooks had copied the instructions onto a new card. This would often be done late at night, at two or three o'clock in the morning while waiting for some preparation to finish cooking: Janni's slow-braising piece of tuna sitting still in olive oil in a barely warm oven, the veal stock reaching the point where the scudding coagulation could be skimmed off. Perhaps Liz Nolan, who worked beside Janni for years and who worked so hard despite her metabolism never adjusting to the demands of fitting five days work into three, would have written it out for him, because Janni did not like writing; he did other things with his hands.

Liz should be remembered for an act of bravery. Taking a stack of plates from an oven when we were cooking the banquet for the Fourth Symposium of Australian Gastronomy in 1988, she was surprised by their scorching heat. We were performing live, our normally hidden kitchen on show for the first and only time, a tribute to the cooks, and she knew that if she dropped the plates it would do damage to the flow. Instead she held on, placed them on the bench and kept on cooking. That night she was in a hospital emergency ward and for weeks cooked with a bandaged hand.

There are cards on which the handwriting places their date more easily than the dish, or part of the dish, itself. The earliest are in the neat hand of

Dennis Morvan, the priest who came to the restaurant in the early eighties when he was nearly forty and trained to become a cook instead. A good person, and a good palate. Many are in the handwriting of Huw Roberts, who trained at Berowra Waters Inn, went to London, then to Italy and a stint in a pastry kitchen in Bologna, and finally to university in Melbourne where he completed an arts/law degree. His writing is extremely neat; a conscientious person and tenacious too, his tenacity somehow a reaction to many sadnesses in his young life. I remember handing him, with amusement, a ruler to measure out portion size when he cut rectangles of panforte, his eye not being as precise as his *mise-en-place*.

There are the cards in my writing, in fact most of them are, either so neat that they were obvious attempts to standardise, or a scrawled adjustment of a measurement. Some are in Virginia Wong See's handwriting, rounded, careful. She had discarded her architecture studies for cooking, but after many years at Berowra Waters Inn went back to her degree. A few are in Janni's hand: these look like a mathematician's indecipherable formulas, the letters somehow pushing themselves into half-formed Cyrillic characters, even though for Janni at that time being in Australia represented a forgetting of Greece. Later, and after the twelve years on the river, he would make use of his culinary heritage; as well as age often increasing sentiment, the restaurant world had moved to embrace culinary differences and the critics probably made more of dishes that reflected his childhood in Thessaloniki than Janni did himself. The first staff meal he presided over (these were unashamed ways of avoiding waste), included mashed potatoes, which we all loved. The potatoes had been cooked with the pods removed from kilos of broad beans. My mother always did this, he said.

If the number of recipe cards is not large, and tells of a menu that did not change easily, then there are far too many boxes of menus. Every time there was even one change to the menu or a change to a component of a dish, or a price rise or a menu for a special occasion, I filed that menu away, wine lists as well. On the one hand they tell a slow story, a chant with rare changes of key, and on the other they are a record of, for the first years, frantic hand-writing (squeezed in between cooking and service), then of the shift to photocopying from the one hand-written menu, and of a last shift to the neat impersonality of printing. The font used for the restaurant name never ceased to please me, even if I had pinched it from *The New Yorker* magazine in 1977 by cutting out letters and taking them to the printer. The glorious 'w'! The 's'!

—

Our indebtedness to the techniques of European cuisines, especially French, informing the use of Australian produce, was a legacy from Tony Bilson, continued and tempered by myself and Janni. It would not be too great a generalisation to say that most accredited, self-consciously, culinarily explorative restaurants of the early eighties fitted into this category. Later we became more eclectic, and more free of self-imposed restrictions, and for many different reasons – travel, reading, the grapevine of local culinary life, a certain intermittent ennui, changing times, independent confidence, competitive spirit, ludic excesses, an odd truly creative shift or two, and the arrival of far better produce. People deeply interested in flavour and produce constituted exactly the same proportion of diners as they always have and will, but a younger group found they were interested in food; and an even younger group stayed with fast and nasty.

Janni and I loved saffron and the suggestion of chillies, cardamom and cumin, salted lemons, star anise, soy, palm sugar, squid ink; a lentil dhal became the base for grilled Coffin Bay scallops; barley replaced rice for a stuffing. But we still loved confit of duck and roasted pigeons, seared duck livers, braised skate, Oysters Rockefeller, slowly baked custards and straight-down-the-line French pastry. And so it went on, macaronic perhaps, as were most of the dishes of this transition. There was a sensation of making something up as you went along (which is what we were all doing in the eighties), forging something that felt original even though we were borrowing from long-established cuisines. But always we held to a formal and, as I resorted to calling it at the time, intelligent, framework.

Oysters Rockefeller
This is my version via ingredients listed in various references and in American cookbooks, including that of Alice B. Toklas, who wrote that in France the dish

'made more friends for the United States than anything I know'. One year, the English chef Simon Hopkinson, having dined at Antoine's in New Orleans where the dish ('as rich as a Rockefeller') was created, sent me a menu smeared with dirty green. The main difference between all these versions and ours is in the refinement of the spinach mixture.

We first served Oysters Rockefeller in 1992 at a dinner held to announce the winner of the Pascall Prize for critical writing in the media. That year the area of expertise nominated was food and Alan Saunders won. The judges were Barbara Santich, Marion Halligan and myself. Because Geraldine Pascall had been a journalist in the mid-seventies, we compiled a menu of retro dishes. The main course was Chicken Kiev which, approached with discrimination, is a fine dish and restores its reputation. The dinner, and much else about Berowra Waters Inn, has been made fictional in Marion Halligan's novel, *The Point*.

This amount of spinach mixture coats somewhere around enough oysters for six, if the portion is around 4 per serve; one cannot be absolutely specific. Pacifics are best for Rockefeller because they provide a deep shell to fill. Sometimes we served just one as an appetiser. Any left-over mixture makes a marvellous green chowder with the addition of a dice of potato, fish stock and, at the last minute, oysters.

SPINACH MIXTURE

For the spinach mixture you will need 50 g chopped spring onions; 75 g finely chopped celery; 300 g butter; 750 g fresh, young spinach leaves (stalks and central veins discarded), roughly chopped; 25 g chopped parsley; 15 g chopped French tarragon; 1 teaspoon Tabasco sauce; 40 ml Pernod; 1 teaspoon salt, or to taste; about 1 cup of fresh breadcrumbs (amount will vary depending on the thickness of the purée); and extra Pernod in a spray bottle. Sauté the spring onions and the celery in the butter. Add the spinach leaves, parsley and tarragon, tossing briefly over high heat until the spinach is wilted and cooked but still bright green. Purée this mixture in a blender until absolutely smooth (a food processor will not do this); if it's too thin to form a mound, fold in breadcrumbs as required. Add the Tabasco, Pernod and salt.

Marrow spoon and salamander

Cover each freshly opened oyster with the spinach purée, moulding it within the shell to completely bury the oyster and make a smooth green mound. Place oysters on a bed of rock salt on a baking tray, burying some of the shell in the salt (this holds the shells upright and, importantly, insulates the oysters, leaving them warm and hardly cooked while the spinach mixture is hot). Bake in a very hot oven, say 220°C, for about 8 minutes. Spray with Pernod before serving.

—

Much has been made of the offal and extremities on the menu associated with the years when Janni Kyritsis was chef. In the interests of arcane scholarship, I once included pigs' kidneys in the almond mixture for Gâteau Pithiviers, but never said so in public. The idea of eating stuffed pigs' ears and trotters, tongue, veal kidneys, sweetbreads, brains and tripe, and especially blood sausage, seemed to titillate some diners but Janni and I shared a genuine liking for these meats; and while we found this predilection was genuinely shared by some, we had to persuade others to find heart for it; a good many stood firm and against. It is unsurprising that Janni didn't think twice about these meats, for he had an obsessive and creative attitude towards waste. For myself, it was surprising: I grew up on mid-loin lamb chops in the forties and fifties, with only the very occasional appearance of 'lamb's fry' (chop, kidney and liver plus crisp bacon).

Pigeon, a glorious red meat, has a flavour suggestive of liver and a texture with a certain faint slipperiness. One of the first impressive dishes Tony and I ate in Paris in the mid-seventies on that first culinary journey was a piece of calf liver, roasted – yes, roasted, fast and short – and sliced to reveal rare perfection. But then we have had a dismal history of butchery in Australia and when at the restaurant we wanted to follow suit, milk-fed calf liver was not available, nor were tender sweetbreads or palatable veal kidneys; they still don't exist unless you have the resources, especially monetary, to find them. If the French still have culinary standing in the face of our growing and pertinent interest in culinary Asia, then it is as fishermen, agriculturists and butchers.

Years after Berowra Waters Inn closed, I received the gift of a box of deep-water fish caught only a long moment before in the waters off the south-east coast of South Australia. As I cleaned and gutted, I encountered a fish I had never seen before. It looked much like the monkfish of Europe, but was, the fisherman's wife said, a 'stargazer'. The flesh was marvellous, but better, a huge liver was found with the guts. We sautéed it and found we were eating something remarkable, approaching the velvet richness of foie gras. Different offal and extremities have different and distinctive flavours and textures; 'variety meats' is a deflective euphemism, but accidentally points to what is so attractive about these cuts.

In 1991, for a banquet organised by Sydney's Mardi Gras director to raise funds for Aids research, we made Tongue in Cheek with a crunch of pig's ear and pickled walnuts as garnish. Braised ox cheek surrounded the veal tongue, which itself was wrapped in roasted red capsicum and the whole held by its jelly as a terrine. The deep-black pickled walnuts, extra produce from a South Australian vineyard and shockingly acid, took the place of black truffles which in France pigs usefully find in pheremonal frenzy. I put my daughter on the table here too: she ran the length of the huge rectangle for two hundred, a table sprite inviting the meal to begin. Damien Pignolet made Fish out of Water, a perfect, poached *boudin rose* of salmon mousseline. Tongue in Cheek and Fish out of Water were upstaged by Phillip Searle's remarkable, immense icecream, Ball and Chain. Sculpted around a steel frame in a very large portable freezer, it took the form of a giant, medieval spiked weapon designed to melt in the mouth instead of kill. The splendid object (weighing in at over 200 kilograms) called for two thousand eggs, ninety litres of cream, forty-five litres of milk and more than five hundred hours of work: it was carried down the length of an enormous rectangle of diners by twelve naked, clay-smeared men and women, accompanied by the *Music for Ball and Chain*, which percussionist Tony Buck had written especially for the occasion. The spikes on this instrument of war were made from biscuit cones filled with raspberry sorbet and vanilla icecream, and tipped in silver leaf. There were around two hundred and fifty of these, each about twenty-five centimetres long. After the ball's slow-motion, Crusade-like entrance, waiters broke away the cones and placed them on plates to become benign desserts.

Marrow spoon and salamander

73

Phillip Searle, an artist of the edible, is, it would seem, a contemporary incarnation of Antonin Carême, *pâtissier* and *cuisinier*, who famously wrote that 'the fine arts are five in number – painting, sculpture, poetry, music, architecture, whose main branch is confectionery'. His caramel parfait is a very grown-up icecream.

Phillip Searle's caramel parfait

The caramel must be taken close to burning so that a slight bitterness is achieved and the sense of sweet sugar is lost. A parfait is extremely rich, made by beating sugar syrup into egg yolks. It is not churned, a great bonus, but you do need to own an electric mixer – my old and domestic Kenwood copes well with this amount of parfait.

For twelve portions, you will need 500 g sugar; 150 ml water; 200 ml cream and, separately, another 750 ml cream; and 10 egg yolks. In a large saucepan (because when the cream is added to the caramel the mass becomes an active volcano), cook the sugar and water to a very dark caramel. Bring the 200 ml cream to the boil and add it to the caramel in the saucepan, standing back from the molten splutter.

Meanwhile, whisk the yolks in a mixer at high speed until they are pale and thick. When the caramel is ready, add it in a steady stream to the yolks in the mixing bowl and continue to beat until the mixture is at room temperature. Whisk the 750 ml cream and fold it through the yolk–caramel mixture.

Having chilled the bowls you want to store it in, preferably the ones you will serve from as parfaits melt easily, fill them, cover with clingwrap, and freeze. This amount fills two 850-ml bowls.

It's only a restaurant, for god's sake

Requiem for caviar

Two memories of the last service at Berowra Waters Inn in 1995 cling as uncomfortably as cobwebs. The most powerful and lasting is a story about portion control and caviar.

One good reason to keep a restaurant open is to avoid waste. At the close of that last service we pulled all produce and left-over *mise-en-place* from the coolroom and distributed it on two benches, one for keeping (to be divvied up among waiters and cooks, neighbours and friends), one for the bin. There was, for the first time since Janni Kyritsis had become chef, a rather large amount of food which had to be thrown away. Janni filled a box with particular left-overs for me, his choice based on the reasoning that as I had paid for all the produce, anything of real expense should be mine. He was always extremely strict about this principle. In that 'owner's' box was a 200-gram tin of Oscietra caviar. My reaction was embarrassment. I have never asked him why it wasn't used: I had bought a certain amount of Oscietra (not as second best to Beluga or Sevruga, but by preference) to use with potato pancakes and sour cream as the last appetiser served at the restaurant. We'd worked out the portions: the extravagance was worth the extravagance, which is to say that the caviar was worth the expense, and there was enough for a mounded spoonful for each 'sandwich' – potato pancake, spoonful of crème fraîche, spoonful of Oscietra, pancake – the perfect mouthful to begin in the days when we were wilfully ignorant of the depleted sturgeon stocks and the pollution of the Caspian Sea.

Did Ben, the young man who prepared and cooked the first courses, simply serve too little, over-concerned that we needed to feed eighty guests from the two tins and so underestimating the amount he could use for each serve? This should not have been the case, as we were extremely good at portioning – of course we were, that's what restaurant kitchens do. Did Janni in his obsession with controlling portions (even though we had a reputation for large portions, this was a trait that helped keep Berowra Waters Inn financially viable) suggest to Ben that he should try to use only one tin, not two? Whatever the case, we had not given enough. I wanted to run to each diner and place a spoonful of caviar in their mouth – to apologise, but it was too late. I didn't want a tin of caviar, had wanted the portion to be properly generous so that the warm, light, white coin-sized pancakes, the modestly sour crème fraîche would only just wrap the salt-crunch explosion of caviar in the mouth, would make a velvet blanket around what I still think is the queen of all produce. Financial viability was not the point any more.

Once, years ago, as the seventies pushed towards the eighties and not long after my first introduction to caviar, I wrote a column for a Sydney newspaper listing ten food-related wishes for what might lie under the Christmas tree. One wish was for a copper pan I could not afford. A distant relation, on reading the column, sent me a copper braising pan which I still use. Another wish was for the one-kilogram tin of Beluga caviar seen at Cyril's delicatessen in the Haymarket. Cyril often had fine foods that couldn't be found elsewhere; he also stocked an Estonian sweet-and-sour bread I still consider one of the best breads to have been made in Australia: deeply moist, fine-crumbed, the smell of central Europe, a bread that did not seem able to go stale. M, a close friend who later became a professional restaurant reviewer and has one of the best palates I know, had introduced me to this bread and to Cyril's shelves. He suggested we buy, with the help of five other friends, that tin of caviar. The cost was $600, which later seemed extremely reasonable. But when I wrote that column, was I dreaming of the intrinsic taste of caviar or of all that caviar represented?

Crime novelist Ian Rankin's Edinburgh policeman John Rebus mused, in *Knots and Crosses*, on how it seemed that 'the more expensive something was, the less of it there always seemed to be: tiny little hi-fi systems, watches without numbers . . .'. French writer Colette averred that if she couldn't have too many truffles then she would do without, and that to have too much caviar was far preferable to having hardly enough. Just this once, my friends and I decided, we would put this to the test at a private table, and we were right: even the largest single caviar egg is the equivalent of a watch without numbers, but if you have too much rather than too little the expense makes more sense. We had taken the flat brown band of rubber from our tin of Beluga, lifted the lid and placed the tin itself, bright-blue and gold and black (the colours Twinings uses to package Russian Caravan tea), proudly in the centre of the table. This seemed bold at the time. M had made blinis (buckwheat-flour pancakes lightened with yeast and beaten egg whites, although many recipes today do not specify buckwheat) and in innocence we had included garnishes of sieved hard-boiled egg, chives, chopped onion and lemon wedges as well as sour cream. Now, along with most other garnishes, I would discard these except for sour or cultured cream.

It is pleasing to have this discarding of all garnishes supported by Alan Davidson's entry for caviar in his 1999 *Oxford Companion to Food*:

> Those with professional knowledge and experience of caviar are virtually unanimous in recommending against providing garnishes such as chopped onion to go with it. Their recommendation would be to open the (chilled) tin only a few minutes before serving the contents, preferably from the tin itself but otherwise from a porcelain saucer and in any case with a non-metallic implement, and accompanied only by very thin toast (or blinis) and a delicate unsalted butter (or sour cream), with the use of lemon discouraged.

The entry for 'caviare' (sic) in *Kettner's Book of the Table* by E. S. Dallas, first published in 1877, is marvellously short: 'If it were not a pleasure it would be an imperative duty to eat caviare, for reasons which will be given when we come to sturgeon, of which it is the roe. It is spread on toast, with a squeeze of lemon.' I turned to the entry on sturgeon; it was once a rich source of isinglass as well as caviar. In Henry Green's 1945 novel *Loving*, isinglass was used to preserve pea-cocks' eggs. Dallas, tongue in cheek, recommended the consumption of caviar or salted sturgeon eggs as a way of containing the species' then-galloping repro-duction rates. The females produce, in season, a weight of eggs sometimes equal to two-thirds of the total weight of the fish: 'At such a rate of reproduction the world would soon become the abode of sturgeons alone, were it not that the roe is exceedingly good, and the lovers of caviare are more general than Shakespeare knew.' This last comment, unexplained by Dallas, is a punning reference to lines from *Hamlet* which John Ayto quoted in full in *The Diner's Dictionary* (1993): 'For the Play, I rememberd, pleas'd not the Million, 'twas Cauiarie to the generall: but it was an excellent Play.' Ayto also mentions that the word caviar has been used to describe the printing over of censored text with a 'pattern of black-and-white diamond-shapes, supposed reminiscent of the appearance of black caviare spread on bread and butter'. His entry is almost entirely centred on the etymology of the word, as are his other 1199 entries. A useful book.

From the 1960s, pollutants were being pumped into the Caspian Sea, and by the early 1990s the legal and illegal harvesting of roe-producing sturgeon had depleted stocks much more drastically and tragically than Dallas could ever have imagined might be achieved by eating caviar. Waverley Root, in his marvellous, albeit sometimes flawed, *Food* recalls how cheap caviar once was in the United States, so cheap in fact that it was served free in saloons – wouldn't you know, its saltiness increased thirst and so more liquor was sold. This was around the close of the nineteenth century and presumably the eggs were collected from American sturgeon, once plentiful.

Novelist Richard Condon, who also wrote marvellously about food (espe-cially the great Sicilian dishes demanded by the Mob), introduces caviar of a sort in his novel *Winter Kills*:

> He remembered the épergne at the center of Mama's table on which she would place the bowl filled with homemade caviar on the day of the month when she would invite the locals in to be enthralled by her music. Mama made caviar out of tapioca, fish broth, squid ink and lemon juice,

which allowed each guest to have as much caviar as he or she wished. 'It would be a cruel thing to give these good, provincial people a real caviar habit,' Mama had explained.

What is it about caviar? Rarity and expense do not explain its luxury. It truly is one of the great 'tastes' among which I would include truffles, great cheeses like Stilton and Roquefort, and great wines such as, to my taste anyway, precious red Burgundies. In fact, caviar stands apart and above all these tastes. It is not made, like a great wine or a great cheese; truffles lift another food, while caviar is complete. When a scientist says things like 'I can't stand to smell it. I can't stand to look at it. It's just not American food' (a scientist who has been isolating DNA from sturgeon roe for the American Museum of Natural History in New York) or 'The more I see, the less I'm tempted' (a special agent with a degree in wildlife biology, who is part of a team policing standards on the importation of caviar into the States and has never tasted it), I can only deem them objective and safe men for their particular jobs, beyond corruption.

In none of the dictionaries of food I have quoted from is there any attempt to describe why we who treasure it do so. Caviar is a combination of salt, fishiness, oil and textural bite, which description does it exact justice but does not explain its seductiveness to the palate. Peter Fuller, the British art critic who died in 1990, published his intense and beautifully written autobiography *Marches Past* in 1986. Juxtaposed diary entries from 1975 to 1978 reveal him naked mid-psychoanalysis; at one point he records eating oysters in France with his French wife's family:

[Colette's mother] puts two short, sharp-pointed rigid knives on the table. The oysters, tightly clenching their grey shells, are alive. One by one, we murder them into our napkins. Fathers fuse with strong, tugging muscles, yielding in each little drama behind my jamming fingers; the salty, mucus sniff of sea-sex, molly-coddling, each time bringing back the first time that the tongue tasted, there. Mothers mingle with that swallowing of a living, whole, bitter-sweet, soft dampness, cool down the throat, into the belly . . . Pleasure and nausea twist together as I skewer the knife into that all-signifying hole. Penetrate. Cleave. Separate. Incorporate. A calcerous crash: the indigestible shell smashes onto the plate. I take another. Close to the tang of briny jelly, a whiff, a hint, of oil or sewage.

No one, as far as I know, has done for caviar what Peter Fuller has done for oysters and analysis.

Caviar is not delicious. I can almost understand why some people don't like it. While I remember the first time I ate a dish with white truffles (shaved over potato gnocchi at Ranieri's in Rome, 1975), I can't quite place my first taste of caviar, although I think it may have been a spoonful from one of the Lalique bowls placed on A's table in Hunter's Hill in 1977. If it was at this dinner, staged and cooked by A, then it is possible that I reacted to this entirely new taste in euphoric gratitude; for its generosity, its flair and its tutelage. A had – still has, of course, it isn't a trait one loses – impeccable taste, an attribute that might seem to be superficial but is, I think, in its most profound form, of great import. In *Kettner's Book of the Table*, Dallas defines taste as distinct from the other senses because, unlike them, it 'is made for marriage, and smell is its better half.' Whereas the other senses increase when one or other of them is deprived, taste works in tandem with smell and sight and touch, it needs the others to heighten its pleasures. He also draws attention to the use of the word 'taste' to describe more than the ability of the tongue to distinguish flavours. This observation is of interest because he includes it in a dictionary of food ('We have one and the same name for the faculty which comprehends a sucking-pig and for that which delights in Beethoven').

So that introduction to caviar included other seductions. I knew that caviar cost more money than I could contemplate spending on food, but I knew nothing about its production and collection – for instance, that the female sturgeon was still necessarily alive when the eggs were taken from its body (nowadays the fish are anaesthetised beforehand). I was still of the 'I don't kill them, I just eat them' persuasion. And I knew little of the mystique attached to these eggs which are produced so prodigiously – which fact caused Nancy Mitford's mother, in response to Nancy having had both ovaries removed, to exclaim: 'Both! But I thought one had hundreds, like caviar!' At A's dinner I was seduced by the table, the beauty, the finesse, the shape, the crafting of the accoutrements, by the production of the whole evening, by A's sophisticated yet charmingly off-hand service, a kind of deliberate dismissal of formality and a flippancy towards the rituals of service which, of course, made them all the more formal, requisite and alluring.

Rereading (a minor bad habit of middle age; there isn't time) Edmund Crispin, who wrote entertaining and erudite thrillers, and who was the right vintage to mix with Evelyn Waugh and Philip Larkin, reminded me in turn to reread a thriller by Michael Innes (an academic known for his detective fiction) in which 'a pea-green undergraduate . . . could be heard incoherently repeating from *Brideshead Revisited* the majestic passage on caviar aux blinis and the hot, thin, bitter, frothy oseille . . .' I reread *Brideshead Revisited* and found that very French meal eaten in a Parisian restaurant very much of its period (*Brideshead* was published in 1945), the caviar playing just the kind of role it always has, lifting the menu a notch or three, adding class and luxury:

> . . . soup of oseille, a sole quite simply cooked in a white-wine sauce, a caneton à la presse, a lemon soufflé. At the last minute, fearing that the whole thing was too simple for Rex, I added caviar aux blinis. And for wine I let him give me a bottle of 1906 Montrachet, then at its prime, and, with the duck, a Clos de Bèze of 1904.

By the time the narrator had come to entertain, with a gourmet's surefootedness, in Paris, the tragic Sebastian Flyte – who had an elephant's foot waste-paper basket and Lalique glass in his rooms at Oxford, and had introduced the narrator to strawberries accompanied by Château Peyraguey – was lost to world-weariness and drink. This, happily, is not how A has ended up. Nevertheless A, it became clear, was my Sebastian Flyte. Indeed A has played Lord Flyte for more acolytes in Sydney than I can count eggs in a deerhorn-spoonful of caviar, but this does not diminish his influence, which is felt by each individual in much the same way that we all, apart, taste food.

Blinis

This recipe comes from an article on caviar by Darra Goldstein in the American magazine *Saveur*, January–February 1998. The omission of the traditional whisked egg whites has little effect on the lightness of the pancake.

You will need 1¼ teaspoons active dry yeast; 1 cup (250 ml) lukewarm milk; ½ cup buckwheat flour; ½ teaspoon sugar; ¼ teaspoon salt; ⅔ cup plain flour; 2 tablespoons sour cream; ¼ cup heavy cream; 2 eggs, lightly beaten; and 1 tablespoon unsalted butter, melted and cooled.

Mix the yeast, milk, buckwheat flour, sugar and salt, then cover and leave for about an hour in order to activate the yeast. Add the rest of the ingredients, cover and leave for another 1½–2 hours, until risen and light.

Melt a little extra butter in a pan over medium–high heat and drop in dessertspoonfuls of the mixture. Turn the blinis once risen and set; the base will be golden-brown after about 2 minutes. Cook on the other side for about a minute.

Keep the blinis warm in a very low oven if they cannot be served at once, although I have sometimes kept them at room temperature for some time and found them still to be light and moreish. They are equally good with salmon or ocean-trout roe, and should be light and taste slightly undersalted to balance the saltiness of the roe.

﹣

When the love interest from the lower deck ate upstairs in James Cameron's big mush of a movie, *Titanic*, he was faced with an outrageously large bowl of caviar offered by a waiter. He had never seen caviar before and lied that it was not to his taste. This is exactly what children do when faced with something they've never had – say they don't like it. One wonders what substituted for the real thing in that bowl (dyed sago?), but the flatware laid out in a bewildering stretch in front of the young man included a genuine and lovely deerhorn spoon.

Tarquin Winot, virtuosic culinary pedant and murderer, the antihero of John Lanchester's black comedy of conceptualism, *The Debt to Pleasure*, asks '. . . if Marmite was as hard to come by as caviar, would it be as highly prized?' In the light of the novel's black humour, it is not wayward to connect this question with the 'scarcity theory of value' posited by Thorstein Veblen. Winot, who spends much of the novel telling us what he knows, tells us that 'Ossetra, whose eggs span the spectrum of colors from dirty battleship to occluded sunflower, is my roe of choice'. 'Caviar', he says, 'is sometimes eaten by chess players as a way of rapidly consuming a considerable quantity of easily digestible protein, without any of the stupefying effects of a bona fide meal.' So another triumphant attribute of caviar is that satiation is not limited by richness, as it is with other expensive foods such as foie gras and lobster, although these chess players are presumably Russian and closer to the source. Caviar remains light, even though it is rich in its own oil-coated way. In this respect it is a fresh and clean food. I adored it. Past tense. Past tense, that is, except for a serve of 'Caluga', the name given to a caviar produced in China and which I ate in Shanghai. It tasted of sump oil and was more mush than bite, but they say the quality varies. And again, past tense, that is, except for a minuscule garnish of Japanese caviar swallowed with the first of the two mouthfuls of a cucumber 'vichyssoise' in a tiny shot glass that began a meal made up entirely of appetisers. This version of a cocktail party was in the very grand and formal restaurant at Te Papa Museum in Wellington at the close of the Australian Symposium of Gastronomy's holiday to New Zealand in 2001. The stolen pleasure, the caviar, was all bite and little flavour, more a pointillist spill of colour on a pale-green miniature pond.

In dictionaries of food, caviar always comes directly after cauliflower, which I find amusing. Cauliflower is so humble and, baked in a cheese sauce, is chiefly associated for Anglo-Saxon Australians with Sunday roasts. But, better, cauliflower makes a fine pairing with caviar and as soup is garnished most successfully with it.

The right potatoes make great sense with caviar too, just as they do with white truffles. When chef Simon Hopkinson turned forty in 1994 he was given a grand and very English party near Bristol. We drove to the house the day before, Simon at the wheel while I shelled French beans (yes, beans) beside him. He cooked for the house-guests the night before the marquee, the pig and the champagne. The first course was a bowl of steamed Jersey Royal potatoes with caviar and crème fraîche; the main course was roasted chicken and the French beans; and the cheese, a washed-rind from Wales, was exemplary.

Years after this lesson in combining the humble and the grand, Keith Lewis, a singer of renown born in New Zealand but living in London, a maker of marvellous marmalade, an old-fashioned correspondent who writes letters in ink from European café tables between rehearsals, and who once posted me a box of *canelés* (small fluted cakes from the pâtisserie Baillardran in Bordeaux), told me about eating, at Vier Jahreszeiten in Hamburg, a dish of sieved potato with caviar; the chef apparently calls the dish, which sounds like a savoury Mont Blanc, *Kartoffel Schnee* ('potato snow'). He uses what Keith thinks must be baked old potatoes, sieved just before the dollop of caviar is dropped on top and a spoonful of sour cream added to the plate; thus, the potato is still hot. In Sydney I surprised Keith with an approximation of the dish as he had described it, calling ours 'Worms and Caviar'.

Requiem for a restaurant

Twenty-five years after what were not so much excesses (it wasn't as if I kept caviar in the fridge with the butter) as exceptional pleasures that educated the palate and played their part in refining a sense of culinary aesthetics, there I was, no longer with boatloads of diners to feed and with 200 grams of Oscietra which I didn't want – not only didn't want, but was embarrassed to have.

The second uncomfortable memory is of standing at the door leading into the kitchen, facing away from the dining-room and the river. The last service had begun. Someone told me to turn around. Chugging past the restaurant was the big ferry that made its living hosting parties and sightseeing tours of Berowra Waters and the Hawkesbury estuary. The people aboard were waving to us, and over the loudspeakers we heard strains of the Maori Farewell Song. The restaurant diners were waving back, laughing, cheering, clapping. I brought my hands up to my mouth in astonishment and some emotion, even crying a little. The whole scene seemed so spontaneous, was so momentarily moving – a theatrical gesture of local solidarity.

C, a painter (of canvases, not houses) who cleaned the restaurant and ironed the waiters' shirts for years, saying he liked the company, and who lived on the river and fought tirelessly for its health and sustainability, had organised this literally moving tableau. The timing was perfect and we were taken by surprise, but I was faking it. Oh, the tears were there all right, but it was more that the moment seemed to ask for them. Milan Kundera has suggested that watching oneself cry, as I was, might be a definition of kitsch. In *Immortality* he writes, 'As soon as we want to feel, feeling is no longer feeling but an imitation of feeling . . . This is not to say that a person who imitates feeling does not feel.'

I chose to close Berowra Waters Inn after eighteen years because I was tired and had lost the passion for the restaurant that gave legitimacy to asking others to work there. I didn't want to cook for a living any more and didn't want to ask others to cook if my heart and hands weren't in it too; this doesn't seem to worry some other cooks I know. Somehow I had always cooked by an accident of finding myself in a kitchen, not because I had headed for the kitchen in the first place. By now I knew that there would never be the money to complete the building to Glenn Murcutt's marvellous plan, nor even to mend every crack as it aged. I wanted to move on and away, not necessarily towards something else but on and away. I wanted to be free of the responsibilities of being The Employer. I wanted no one else but Janni Kyritsis to lead the kitchen and yet had no idea how long Janni would want to stay. Our professional partnership, which had been a glorious one for so many years, was tired, jaded, cranky. So, for whatever it was worth, those public yet perfectly modest tears in the dining-room on the last day of Berowra Waters Inn were, at most, a display of loyalty to those who worked there and to those who ate there. P, the waiter who, when he first arrived at the restaurant, seemed too old-fashioned to fit in with the other waiting staff and who became one of the most valued and loved of all of them, was overcome by emotion during the last service and cried real tears. He had chatted beforehand to the *Bulletin* journalist Lenore Nicklin while picking over salad leaves with another waiter, and she later said that he had worried about the effect on Janni of closing the restaurant, for he had now been there for twelve years. I knew, or perhaps I only really know in retrospect, that Janni would simply shift his loyalty to another place, without undoing the years of dedication to Berowra Waters Inn. This wasn't a case of a factory closing and unemployment looming: the credentials of all the people who worked at the restaurant were impeccable; they could choose where they wanted to work. Instead it seemed more like giving them back their lives, their weekends, their privacy. And, selfishly, it gave me freedom from my responsibilities to them.

In retrospect, and despite overseeing the revitalisation of Bennelong Restaurant at the Sydney Opera House for three years after leaving Berowra Waters Inn, I realise that I didn't really want to work with anyone else at all, not any cooks, not any waiters. I'd had enough of restaurants. I'd lost my heart and ego to one, and one was enough. It wasn't just about cooking – the food was, I honestly think, the least of it. You don't lose your heart to making meals for a living but to a larger idea, even when that idea is centred on cooking good food. And you don't lose your heart to caviar, or to any food. You accumulate memories that include the myriad other details of the senses. The last menu:

Potato pancakes, Oscietra caviar, sour cream and chives
Brioche with bone marrow, échalotes and red-wine butter
Roasted pigeon, pigeon liver, mushrooms and pigeon sauce
Peppered kingfish, celeriac and smoked fish roe butter
Warm salad of grilled witlof and roasted onion
Tomato consommé
Desserts
Coffee and macaroons

26 March 1995

Cooks: Janni Kyritsis, Ben McIntyre, Christine Osmond, Oonagh Loftus

It was an unpretentious meal. Nothing fancy, nothing precious except the caviar, and central to its structure the deliberate, inverted gradation from rich meat through fish to vegetables and then clear vegetable (tomatoes are a very vegetable-like fruit) soup. With more conviction on my part there would have been no dessert, but most people, for reasons completely incomprehensible to me, want to bury the savoury under a sweet decay of sugar. I've a theory that one way to address the sugar problem might be to offer a glass of a complex 'sweet' wine at the menu's commencement – a Barsac, say, or a remarkable Austrian *Trockenbeerenauslese*; and even, if one has to, include sweetness at the close by doing the same in abstemious portion. After all, someone once described Château d'Yquem as 'Crème brûlée in a glass'.

Potato pancakes

This is the Berowra Waters Inn version of Crèpes Parmentier in Georges Blanc's *Ma Cuisine des Saisons*.

Take 500 g steamed potato flesh (Désirée work well), weighed after peeling, and passing through a fine mouli. Mix in 25 ml milk, 3 tablespoons sieved plain flour, 3 whole eggs and 4 egg whites (½ cup). Finally, add 3 tablespoons thick cream and season with ½ teaspoon pepper and 1 teaspoon salt (or salt to taste).

Melt a little clarified butter in a pan, drop in spoonfuls of the mixture to form little pancakes about 5 cm in diameter, and cook for 3–4 minutes on each side. Keep warm in a low oven, although best eaten straight away and as hot as possible.

Peppered fish with smoked fish roe butter

These are Janni Kyritsis' recipes. At Berowra Waters Inn our preferred fish for this dish was mackerel, which is quite oily; you could substitute a firm white-fleshed fish.

THE FISH

For eight portions you will need eight 200-g, thick fillets of fish, skin left on; olive oil; 4 teaspoons freshly ground coriander seeds; 4 teaspoons freshly ground fennel seeds; and 8 teaspoons cracked black peppercorns, sieving out any powder. The oven should be preheated to 180°C.

Coat the fish on all sides except the skin – aim for a thick crust of spices. Sear the fillets on all sides in very hot olive oil and then place in the preheated oven for 10–15 minutes. The fish should be only just cooked through.

SMOKED FISH ROE BUTTER

You will need 100 g smoked fish roe (we used orange-ruffy roe, but I believe this is now unavailable), weighed after scraping away from the membrane; 2 tablespoons lemon juice; 2 tablespoons water; 2 cloves of garlic; 1 teaspoon ground white pepper; 400 g softened, unsalted butter. Using a blender, proceed as if making a mayonnaise, adding the butter as you would oil. The resulting mixture should be very smooth. Serve the butter as a hot sauce by whisking it over medium heat. Alternately, spoon some of the room-temperature butter onto the fish.

A good vegetable to serve as a bed for the fish is blanched matchsticks of celeriac. If you are serving the butter as Janni did, spoon some over the vegetable and then place the fish on top. This leaves the spice crust crisp and best flavours the celeriac.

—

It had long become clear to me that, in making the main course the most filling of the progression of dishes in a European menu, too much is asked of the appetite. Like a short story, a menu needs to be going somewhere but it should also release the diner with a satisfaction that does not lead to satiation. That meal of tiny portions in Wellington, the meal disguised as cocktail nibbles, by never reaching a main course made one ponder the place of a central and filling dish. It was not a persuasion for a succession of mouthfuls instead of more substantial dishes, but was food for thought.

Possibly the greatest cuisine is that developed by the Cantonese, and its menus lead one away from a central climax. One might say that the progression is one of undoing satiation: the menu is the sum of its digressions and the digressions follow an order, within the apparent arrival of everything at once, which is so much more accommodating to the appetite. To have fish after meat and a broth after the fish is a supremely intelligent progression, yet in the West the menu follows a set rule that puts the soup before the fish and the fish before the meat, the exact opposite. Wanting to leave the table still hungry is a perverse desire but if, instead, the elements become less filling as the meal progresses, appreciation is extended.

There is another difference between French and Chinese cookery that fascinates me: the French place paramount importance on stocks and reductions – the *fonds de cuisine* – as a foundation for last-minute cooking, while the Chinese begin from scratch. Their *mise-en-place* is more to do with fermented, pickled, salted and dried stores, and a broth might only be made after the meat has been taken from the bones and eaten, as in Peking duck. Japanese cuisine takes a different approach again. In 1982 the Australia–Japan Foundation brought a great Japanese chef, Masaru Doi, to the food school in the Sydney suburb of Ryde. He made two stocks, 'primary' and 'secondary': the first stock, *ichiban-dashi*, is the result of only two ingredients, kelp and bonito; and the second, *nihan-dashi*, reuses the ingredients from the first. It is the first stock that is the most prized and the most clear. Classical French preparation works in the reverse order; clarity is achieved with the final, prized consommé. The last menu at Berowra Waters Inn spoke, via its structure, to the future, to a different way of approaching the table from the kitchen. The dishes celebrated the past and the present. The written menu included the exhortation 'For the good of all', a misquote from something read not long before but which made different and good sense in the context of closing the doors. This river guide acted selfishly in order to be released from a profession that had begun to pall. Pulling the outboard from the water for the last time released those who worked there to different lives. Handing the last menu (an irrelevance, as it allowed no choice) to the last diner after eighteen years brought a sense of relief for which the tears might have been real. And by closing, instead of struggling on, the memory and myth of the place was secured.

It's only a restaurant, for god's sake

Clearing the table (Bennelong Restaurant)

Having put Berowra Waters Inn to rest, still unsold and an albatross of debts around my neck, I became that part of Gardner Merchant Australia's tender for the catering contract at the Sydney Opera House which was supposed to seduce and giddy the trustees with visions of perfect food, perfect service and a bustling Bennelong, the righting of past catering wrongs in the face of Sydney's growing confidence in itself.

Gardner Merchant executives, the company's consultant Anders Ousback, the architect Leigh Prentice, and their female representative of restorative idealism marched into the boardroom and the oral examination. I wouldn't have to say anything much, Anders had said, but of course I did have to say something and made the short speech of my life on the run. Later Anders said he'd reckoned I'd probably do a better job if I had to rise unprepared. I told them that in Australia we have been guilty of hanging Tiepolo on the wall and plating under clingwrap, a reference to the National Gallery in Canberra at the time (and since more than rectified), and that we had never included food in our prescriptions for high culture. I also told the truth when I said that the only space which would ever bring me back to the city was Bennelong.

Gardner Merchant won the contract and I took on the role of hands-on consultant, back in the CBD after eighteen years of river-crossing. Somewhere into the abyss of the undoable which doing Bennelong Restaurant soon became, I used to daydream that it had become detached from the rest of the Opera House and floated into Sydney Harbour. At the time this dream was a result of the frustration of shared work spaces in a building which, extraordinary as it is, was never made to function well below stairs. Now I realise that I wanted to transform Bennelong into Berowra Waters Inn: I'd got too used to taking a boat to a restaurant, to the privacy and autonomy of a dining-room that was in fact a private verandah and a home. Dragging Bennelong away from the Opera House precinct was also a dream in which its visibility – all glass, and the only sign of working life as one walks towards the Opera House from the quay – might be clouded and made private. The more I consider the whole idea of restaurants, the more I believe they need to be intimate spaces rather than places to be seen to be seen in. This doesn't undo the sense of intimacy one experiences in huge dining-rooms like La Coupole in Paris, because its blocks of banquettes divide a large room into cosy spaces for conversation; and even when the French dine side by side and face the dining-room, they seem to know how to retain their privacy. This is more a comment on Australians than on the French: we are still self-conscious when dining in formal restaurants and are yet to treat grand public dining-rooms with the irreverence they need in order to become comfortable spaces. The fact that Bennelong is an apparently autonomous glasshouse so close to the opera theatre and the concert hall exacerbates the problem of privacy, allowing those outside to watch the diners, even though dining itself is already a form of theatre. In between services, the interior is always on show. It is as empty as the concert hall in between rehearsals and concerts but, unlike the concert hall, is still on show. If fine dining is an intimate, private and participatory experience, the marvellous cathedral that is Bennelong does everything it can to undermine this, although acoustically, like a good cathedral, it was glorious.

The embarrassment of the interior's last embellishments – plant boxes disguising the boldness and strength of the granite dividers, a bar in the central space that divided the southern and lower dining area from the one above and which did all it could to disguise the strength of this middle platform and its relationship to the built landscape (the way, for instance, the stairs continue through the restaurant from the outside, the glass simply making an enclosure without interrupting the steps) was an embarrassment that in some part I began to understand but never had any sympathy with. You can't domesticate a cathedral and, of course, shouldn't want to. Cathedrals support public worship and traditionally demand

Clearing the table (Bennelong Restaurant)

human discomfort – there are no 'swan' chairs by modernist Danish designer Arne Jacobsen (Leigh Prentice's inspired choice of seating for Bennelong's bar and upstairs area) in Rheims or Chartres. I keep using French examples of dining and awesome religious spaces only because the French have done both so well for so many hundreds of years.

Leigh Prentice exercised creative respect for the space and its context by the restraint of his restoration. Restraint, of course, doesn't come cheap; details show. We had seen Joern Utzon's plans for Bennelong and he had marked the northern, upper level a 'grill room', which was, I think, to misunderstand his own work or the definition of 'grill room' but did suggest that we were in agreement about the kind of function it might serve. I saw this space as the one most easily reached from both theatre foyers and so a casual, easy, convivial area, and I suspect Utzon did too. We tried containing the work of cooking and serving to what amounted to a service island in this area, which was far away from the kitchen, but we were defeated. Wherever the food came from, it still involved marathon running on granite stairs: the low rise and the width of each step created pleasing proportions and easy climbing, but they still hurt. I date an arthritic left foot from this long-distance service.

The tables and the Jacobsen chairs, by being so much lower than normal dining height (the same height, in fact, as the tables at the equally iconic but intimate Harry's Bar in Venice, and a reminder of part of the original foyer of the Windsor Hotel in Melbourne), suggested the casual yet celebrated the formal. They made of that space, as far as it might be made, a comfortable place in which to lounge and dine. It was gorgeous, if gorgeous might describe clean low lines, and I think it can when a certain sensuality of material and of comfort are included. I had envisaged a successful Bennelong drawing people to the Opera House to eat and drink even if they were not going to the theatres – a way to make the precinct approachable, a way to bring the public inside and to feel welcome, but we were driven crazy by the compulsive touching and smearing of the outside of the glass. The site itself defeats any idea of easy conviviality because it sits outside Circular Quay and is a kind of Vatican City (and like that enclave too, is a law unto itself) with a monument to walk around. The bustle of the harbour always won.

Downstairs, which was closer to the kitchen but still too far away, Leigh Prentice made reference to a drawing of Utzon's which detailed intimate islands of banquettes surrounding tables. Again Leigh's solution was a combination of elegance and plushness, courteous to the original idea, the proportions and plan beautifully organic. Looking at the floor plan as I write, I can almost transpose the layout to that of a formal garden, not something I would have seen before leaving the city for a house in the country. On a tour of Castle Drogo in Devon two years before, I had seen in the kitchen a large circular beechwood table designed, as was much of the furniture, by the property's famed architect Edwin Lutyens. While seemingly having nothing to do with this table, the central waiters' station in the lower formal dining area of Bennelong took its form from it. Three other aspects of Castle Drogo seem strangely connected to Bennelong and the problems it presented to architect and restaurateur. First, the dining-room was a great distance from the kitchen; and second, according to his daughter, Lutyens' patron Sir Julius Drewe placed 'an electric cloth under the damask cloth and put candlesticks at the four corners which pricked in with little connections into the electric cloth for lighting the table candles'. Light needs a surface off which to reflect, and Bennelong's vaulted ceiling is so far away; lighting the dining areas called for lamps for each table. So while Bennelong as cathedral needed lighting that kept one awe-struck, dining, including its formal service, needed the practical and the intimate. Leigh addressed the splendour with three Poul Henningsen 'artichoke' lights. These can be suspended or turned up the other way and used as lamps: choosing the latter alternative, and using only four, one on the upper level and three in the much larger and formal dining area, was Leigh's master stroke. Less *is* more, especially in the case of these iconic lights, which would be ridiculed if used en masse. I walked around Bennelong not long ago and they have been removed.

Another detail I had loved at Castle Drogo was a pair of enormous, shallow wooden sinks in the scullery, the cedar as smooth as velvet and presumably used to wash the glassware and finest dinner services, for they are in the butler's pantry. Bennelong's kitchen was also the preparation and dishwashing space for a café and for catering in public areas. With good grace, Gardner Merchant had

Clearing the table (Bennelong Restaurant)

93

bowed to the expense of acquiring delicate porcelain from Limoges, to David Mellor cutlery, and to jugs and bowls Arne Jacobsen designed for Stelton. In redesigning parts of the kitchen, we allotted a corner to the modern equivalent of Lutyens' cedar sinks.

—

While the powerful effect on me of touring Castle Drogo had not played any real part in the restoration and reinvention of Bennelong, and many of the connections made above only occurred in hindsight, they do help illuminate our responses to the space and explain why at Bennelong I cleared the tables.

By the early nineties at Berowra Waters Inn, I had begun to ask questions about the the table's surface and what we unthinkingly place on it before dining begins. It began with the napkin: if the waiter takes the folded napkin from the setting in front of the diner, where he has carefully placed it before service, and opens it to be placed on the lap, why isn't the napkin brought to the diner on being seated instead of marking the place of arrival? The etiquette of whether the server or the diner places the napkin is a different thing altogether, but all waiters have experienced the frustration of having to ask the diner to take up the napkin so that the plate of food might be put down on the table. One could go on and on, post-Emily Post, about these ridiculous formalities: what is the point, and after that, what is the point of the setting itself? If culture is the result of memory fading, as stated by artist Michael Goldberg some years ago ('When memory fades culture takes over'), the culture of European fine dining might be said to be the sum of social aspirations expressed through rituals that no longer have meaning. We may understand, by reading, why the French, for instance, see it as *de rigueur* to always have a plate in front of the diner in a formal restaurant whether there is food there or not, but this is no reason to retain the practice.

I had begun to see the tabula rasa as the theatrical starting point of the unfolding revelations of dining and its service. To set the table before the diner chooses began to seem discourteously presumptive: the red-wine glass that needs to be removed if only white is chosen; the side plate and knife that are removed as a courtesy if a diner declines bread, which in turn makes an efficient signal not to offer bread to that person. I wanted to remove the need to undo the setting, and in removing it give a greater sense of thoughtful service, of subtle performance. So I cleared the tables at Bennelong, but found that most diners were not ready for revolution. And even I, in the event, found the clear white table confronting. We pretend to classlessness in Australia, but when the little signs of class disappear we are put out; while the bare table is acceptable in a cheap restaurant, it unsettles expectations as the price rises. This is connected, I think, with the urge to show one's worth through what one owns; a step across from Brillat-Savarin's 'Tell me what you eat: I will tell you what you are'. The set table is a display and the display proves the need for service. Aside from the legitimacy of clearing the table for theatrical purposes, I suspect I did want to unsettle things, to ask diners to think more deeply about the meal, to think beyond and around the examination of the Mellor knife or the wine carafe's mark (in our case, the carafes were laboratory flasks and defied desire), even the food. In some absurdly roundabout way, I was pushing for the examined life via the table.

➤

The menu at Bennelong was the Berowra Waters Inn menu, the country mice visiting the city for the first time and planning to stay. Placing the brioche, bone marrow and red-wine butter on the fine and modest-in-size Haviland dinner plate with its pale green line around the rim asked only that the brioche be made slightly smaller to fit the proportions, the Tripe Lyonnaise sat just as comfortably in the Haviland 'pasta' bowl, the pot of crème brûlée did not quarrel with the dessert plate; but the food seemed different, tainted by the troublesome kitchen where for the first time in twenty-one years we found it necessary to lock the doors of the coolroom, the fridges, the cupboards in which the flatware and crockery were stored, the wine racks, and everything else that lived in the service area.

A cook's knives were stolen, deep finger lines were found in bowls of a chocolate dessert the day after it was made. The kitchen was not private; it acted as a kind of public thoroughfare. The greatest indignity, and this was a fault of

Clearing the table (Bennelong Restaurant)

some of the new troupe of sometimes dedicated and sometimes only curious and ambitious cooks, was the casual attitude towards the boxes of recipe cards we had brought with us from the river. As cards began to disappear Janni Kyritsis, who had come to Bennelong only to help the kitchen find its feet, photocopied every one of them and kept the originals in a separate and private place. These were not an alchemist's formula but a history of years of work and relationships. He and I were profoundly depressed by this situation where, in general, trust – which was the unspoken absolute of life on the river (even the building itself was never completely locked) – hardly existed and motives were muddled. After the months of design and restoration, of decisions that were the result of a dizzying creative excitement and collaboration with Leigh Prentice and Anders Ousback, I realised with horror that I had strayed into a world I had no wish to be part of, and everything from there on confirmed this sense of foreboding.

If a personal disenchantment with restaurant life had begun to take hold some years before this, it had simply been the result of trying to retain enthusiasm for what I wasn't passionate about any more. This was not a falling-out with the river or the building or the people who came to work there, or those who came to dine, but it certainly included a weariness at the thought of one more boat engine in need of repair and one more dish in need of revitalisation. Bennelong might have worked like a tonic for six months, but the sum of its dysfunctional parts only deepened the disenchantment. I have already pointed to the separation of the Opera House precinct from any sense of city life, and the inadequacy of the underneath-and-behind-the-scenes working spaces and the rabbit warren of corridors. Add to this the necessity for diners to use the public toilets in the box-office area (they might have to queue for ten minutes or more if they needed to use them during a performance interval, and we used to joke that we needed cloches to place over the food if it arrived at a table just when the diner needed to leave, because it would have taken so long to return the dish to the kitchen and then to the table again). Bennelong's lack of working autonomy was something we could not get used to. We were one part of a group of cafés and restaurants that Gardner Merchant had tendered for and we were asked to be part of a single team. At the same time we were deemed to be the flagship and the glory. Yet we had no real autonomy over our systems of work and agreements with staff. Janni and I had come, by company standards, from an eccentric and private place on a river. We did not adjust easily to having an office long underground corridors away. They expected to solve the problems of our space in the same mode they approached all others.

This most glorious public space, although apparently reorganised to work as efficiently as possible while paying absolute courtesy to its soaring sight lines and aesthetic imperatives, left no place except the connecting 'tunnel' to the kitchen in which to be *not* on show. The space I had tentatively put aside in the kitchen for a desk and some reference books (all needing a lock and key) died because, rightly, the priority went to the Lutyens scullery. A review of the restaurant (now in the latest of its incarnations and with a highly reputed chef at its helm) in a national newspaper in 2002 damned the service for being 'lost in space' and made me grimace in sympathy, although one supposes it is possible that it was simply as outrageously offhand as the journalist reported. The formal dining-room (that is, the southern, lower space) seems to present every obstacle to gracious service that a beautiful and inspiring room might include. Because of the severe distances to kitchen, to service 'tunnel' and to waiters' stations, any setting up or putting down, removing or replacing seemed to cause an exaggerated amount of attention, which distracted from the conviviality of dining, whether at the first point on the cleared table, or throughout the meal. The dining-room felt either policed or as if no one was there to care, however hard we tried to do our best by it.

The finest service is surely that which collectively has the eye of an eagle, the invisibility of the tiniest of birds and yet leaves the sense of care hovering over the table. In this dining-room there was nowhere to wait which might have given waiters a subtle observation point from which to appear at the table as if on cue. The service 'tunnel' encouraged being away without leave; the room itself resembled a set for an identity parade. Then again, when the dining-room was crowded and the waiters busy, the patterns of flow were lovely to follow.

Sydney seems to have produced a confederacy of elite waiters who, while they

Clearing the table (Bennelong Restaurant)

97

are very good at what they do – which is to take orders, deliver food and wine to the table, and in time, remove the emptied receptacles – demand very high wages. What is it about this job which causes those who do it to want greater financial reward than young cooks receive? After all, waiters might be seen to be no more than those who deliver what the cook makes. This is not to deny that the very best waiters bring other, more complex, skills to the table along with a knowledge of food and wine. Perhaps there is something abject in their self-image that demands extra compensation?

If Janni Kyritsis was made ill by the regulations and misbehaviour in the kitchen, then my sickness of the heart was caused by a hospitality industry form of iatrogenic infection that this difficult dining-room seemed to breed. Many waiters who had been working at Bennelong under a different regime, before its renovation, and who had been promised their old positions when the restaurant reopened, joined the new guard. This caused a certain amount of friction, but was also a lesson in the differences in attitude towards the work all waiters do. The old guard made no judgements about the food; the new had come to Bennelong for the anticipated glory of their association with fine food. The old guard wanted continuation of employment; the new, glamour. At best, this clash of values provided an opportunity for tolerance and compassion. I think both groups benefited. The immensity of the dining-room space and its distance from the kitchen suited the old guard better than the new: they simply did their job well and took home their wages and tips. The young turks, differently, wanted an intimate relationship with the kitchen, reflected glory, and a workplace integrated with their gregarious lives. On all of these counts they felt short-changed.

Just as Bennelong turned out not to be the place to clear the tables, it was not the place to question the attitude of the workforce and, as well, I did not have the strength or courage to do so. The restaurant belonged to a very large company who in turn answered financially to the Opera House coffers. The bottom line was that I didn't believe in this restaurant and, ipso facto, no one who worked there believed in it. Janni had once told me about a Greek saying, 'A fish smells from its head'. This is the pivot around which a good restaurant works.

In many ways the most frustrating impediment to the success of the Bennelong space, or for that matter any fine dining-room in a significant public precinct, is that the Sydney Opera House is seen to be, and indeed is, owned by the taxpayers. Being 'ours', it is considered obliged to please everyone (except perhaps for the opera theatre, exempt because every opera house needs opera to fulfil its nominal, fantastic role), and dining-rooms are expected to do the impossible and satisfy all tastes, all purses. This is an absurd requirement for any business, but especially so for a fine restaurant, which depends on an unspoken accord between the restaurateur and the customers. The best restaurants are expressions of personal taste, a term that covers everything from food to conviviality, and in this sense they are private worlds.

On one of our first nights, having turned the parts of a traditional prawn cocktail into a fine little dish for supper, we received a complaint from a diner. 'I can smell prawns!' he cried. A French politician once said something like 'Politics, like a good andouillette, should smell slightly of shit' and this is what I wanted say to that diner. Instead, I explained the presence of a reduction of prawn heads and shells in the mayonnaise: I wanted to cajole and persuade and ask him to walk down another path. (I've a theory that some of the greatest cuisines are the ones that perfected composting, turning little fish into high rotting flavour.) He listened courteously but did not change his mind. He was not persuaded and was not charged for the dish. We also served a caesar salad in the upstairs area, rescuing it from the doom of overlarge bowls lined with spikes of overlarge lettuce leaves, the usual presentation in cafés that think this salad is a cheap and easy impression of plenty.

Caesar salad

These quantities will serve eight people. Take 4 cos lettuces; 8 very fresh free-range eggs; some slightly stale white bread, cut into 1-cm cubes; garlic and olive oil for frying the croutons; a piece of bacon weighing about 500 g; and about 30 anchovies (Spanish are best but expensive), rinsed and patted dry if they are too salty.

For the dressing, you will need: 1 egg yolk; 1 tablespoon Dijon mustard; ½ teaspoon each salt and pepper; a pinch of fine sugar; 40 ml lemon juice; 1 teaspoon Worcestershire sauce; ¾ cup olive oil (extra-virgin would provide too dominant a flavour); plus about ½ cup finely grated parmesan.

Take only the crisp, pale inside leaves of the lettuces. Poach the eggs, taking them from the water when the yolks are still very runny, and immersing them in

Clearing the table (Bennelong Restaurant)

cold water. Smash 2 cloves of garlic and add them to the olive oil in a pan. Fry the bread cubes in the hot oil until golden and crisp – you will need a small handful per portion. Cut the bacon into quite thick matchsticks and fry these until crisp and brown; each portion might take eight of these pieces.

Make the dressing in the usual way, but do not add the parmesan until just before adding the dressing to the salad.

When you are ready to plate the salad (here the verb is literally correct – use a plate, not a bowl), lower the poached eggs into very hot water so that they heat through but the yolks remain runny. Toss the leaves in most of the dressing and then stack them on each plate so that you have a leafy nest for the egg. Scatter with the bacon pieces and croutons, then gently remove the eggs from the hot water with a slotted spoon, drain on paper towel and then lower an egg into each nest of leaves. Lay the anchovy fillets over the salads and finally pour over a little more dressing.

Of course, you might happily toss the lot (except for the egg) – just make sure the dressing reaches every ingredient and that each serve has a fair proportion of the separate ingredients. The point of a caesar salad is the spoilage of the whole by the spilled yolk. Old hat it may be, but a remarkable combination of flavours and textures when prepared with proper attention to the ingredients. Rustic in McLaren Flat now, I grow cos lettuces for this very purpose and call to the chooks next door to lay.

There are sweeter stories of Bennelong to offset the ones that hurt. A grand and well-known Sydney interior designer told me that he longed for Mont Blanc because it was the dessert he remembered from his student days in Paris, and so we found the chestnuts and perfected the dish. Our Mont Blanc gave him pleasure and we kept it on the menu. To include a dish on the menu because it is the central ingredient of a story told by a customer to the restaurateur is to increase its meaning. When those who are not part of the story choose to eat it, they too become part of the reason that dish came to stay.

Mont Blanc

This amount will give up to eight serves. You will need 500 g chestnut meat (peeled and frozen chestnuts work well for this dessert; very fine ones are available from a Victorian grower); 500 ml milk; 1 vanilla bean, split and the seeds scraped into the milk; 1 cup (250 ml) caster sugar; 2 tablespoons fine brandy; cream whipped with a little extra sugar and brandy.

Simmer the chestnuts in the milk with the vanilla bean and caster sugar until the nut meat is tender and very soft. Add the brandy and purée in a food processor until very smooth. Make a mound of the purée by pushing through a sieve, or use a piping bag with a very fine nozzle (if you are making one large Mont Blanc, a mouli-legume with the finer holes does a good job if held steady); the mound should have the appearance of loose vermicelli. Pile the whipped cream on top so that the 'mountain' of chestnut purée is hidden in 'snow'. I like to lean a paper-thin shard of dark chocolate on the side of the mountain. Paul Bocuse, in his *La cuisine du marché*, flavours the cream with Chartreuse, about which I have no opinion. Whatever you do, do nothing to trick up the mountain and snow.

I remember a dinner organised for US journalist R. W. Apple Jnr and his wife Betsey, whose high southern accent was used by Ken Burn as one of the voice-overs in his Civil War documentary. Apple's appetite caused the food writer Calvin Trillin to dub him Eighteen Lunches Apple (an upgrading from the nickname Three Lunches Apple, which he was given much earlier in his long career) in a profile in *The New Yorker* in 2003. He had, one summer in Pennsylvania, pan-fried shad roe for me and another guest and then taken us to Gettysburg and told the story. It was early morning, a fog was lifting, his voice was perfectly pitched and he held us spellbound.

Christopher Hogwood, conducting performances in the Opera House, was another guest at this dinner. Also invited were Leo Schofield and his daughter Tess, a costume designer, and Noel Staunton, then technical director of the Australian Opera. Noel had been one of the most constant and supportive patrons of Berowra Waters Inn; Johnny Apple loves opera as much as he loves food. The service was brilliant, the food was as fine as the kitchen under Janni ever turned out, the table felt alive, the guests were comfortable and pampered. They understood;

Clearing the table (Bennelong Restaurant)

they understood the place and the table. This is what I had come to Bennelong for: to promote the art of dining in a building devoted to the arts.

We served tiny pots of a cold, baked chocolate cream at this dinner. They were completed with a large shard of very crisp and thin florentine biscuit as a rakish hat.

Pots of chocolate

This will make about ten pots of 100–150 ml capacity.

Set the oven to 170°C. You will need 500 ml milk; 500 ml thin cream; 70 g caster sugar; ½ teaspoon freshly ground cinnamon; ½ cup coarsely ground, fresh coffee beans; 1 vanilla bean, split lengthwise; 10 egg yolks; 250 g very dark cooking chocolate (at least 66% cocoa butter is best), melted and kept warm; and, if possible, 3 tablespoons good-quality walnut liqueur (cognac or armagnac as substitute).

Combine all ingredients except the yolks, chocolate and liqueur, bring to the boil and then strain through many layers of muslin. Whisk the resulting cream into the yolks, then add the melted chocolate and the liqueur. Ladle into small pots (the custard is far too rich for large serves) and bake, covered, in a bain-marie for about 35–40 minutes or until just set – your finger should just pull away from the surface without disturbing it.

Florentines

Florentines are my favourite biscuit, but to live up to expectation they must be made very thin as explained below and with due attention to the exact ingredients. We refined the recipe at Berowra Waters Inn and I still often make them at home, intent on explaining by example to all guests that florentines do not have to be the biscuit they thought they knew. The basic ingredients and most of the method come from *The Art of Fine Baking* by Paula Peck, a book published in 1961 and bought while I was living in America in the early seventies. In 1995, a young woman who had been making desserts in the Berowra Waters Inn kitchen for some time and who then contentedly ran away with a gentle and handsome waiter, brought me a present; another book by Paula Peck, *The Art of Good Cooking*, which she had found in an antiquarian bookshop.

The instruction and explanation is necessarily long, but if you follow it well and do it again and again it will have been a good lesson in working with this kind of biscuit. These quantities will make four trays of spreading florentine batter, which will then give you about fifty large biscuits. Working with any less mixture would be far too fiddly. Despite the coating of chocolate, and the near-caramel reduction of the sugar mixture, florentines keep well.

You will need 1 cup (215 g) sugar; ⅔ cup (250 g) honey; ⅔ cup (180 g) thick cream (e.g. 45% butter fat); 4 tablespoons (55 g) unsalted butter; ½ cup (100 g) candied peel, which you must chop much more finely than it is when purchased; 3 cups (270 g) blanched and sliced almonds (it is essential to purchase almonds that have been finely sliced, not merely chopped); and 6 tablespoons (50 g) sifted flour. You will also need about 250 g best-quality couverture (chocolate especially for chocolate making and coating).

Place the sugar, honey, cream and butter in a saucepan and take the mixture to 116°C or 'soft ball' stage on a jam thermometer. If you don't take the mixture to this temperature, it will take too long to spread and brown in the oven. If you take it further up the scale, you will not be able to spread the mixture.

While this mixture is cooking, line four baking trays with non-stick baking paper and set the oven to 190°C. Having combined the candied peel, the almonds and the flour in a bowl, pour the sugar mixture into this and combine. Immediately divide the mixture onto the four trays and push it about a little to help it spread thinly. Most of the spreading will happen in the oven. Bake for somewhere between 10 and 15 minutes, until the mixture has browned, spread and is bubbling furiously. With a fan-forced oven, you can bake more than one tray at a time, at different levels.

Remove from the oven, slide the baking paper with the mixture off the tray, cover with another sheet of baking paper and, using a rolling pin, roll the biscuit until it can be no thinner. This is the step that ensures a very thin, very crisp florentine, as long as you have used thin almond slices and chopped the peel finely. Take off the covering sheet of baking paper and allow biscuit to cool, then turn over so that the base is uppermost. Repeat with all the sheets of florentine mixture, trimming the edges to square while the sheet is still slightly pliable and before it sets hard.

Clearing the table (Bennelong Restaurant)

Melt the chocolate over hot water and spread it over the underside of the four biscuit sheets – a spatula works well. Allow the chocolate to set. If it is 'tempered' it will retain its sheen and set well, but tempering is something of an art and simply melting it carefully works well.

I like simply to break the sheets into shards, which means you have no waste of the most perfect biscuit there is. If you do want perfectly shaped biscuits, you need to cut the sheet while it is still yet to set hard, dipping the knife or cutter into milk so that it doesn't stick to the mixture.

———

Because Bennelong is such a visible part of such an extraordinary public building which is not easily perceived as issuing an invitation to enter, it seemed to be a space people would cautiously tiptoe into, simply to look, even though it has no easily found entrance either. Architect Greg Burgess has spoken of a building that might be entered from all sides, a reference to his work with indigenous peoples and a philosophical stand the Sydney Opera House firmly opposes. This problem is currently being addressed as part of major work on the building, with Utzon's approval.

Joern Utzon gave Sydney, despite the city's initially reluctant involvement both imaginatively and financially, a building that not even Frank Gehry's Guggenheim Museum in Bilbao eclipses. Buildings like these are notoriously difficult to humanise (anyway, we might even ask why they should be) because they are symbols and signposts before anything else. With Utzon's gift came the challenge of use and definitions of use.

I came away from three years at Bennelong believing that it never will be a viable space for dining. It needs another use or, at the very least, an extended, more three-dimensional one. The best we did was a three-night season of Not a Lieder Recital, which was supported by the 1996 Sydney Festival and which gave me cheer. This bravura and witty show by pianist and composer Jonathan Mills, countertenor Hartley Newnham and actor David Wicks plays intellectual and performative games with the idea of intimate recital; it was devised as an interlude for a fine meal (or the opposite way around, where the meal plays similar games), wickedly amusing, beautifully performed and thoroughly charming. In 1998, Jonathan, Hartley, David, chief Craig Willis and I took the show to Magill Estate Restaurant (possibly the most beautiful dining-room in Australia, designed by Keith Cottier) for the Adelaide Festival and it again romped home with a less witty but far better menu.

The audience at Bennelong adored the occasion and the staff loved playing host to it. We presented the trio with large bunches of flowers at the close of the season. These turned out to be pineapples, which surprised the performers and caused the audience of diners to laugh with them. I even began to believe for a moment; but the separate and smaller cathedral that is Bennelong remains, its problematic space damning any attempt to tune its interior. In a last effort to love-before-leaving this cathedral with its umbilical cord to the bowels of the Opera House, we hosted a performance by the young tenor John Heuzenroeder, accompanied by the pianist Michael White, of Schumann's *Dichterliebe*. Theirs was a marvellous concert, but even a serious lieder recital, which transfigures the air, does not cause the concrete arches of Bennelong to become any more hospitable.

When the scaffolding was in place to vacuum the ceiling and clean the glass after the completion of Leigh Prentice's restoration and renovation, not long before we opened, Janni Kyritsis and I climbed to its very top, close to the point of the concrete arch at the southern end of the room. Make a mark, the builder said, but we declined although we saw there the signatures of workers from thirty years ago. That scaffolding looked extraordinary: it seemed somehow to be at home in that place, as nothing else has ever been; it exaggerated, yet made comprehensible, the beauty and unreachability of the arch. One night, late, a workman high on the scaffolding took a mouth organ from his pocket and played the blues.

I failed Bennelong and Bennelong failed me.

Clearing the table (Bennelong Restaurant)

Food

Of middle age, the Canadian novelist Margaret Atwood once wrote that 'the mind's eye grows sharper but you need glasses to read the menu'. Most of these digressions on produce and cooking are the result of a shift from writing menus in a city to a more thoughtful middle age in the country. Running a restaurant seems, in retrospect, like accidental tourism. Easily distracted, I have always felt most comfortable when cooking alone. This also precludes the notion of competition, except with oneself. Cooking for curiosity's sake rather than for a living also means there is no deadline unless an invitation has been issued, and even then it is a pleasure and a chance to give and receive without being troubled by putting a price on one's labour.

Australian writer and poet Eric Rolls, asked (on turning seventy-nine in 2002) what it was he loved about living on the land, said that it defies any sense of self-importance. I live not far from a small capital city but far enough to understand what Rolls means. To have exchanged, serendipitously, city and restaurants for country and plantings, with a well-stocked bookshelf for support, is to have cut myself down to size, to have found a little perspective, and to have seen that the birds, seeming at first to be flying with free and playful spirit, do so with an exhausting, constant vigilance.

Nothings

An American friend who likes to explore the flawed idea of paradise came to lunch at La Huerta. He stood at a quince tree recently planted for him and said the property must have a name. Oh, it has, I replied, but the land is not at ease with its name yet. *La huerta* is Spanish for 'orchard' and 'market garden' and, with a stretch, refers to my rule of growing only plants that produce food. A little pretentious, perhaps, but with use its gloss will fade to fit, even though I have no intention of ever taking money in exchange for produce. Just to make sure that this, one of the few Spanish words I am able to pronounce with any fitting cadence, was at least appropriate, I asked Alicia Rios for advice.

Alicia, who creates performances involving food and is an expert on olive oil, 'got drunk [when young] on Franco-Germanic philosophical jargon and became a vitalist, voluntarist, gestaltic rupturist existentialist devotee of Bergson, Bachelard, Fischer, Chiva, Calvo . . .', and a lecturer in psychology. She told the historian Theodore Zeldin, who writes about her in *An Intimate History of Humanity*, that her religion is the 'cult of daily life'. While still an academic she opened the first vegetarian restaurant in Madrid and and called it The Garden of Delights. She spent a large part of each of her childhood years 'in a paradisiac, wild place'. Alicia would tell me if La Huerta was the right word for this sometimes dry, sometimes inhospitable land on which I planned to grow food to share.

'*Sí, estoy de acuerdo. Una huerta, La Huerta, se asocia a un espace paradisíaco!, como en la miniaturas persas y turcas. Es un orchard, y puede tener el carácter de Mercado o no.* You can have an orchard for your own enjoyment, and produce your own vegetables, plants and even flowers for yourself or to provide your customers – who, by the mere fact of entering into La Huerta get enchanted and become fairy friends. Not in vain are you introducing the magic and energy of La Huerta into their bodies and souls. You are not getting romantic since you are also taking the care of nurturing the produce of La Huerta, and nothing more real and touchable and smellable than this! And! Remember Gaycilla, that I've already been involved in your Huerta and been imprinted by her, and there I'm just seeing Nature in a huertana way, that means, inspiring and poetic.' I have dedicated the pomegranate tree (*la granada*) to Alicia.

A line of four different quince varieties became trees dedicated to mentors. The American friend who began life as an Egyptian has been allocated the Van Diemen's quince as he seems to be taking to Australia by osmosis; and his wife, next to him, the Portugal. The next one along is a pineapple quince and when I offered it to Michael Symons, whose writings on gastronomy have had the most profound influence on my own, he replied that a ham-and-pineapple pizza is something he is rather shy about liking, but nevertheless he does. The next one along, an orange quince, is for another influential friend who, if he is to be in Mentors' Row, must simply accept it. So it is a strong row of trees, planted this winter while dormant and from bare-rooted stock, which will begin to fruit in the next two years, during which time I shall work out ways to keep the cockatoos and rosellas away. James Boswell wrote that 'in an orchard there should be enough to eat, enough to lay up, enough to be stolen, and enough to rot on the ground'. Stealing is not quite what the voracious birds do, but it is close enough to self-interest. Another two quince varieties, Fuller and Smyrna, will fruit for birds and myself in a different place, the sun reaching them at a different time of day: it will be interesting to see which location favours quince best.

For now, last season's fruit having been jellied and jammed and dried, different produce demands some attention. I have been labouring pleasurably over yoghurt, pumpkin, chestnuts, dried figs and sourdough, smoked eel, pasta and 'Nothings'. Late autumn settling into winter provides crisp, clear days and cold nights in which to dig and knead. One wants to work physically. Arriving late at the gate of gardening, I still find autumn's invitation to dig and clear and mulch a marvel of conjunctions. The body wants to be part of the land. The soil may go to sleep in the winter, but it invites participation in its dormancy.

Yoghurt

We might start with yoghurt because it is a constant, not seasonal, although the percentage of cream in the local (nearly) milk changes with the colour of the grass. This milk comes from a dairy near Lake Alexandrina and the tight-lipped mouth of the Murray River, south of McLaren Vale. It is biodynamically produced, full-cream and not homogenised: a two-litre container of the boiled and cooled milk needs only four tablespoons of yoghurt from the last batch, and tender coddling, to transform it into a mild creamy mass with a thick layer of yellow cream on the top.

Now that I stay at home and everything is DIY, the combustion heater provides the even heat to nurse the two litres overnight, wrapped in a towel. A friend in Sydney lights a pile of wood in her fireplace long before others do in the Blue Mountains, which is so much colder. I am with her, and do not wait for frosts. Once I looked from the kitchen across to the heater and saw four bowls of varying sizes sitting near the warmth as though the heater were mother and the bowls her children. I am not motherly, or at least I have deflected motherliness towards foods. One bowl held sourdough starter lively with fermentation, another two very large bowls each held a one-and-a-half-kilo loaf of sourdough beginning its first and fermenting rise (mostly spelt flour, with a small percentage of rye for moisture and flavour), and the fourth bowl held the yoghurt. It was an image of a family group, cosy, at fermenting peace. Late at night I would make the bread, feed the starter and check the warmth of the yoghurt, which is to say that mothering, even of foods, is not something one can simply leave to a heater; and even the heater needs to be fed.

Most of us have foods that are central to our sense of health and wellbeing. I know people who dismiss yoghurt with a shrug, whereas I feel my body depends on it. In an interview, the revered Alan Davidson (the 79-year-old compiler of *The Oxford Companion to Food* who has recently published *The Wilder Shores of Gastronomy,* a collection of articles from the food and history journal *Petits Propos Culinaires*) admitted to a fascination for the foods 'which have swept the world' – pizza, for instance, and yoghurt. One of the attributes of yoghurt, I would think, is that, unlike cheese, it produces little whey and keeps, while cheese needs large quantities of milk and produces huge quantities of whey. Yoghurt, even yoghurt made from full-cream milk, is wonderfully clean and not rich.

Ubiquitous in southern India is a dish of yoghurt rice called Masura Anna in Karnataka. A clean, creamy dish to be eaten at room temperature on hot days, flecked with green chillies and ginger and fresh coriander. There is an Indian bread I make that calls for the dough to ferment a little overnight with the help of yoghurt; it is called Moti Roti and only recently the baker John Downes, who lived in India for some time, told me that *moti* means 'pearl'. This makes sense: the dough is so smooth, the colour pearly white. The flavour, once the bread has been slapped onto a fiery-hot cast-iron surface to blister and cook, is slightly sour and all the better for this. You can stretch the dough once it has rested, as though it were filo pastry, but this bread is best rather thicker than that.

Pumpkin

A dollop of this yoghurt (there is a fine chapter on yoghurts, panir and other Indian dairy preparations in Yamuna Devi's *Lord Krishna's Cuisine*) is an optional addition to pumpkin soup. Autumn saw the street stall (which looks like a battered bus-stop) just down the road from La Huerta fill with pumpkins, first butternuts and now a seemingly endless supply of whoppers called jarrahdale. At three dollars for the largest, one is tempted to use them for a garden wall instead of stone. Instead, I buy too many and hand them over to friends and, when I haven't enough money to pay him, to the farmer who brings the wood for the combustion heater. Roasting them, skin on, is all one needs to do to appreciate the sweetness, but using pumpkin for Indian vegetarian dishes is to expand your repertoire considerably.

There is a cake in Rose Levy Beranbaum's *The Cake Bible* that was worth all the measuring. Having so much pumpkin to hand, I tripled the recipe quantities. Pumpkin is mostly water and it is worth reducing the purée of cooked flesh for some time before measuring it into the batter. Dark sugar, toasted walnuts and walnut oil (instead of butter) are three of the other ingredients; the cake is homely, moist, keeps well and is utterly delicious. Making three of something is not just labour-saving, it means there is also cake for the neighbours – which, of course, whittles down the supply and calls for further labour.

Using another jarrahdale to make soup for the freezer brought on a little fiddling with cuisines, as weeks before I had made Thai red curry paste in some quantity. Frying rather a lot of this paste with onion and then adding the pumpkin with a modicum of carrot and celery and potato, covering generously with rabbit stock (not by preference, but because it was there), this combination turned out to be marvellously lively and legitimate. We have all suffered through pumpkin soups one can stand a spoon up in and which taste of nothing but pumpkin and water. The central problem of puréed vegetable soups is that they are usually left too thick, and in the case of pumpkin are more like pale-orange plopping mud. There is a viscosity somewhere between too thin and too mudlike that turns a simple purée into velvet for the throat. After blending, you will see the tiny flecks of curry paste whose blachan, galangal, turmeric, garlic, lemongrass and so on scent the sweet pumpkin into a soup far grander than you would have anticipated. Young and green, I was always attracted to a prawn and pumpkin soup in one of Elizabeth David's books. I still like it, but want more spice.

When I write of puréeing, I do not mean a quick whizz in a food processor. If one is careful of the size and whizzability of the initial ingredients, a blender (what we used to call a 'vitamiser') will make a perfect aromatic puddle of the soup, as smooth as a baby's bottom or Moti Roti. With sorrel, for instance, I take care to tear off not only the stalk above the leaf but the vein of stalk that is part of the leaf itself. This attention to detail either impresses or seems a crazed waste of time. Those who understand that it is essential know that good cooking is some-times akin to a jeweller's craft.

Chestnuts

Your born-again rustic correspondent went to Sydney recently and ate out three times, which was almost too much for the heart and purse to take, except at Claude's where Tim Pak Poy's food and some of the tableware were so extraor-dinary that no monetary value could be given the experience. Anders Ousback had made small flat-based bowls and tiny beakers from a porcelain clay: they are so thin and the colour so neutral that it is hard to know where the bowl or beaker ends and the food begins; the container seems to be edible. When I told him of this reaction he was pleased and said that that was exactly his intention. The beakers had originally been made as 'take-away' containers for Tim Pak Poy's fabled smoked salmon consommé, which was served at an outdoor food festival. Ousback watched with amusement as many of the beakers were thrown in the recycling bin.

At a different meal a roasted-chestnut soup began the set menu, its flavour, well, that of chestnuts, but its consistency far too thick. This purée was served in a low wide bowl, which allowed it to go cold far too quickly. Bowls this shape are elegant but are suitable only for pasta and salads. It was the end of May in Sydney and chestnuts were in high season. The first food I ate in Europe in the early seventies was chestnuts roasted over charcoal by a street vendor in Rome. It was December and very cold. More recently and closer to home, at the Willunga farmers' market, a stall was selling them in June when the greengrocer in town had declared them finished. When a purveyor says something is finished, interrogate, especially when he is selling cherries for thirty dollars per kilo. When a farmers' market holds fast to its constitution and becomes the sum of providores selling local produce to be cooked after purchase, it becomes a true indicator of the seasons. In the kitchen, this restriction leads to celebratory culinary confinement.

Peeling chestnuts is a chore occasionally interspersed with the wonder of the odd nut that succumbs with a generosity that takes my breath away. These, with the first sharp pull of a paring knife, show that the internal skin is much happier keeping company with the outer shell than with the meat. Glory be to God for these, which are always the most fresh. Alone, peeling three or so kilos, there is space for puzzling over the void. Listening to Cyril Cusack reading the sublime poetry of Gerard Manley Hopkins when I take on these repetitive chores exaggerates the achieve, the eventual mastery, of the actions.

While I was still at Berowra Waters Inn, a friend arrived one day for lunch with a present that was mine if I knew what it was for. I didn't, but took it anyway: a chestnut knife, a lovely thing, a wooden handle with a small, short, curved blade that easily makes the requisite cuts into the base of chestnuts so that they may simmer or roast without exploding and the heat creates steam, so separating the inner skin from the meat. I am deft with this tool now and deserve it. Some of my last lot of chestnuts peeled so perfectly that, despite knowing there are some things best left to professional *confiseurs*, the *marrons glacés* I made, which would not have passed muster in Florence, are good for nibbling with coffee (something I do not drink). The rest were braised with butter, a light meat stock, shallots (these, too, are doing well in the vegetable beds) and brussels sprouts with lots of ground pepper – the traditional and best way to treat them, which is as floury vegetables.

At the lunch in Sydney that began with the chestnut soup, I had talked to the writer David Malouf about *castagnaccio alla Toscana*, a savoury cake made from chestnut flour, oil and rosemary. He misses it, having once lived close to *castagnaccio* country. I want to post him one, but fresh chestnut flour is hard to find. I have grown rather fond of packing food for the mail – the first eggplants to someone who would understand their blush; jerusalem artichokes because they surprised me; protected biscuits and breads of varying sourdough kinds. Giving food is a different thing altogether from putting a value on it and charging for it to make a living. Poorer but released, this liberation is central to my post-restaurant contentment.

Dried figs and sourdough bread

I have an aversion to fruit-and-nut breads, but one bread I have grown to like very much is a loaf with a purée of moist dried figs incorporated into the dough as well as large pieces of fig, some crushed aniseed and a little olive oil. Do not try to make this bread with mean, inferior dried figs, which are more common than the perfect kind. Sliced finely and grilled on a barbecue, the resulting aromatic toast is marvellous with blue cheese. It is a keeping bread too, a fine winter bread, its central attraction to the palate, eye and nose being the fig kneaded into the dough. The recipe is in an instructive book on sourdough culture and breads by Nancy Silverton, who founded the La Brea Bakery in Los Angeles. The temperatures she gives for baking are extremely high, so one should fiddle slightly with her otherwise faultless advice at the baking stage, especially as this bread has a high sugar content. I have sometimes added toasted walnuts to the dough as well as figs, but

I think this loaf would be just as good if the pieces of fruit and the nuts were left out and only the purée of figs and the aniseed added to the dough.

Smoked eel

The closest major shopping centre to La Huerta is some kilometres away and a third of the way to Adelaide. It is one of those frightening places where the poor entertain themselves by spending the money they do not have.

Deep within the bowels of this fluorescent 'paradise' is a Polish delicatessen that sells smoked eel, fished from Victorian lakes and smoked close to home. Sometimes it is smoked for too long and seems to be all fat, but most of the time it is a very fine product indeed. When it is good it is very very good, and I think it might be used to make a variation on Tim Pak Poy's smoked salmon consommé; smoked eel has a pleasing pungency that makes it distinctive. Apart from simply serving it with a fresh horseradish cream, and adding matchsticks of the vegetable I hold in highest regard, celeriac, if you want to get fancy it is very good tossed through a cross-dressed salad made with fresh squid-ink pasta, cucumber, lots of coriander, finely sliced green chillies, and pickled ginger (easy to make your own when young ginger is in season and if you have one of those cute Japanese instruments that are sharp enough to slice your fingers off and whose instruction sheet is a lesson in comic translation). The dressing needs sesame and peanut oils, and soy.

Pasta

The winter displays of mothering inside La Huerta include a long piece of thin dowel with fine black pasta hanging over it like Anna Magnani's hair on a melancholic day. It is best not to use your broom to hang the pasta from. A piece of dowel at least two metres long is a handy thing in a kitchen.

One of the things I like about making pasta (apart from the obvious, which is that it is an entirely different product to the dried) is that the task is finished without the cooking. The pasta keeps well if dried properly and even in that process does not become 'dried' pasta. This pause in the production process is in keeping with the joy I find in measuring out the egg whites, weighing the sugar, weighing, skinning, toasting and chopping the almonds, and setting out the lemons for grating, for instance, the night before making trays of meringues. This separation of steps has the effect of a beguiling, albeit fake, shortcut when you really get down to the making: it is as if one has had help.

'Nothings'

A friend (the dedicatee of the Portugal quince) arrived from Milwaukee with a cutting from *The New York Times*. It was an obituary for Elizabeth Coblentz, 'an Amish homemaker' who for decades had written a syndicated cookery column. Homely and syndicated might seem oxymoronic, but in an age where the food of a restaurant in New York City is described by a reviewer as 'homely yet nouvelle-pretty' we seem to accept such things. Coblentz, admirably, refused to be photographed and posted her handwritten columns from a house where there was no electricity, telephone or running water.

One of her recipes was reproduced in the obituary: it is for biscuits called 'Nothings', often made by the Amish for weddings and celebrations. I used to make biscuits called Troubled Thoughts, but Nothings are much closer to Schopenhauer and the 'philosophy of pessimism'. Making them is far less time-consuming than doing nothing, except that standing at the pan of pure lard (hard to come by; render your own) or oil in which they are deep-fried needs your undivided attention. However, they do cook in no time. Flour, a little egg and a little cream all mixed to a stiff dough, rolled thin, cut into rounds, a couple of slashes and then into the pan, the resulting light, puffed rounds finally dusted with icing sugar. A relation, one sees, of the generic doughs for deep-fried biscuits: the French *bugnes* or the *cenci* of Italy, for instance. I did what I presume no self-reliant Amish woman would do and ran the dough through the pasta machine, which makes things even more simple and the biscuit even closer to non-existence or paradise, whatever you want to call it.

Apple to rabbit

In the past weeks I have been immersed – in alphabetical order – in the practical considerations of apples, prickly pears, quinces and rabbits. All this produce is local: the apples from newly inherited trees, the prickly pears from giant stands of cactus on the roads leading out of McLaren Flat to the Adelaide Hills; the quinces stolen and then begged from a tree that might have been on public land but wasn't; and the rabbits with their offal purchased from the grower at the Willunga farmers' market. Complicit in this seasonal education have been two friends who were independently guests at La Huerta, and a third friend who has been involved even though she lives in England and is so far away.

Out of the schoolroom, we surely must begin with quinces, for their perfume, their first and most prized quality; it will then pervade the kitchen. Waverley Root, in his 1980 *Food*, a marvellous dictionary in which I file torn-out addenda to what he writes, begins his Quince entry with 'The appreciation of taste is, I suspect, an artificial phenomenon acquired by education, like the appreciation of Western music, also an artificial phenomenon acquired by education'. I remember watching chef Janni Kyritsis eating raw quince and finding my mouth puckering in distaste. And yet I remember peeling an apricot for him because his mouth puckered at the thought of the skin. Root suggests that the quince perfectly betrays 'the subjective and artificial nature of our responses to the stimuli of taste'. I, too, think the palate has a culture-specific scale.

We saw laden quince trees everywhere as I took K, visiting from London, along roads connecting the Southern Vales to the Adelaide Hills early in March. None of the fruit was large and although size of fruit does differ from variety to variety this had more to do with the drought than with inheritance.

On the road leading to the sea from the small township of Willunga I have watched a small quince tree for the past few years. It is ignored by its owners and the fruit begs to be picked, which I do. Wild, ignored and undernourished, this tree offers less-than-perfect-looking quinces but enough to show it is more than alive. One could not cook them whole for eating, even if washed, as they are always partially spoiled and gashed with hard brown marks, sometimes a little rotten in one place and into the centre. They have little fur and, as with size, this coating differs from variety to variety. The pleasure of growing or finding produce includes relegating visual perfection to a lesser basket, and I take from them whatever flesh might be used. I think of hartshorn when I feel a furry quince. Hartshorn, the furry down from deer antlers, was once used as a setting agent, in the same way that pectin from fruit sets the jellies we make.

It was not coincidence that saw a letter arrive from England the day we picked the largest basketful. I had been deep in correspondence with J, who grows as many varieties of quince as she is able to locate. In this turnabout world she had put me in touch with a man in Victoria (Australia) who sells many varieties of quince trees. Her house is more her castle and her garden her grounds, but she makes jams and jellies like the best below-stairs cook even though it is her husband who is the everyday cook in their household; preserving is somehow a separate skill. Her letter included a simple recipe for quince jam from Margaret Shaida's recently published *The Legendary Cuisine of Persia*. This jam is made in exactly the same way we still make jam, but includes cardamom in the final stages of reduction and asks that the quince flesh be sliced extremely thinly, which is its charm as the slices hold their shape while the skin seems to disappear. I think it needs some lemon juice towards the end, too. On the way to jam it passes through that colour I have grown to prefer above the opaque deep ruby produced by reduction and slow cooking. It is, at this earlier stage and some time before setting, translucent and a delicate apple-like rosy pink. With the next batch of quinces I stopped here, added a little lemon juice and the crushed cardamom pods, and served it with yoghurt. Only the addition of muesli restrained a Persian delirium.

At Berowra Waters Inn we often baked quinces with star anise, which, used sparely, adds wondrous faint hints of liquorice. When poaching or, best, slow-baking them for a fruit compote, leave the core intact and remove it at the cooled close of cooking. This best sorts out the woody interior from the flesh, wastes less quince, produces a better-shaped piece of fruit and is, triumphantly, so much easier. A friend in New York wrote last November to say that she was cooking quinces with Gewürztraminer and honey, that she would add this preparation to a pie of Granny Smiths and raspberries for Thanksgiving. This was to be reminded of a filling of grated apple cooked with butter and eggs that we used to make at the restaurant for a *chausson*, a puff-pastry turnover, and which I still enjoy making. Made with half quinces (which grate well) and half apples, the filling set well and the colour was marvellous.

Quince and star anise and rabbit commingle marvellously. The farmers' market at Willunga is now a year old and edging towards legitimacy, which is to say that the number of growers with their raw produce is increasing in relation to the makers of profit-added ('value' is the wrong word) foods in little jars. One of the best stalls is that taken every other week by a couple from Meningie, south-east of Willunga, who breed rabbits for food. They (the rabbits) seem to have had a stress-free life and the flesh is pale and succulent, so moist, in fact, that the legs happily grill to pink on the barbecue over charcoal. One saddle I boned and stuffed with a loose filling of some seared livers, the kidneys (oh that rabbits had at least eight kidneys, instead of two), only enough fresh breadcrumbs to bind, a slop of egg and lots of basil and parsley, although I know that tarragon will be better when it has grown enough to be picked. I rub *quatre épices* or, better still, *ras el hanout*, indiscriminately over all meat, from beef to duck to rabbit. You need to make enough of either mixture to ward off the weariness of having to make more too soon – but only just enough, so that it is always close to freshly ground. The long flaps that continue to the belly from the saddle of a rabbit are designed to enclose; wrapping the whole in thin slices of pancetta enhances flavour and wrapping again in caul ensures a tight parcel and makes a pretty, fat, transverse slice for the plate when the boned saddle is served.

As a prelude to the saddle, I grill the best livers from a large package handed over by the growers with generosity and with gratitude for my having wanted them at all. Some are as pale as the best goose or duck livers; the texture, if less creamy, still good and the flavour gutsier. Like poultry livers, the rabbit's is also prone to spilled bile, but these greenish stains are easily cut out. With the livers a jar of apple jelly made from Granny Smiths, which have ripened earlier than the other two varieties, is very good. As with the quinces, the imperfection of the apples is no impediment to making a good jelly. In the same way that quinces cook through a pale-rose stage, apple jelly – even from the greenest apple there is – reaches an amber that suggests a rosy pink. It is not for nothing that these fruits belong to the family Rosaceae, even when the flowers and their hips might argue that they existed before becoming a colour.

Over tea one morning (a fine Darjeeling that hints in its liveliness to rose-pink as well), K and I quibbled over the imprecise instructions given by May Byron in her 1927 book on jams and jellies; I am honoured to own it, but wish she were still alive to cook with and question. When Byron says 'boil' I would say 'bring to the boil and simmer fast'. When Byron gives times for her 'boiling' I want to know what diameter her pan is. Still, she is the heroine of my jelly-making middle age and the addition of cayenne to an apple jelly made from what I think are Cox's Orange Pippins suspends tiny dots of red in the rosy jelly and adds vitality, even on toast. This is Apple Jelly No. 3 in her book; her jellies run on and on like rasp-berries, as Sylvia Townsend Warner once wrote about Schubert's songs.

I began again to make sourdough about three years ago and haven't bought commercial bread since, preferring to run out than to relax, liking the discipline in an undisciplined middleage. I gave myself about two years to begin to understand the interaction of temperature, humidity, the health of the culture, different flours, different ovens, and many more variables, but even now I know I am only just at the point where I might start to say I make bread. With jellies there is a point at which the imprecision of Byron's instructions matters not at all. The jelly itself will tell you everything: when a fine one has finished cooking and is tipped into a jar, its urge to set will be so strong that you store the information on its making for future jellies. That's craft for you, I guess, the accumulation of practical knowledge, even when this simply means combining fruit and sugar and skimming scum. South Australian academic and food writer Jennifer Hillier, whose deconstruction of recipes and cookery she bases to a large extent around the notion of *metis* (an ancient Greek term commonly translated as 'cunning' or 'cunning intelligence', and taken up by development theorist James Scott), would be smiling in triumph at the talk between K and myself.

He, alarmingly, makes jams and jellies with skill and high standards, as well as managing to maintain a career as a leading tenor in Europe. By a curious coincidence he once sang in a production of *Arabella* at Glyndebourne designed by my quince-growing correspondent J. K thought highly of the apple jellies when he came to stay on one occasion after singing, aptly, Mahler's *The Song of the Earth* in Sydney. He recommended little tricks like saving the water which has been poured over the skins and cores, and using it to top up the simmering fruit if needed. Later I found that May Byron recommends the same practice, and another friend stores pips from juiced oranges in his freezer as a supply of pectin for his annual marmalade days. In the volume on preserving in Time Life's ever-explanatory and comforting series *The Good Cook,* there is a lovely jelly called 'Paradise' reproduced from Irma Rombauer's *The Joy of Cooking* (1931). It is made from apples, quinces and cranberries, and you can imagine its utopian glow. Can one buy fresh cranberries in Australia? Might I replace them with dried barberries from a place far closer to Paradise: Iran?

When the rabbit grower gave even more livers, I promised her a terrine and a 'parfait' of livers. For the terrine, chicken livers in a recipe from Michel Guérard's *La Cuisine Gourmande* were replaced with the rabbit's own and everything else was left as is – the pork and veal, the back fat, the alcohols, the seasonings. The Swiss butcher in Willunga provided what he calls pancetta, which is smoked as well as cured and all the better for wrapping the terrine in. Had I more rabbit meat I would have used it instead of veal for the forcemeat. It takes at least two full days and nights for a terrine to settle itself and mature; then it is superb with Apple Jelly No. 3. On the property to the north lives Herb who is ninety-two, (though he is prone to exaggeration and sometimes boasts that he is ninety-five). I gave him some of a terrine, calling it meat loaf to keep him calm.

K and I drove into the hills behind McLaren Flat and got lost among some gigantic prickly-pear cacti. They were all close to the road and the pears ripe-red for the picking, like swelling boils in rows on gigantic mittens. Without the secateurs and gloves that should stay in the vehicle of anyone interested in the stealthy collection of produce and cuttings, we folded a towel in four and were able to break off enough fruit to do something with. *The Oxford Companion to Food* records that desert-dwelling American Indian peoples picked prickly pears early in the morning, when they are still damp with dew, and then rolled them in sand to get rid of the horrendous little tufts of spines; here in the 'civilised' world, I am still finding spikes in thumb and towel. Even this plant's other common name, the Barbary pear, sounds dangerous. The spiked grenades we picked were relatively bland-tasting when raw, but the colour of the jelly (hold them with a fork to peel) is a clear shiver of golden-red, like stained glass. March was a cruel month.

Postscript

I began to spend far too much time making jellies and, ever hopeful, have planted a medlar (another member of the Rosaceae family). I watched on television a British murder mystery in which the medlar was the symbol of evil. It is a strange fruit that only ripens for eating after lying about on straw or sawdust for a few weeks. The policeman in the story, reading from an unsourced book, said that the medlar 'ripens only by its own corruption', which might also describe our bodies' decay and simultaneous sharpening of the mind. This slow ripening is called 'bletting', and is the only word I have ever looked up in the two-volume *Shorter Oxford* and not found there. It is, however, in the *Complete Oxford*. The fat French–English dictionary, acquired at a library sale because its spine could not take the strain, translated the verb *blettir* as 'to grow drowsy'; I now use 'blet' quite often.

And there they were, in the final frame of the murder mystery: two dozen jars of medlar jelly looking more like jam. Translucence, like ripeness, is all.

Sour wings

Sorrel soup travels well. I planted sorrel last April and it wasn't long before the bugs and I were sharing the leaves; no strings or stalks for either of us. Enough for omelettes at first: a chiffonade of sorrel and just a little black olive meat, lots of black pepper, which pairs perfectly with sorrel, and all laid across the centre of the omelette before closing the whole as a roll when the eggs have barely set. The lemon flavour of the now-dull chiffonade makes a splendid contrast to the richness of the eggs.

Soon there was enough growth (one gardening book instructs that the leaves can be picked after the first five appear; I counted) for sorrel soup, which takes a pretty large colanderful to make enough for six or so. The first time, the guests travelled to the soup. We were surprised by the class of it, the velvet texture, the lemon flavour; an adult dirty-green hot smoothie of a soup and uninhibited by other flavours – just the sorrel, some butter, a little flour to bind, some very light chicken stock, a dice of potato and a whirr in the blender, a little milk to stretch it further and lots of ground pepper. The clumps of sorrel produce more bright-green elongated leaves, I make more soup, the clumps respond and so it goes: in equilibrium, a good relationship, each seeming to benefit from the other.

I drove to Melbourne some months into take-it-for-granted sorrel season. Friends from London had come to Australia, but couldn't come to my house to eat, so the food went to them. I missed the recital given by the one with the voice, but managed to make it for lunch. Always prepared, I had most of the ingredients with me, including snips and cuts from the garden and an absolutely, completely finished and tasted-for-seasoning, you guessed it, sorrel soup, all packed snug and cold in the boot. It travelled well, went straight into the fridge and that was one course I didn't have to think about; except, hell, I forgot to serve it. If there'd been one less course I might have remembered. I blame the ex-ex-husband, a scientist, who'd made some pretty damn good grilled octopus and what with the olives and the salmon and the sausage and the rice pudding and a couple of Irish songs to melt the heart and the sorrel soup standing by, I decided to stay two more days so that at least I'd get to one Melbourne Festival concert if I could cadge a ticket.

So I had one day to myself in country outside Melbourne, a lazybones day of cleaning up and doing the dishes and the odd nap and never getting out of a nightshirt, which I've never thought was letting things go anyway, and the phone rang. The Russian maestro, said the important young man who had invited him and his orchestra, wants to go to the country and see kangaroos. No problem, kangaroos à la minute are my forte, I replied, and I took the maestro on a wild kangaroo chase at the edge of the city near Yarrambat (which is where I was staying), and we watched at close range – cross my heart and hope to die – a herd of over forty of them watching us, and then, as graciously as kangaroos can, loping away, stopping every now and then to check that we were still looking. And had the maestro and his entourage eaten lunch? No problem, there was sorrel soup in the fridge.

Robert Landry, in his 1970 *The Gentle Art of Flavouring* (a translation of his original *Les Soleils de la Cuisine*) writes that 'borscht water', a fermented water flavoured with lovage, which is used to make the Romanian and Balkan versions of borscht (no relationship to the beetroot, cabbage and beef borscht of Russia), can be made by adding lemon juice to the water sorrel has been blanched in. Is this what the maestro was alluding to when he commented that sorrel is used to make green borscht?

⁓

Back in South Australia the sorrel had been doing well without me, which is one of the glories of an advanced salad bed and a little rain but which also galls my need to be needed. There was chicken stock in the freezer as usual, free-range of course, and when someone else rang from Melbourne to ask for the recipe I went for surprise and posted her a containerful of soup: aluminium foil for insulation, bubble-wrap, sticky tape and a prayer for a safe overnight journey. There was the odd stomach-wrenching turn when I thought about what other people's mail would look like if things went wrong, but once again sorrel soup proved its travelling credentials.

By late December the clumps of sorrel were fighting to go to seed. I let one have its head so that the crop might be perpetuated and I might legitimately call myself mother. I'd just got back from listening to a little music near Mudgee, which involved a round trip of 4000 kilometres, when I was told that two friends from New York were going to be in Sydney for Christmas. I hadn't seen them for years. For a moment I thought about packing up again, but came to my senses. I do love those long lone drives, though, and am adept at dipping sourdough Melba toasts into scrambled ostrich egg as I drive between, say, Junee and Narrandera while John Cage on tape reports that when Sri Rama Krishna was asked why there is evil in the world he replied 'To thicken the plot'. But enough is enough.

This time I picked the sorrel so early in the morning that it was wet with dew, made the soup, chilled it fast and then froze it, snatched it out, bound it up, coddled it in insulating foil, did the thing with the overnight bag at the post office and the thing with the stomach and worry about staining other people's mail. But I knew it wouldn't let me down: it's well travelled, a long-distance soup, and it has fed some of my best and distant friends.

If you haven't tasted sorrel soup, it's possible you think I'm making a silk purse out of a sow's ear, emeralds out of leaves. To look at fresh sorrel you would never guess at the transformation of the delicate (even when quite large) crisp leaves into the strangely glutinous dull-green reduction that results from melting it over heat with oil or butter. At its thickest and darkest it reminds me of laverbread, the thick purée of low-tide seaweed beloved of the Welsh and Irish. Spinach, although it melts down in the same way, does not acquire that gel-like quality. Sorrel is a member of the dock family (the docks and the sorrels: sounds like a folk-music group), but having never tasted its relatives I don't know whether all of them share this characteristic.

If you do know sorrel then you will wonder at my leaving it at soup and omelette, for it is the basis of one of the best sauces in the nouvelle cuisine repertoire and makes perfect play for the palate with fish and white meats. I am cautious about attempting to list everything it might be used for. Culinary knowledge in our mostly urban comfort zone is a fraught, post-modern, open-ended encyclopaedia; there is an aversion to cooking anything twice, a shift from cooking as work (though never without its pleasures) to an indulgent hobby. So let's leave it at soup and omelette, with a nod to the sorrel sauce made famous by the Troisgros brothers in Roanne, near Lyon.

A sorrel soup

The recipe I use is from Simone Beck's *Food and Friends* and she calls it Soupe à la Suraile, translated as 'Norman sorrel soup'. Is *suraile*, then, a regional name for sorrel, a combination of *sur* ('sour') and *aille* ('wing')? Sourwing, a lovely name if I'm right, or even if I'm wrong. The English word sorrel comes from the old French for 'sour', and the French word, *oseille*, is thought to have been derived from 'oxalis', oxalic acid causing the sourness of the leaf (it is also the toxin in rhubarb leaves). Complaining to a friend about the soursop which disfigures the land from autumn through winter, he pulled one out and showed me the long white tuber he said he used to eat raw as a child, even though it is full of oxalic acid. Trying to love soursop, I blanched some of the tubers and dressed them as though they were asparagus, to no avail.

You will need, for six or so portions, a large colander packed firm with sorrel leaves (all stalks and central veins removed); 3 tablespoons butter; 2 tablespoons sifted flour; 6–8 cups light chicken stock; 3 medium-sized potatoes, peeled and diced; salt and freshly ground pepper; a little cream or milk to finish, if you so wish.

Melt the sorrel in the butter in a non-aluminium saucepan until it is completely wilted, add the sifted flour and stir over heat until the flour is cooked through. Add the stock and potatoes, and bring to a simmer. When the potatoes are cooked, purée the soup in a blender. Season with salt and pepper to taste, and add cream or milk at the end if you like and if the soup needs thinning – just a touch will enhance the colour, too much will lessen the flavour. The soup should be absolutely smooth, so a blender (rather than a food processor) is the best tool, and the reason for removing all sorrel stalk and vein.

Kettner's Book of the Table includes a soup called 'Bonne Femme', which is exactly the same as the soup above except that it is thickened and enriched with a liaison of egg yolks and cream; it is not puréed. 'There is a gracious sauvity [*sic*] in the soup, with a sub acid flavour.' I'd call it 'suavity', but won't argue over the order of a couple of letters. It's anyway a good word, suggestive of smoothness and sophistication. (In French cookery, *à la bonne femme* traditionally refers to humble or rustic dishes, such as potato and leek soup.)

The sorrel soup known as Potage Germiny is above all a *potage* and not a *soupe*, according to Robert Courtine in *The Hundred Glories of French Cooking*. 'When a *soupe* moves up the social scale,' he writes,'it becomes a *potage*'. Here, fresh sorrel is cooked in strong beef stock and when this has cooled a mighty amount of cream is mixed with a mighty number of egg yolks and added to the sorrel–bouillon base. Heated through without being allowed to boil and so curdle the yolks, it is then seasoned and, in this version at least, allowed to cool and ultimately served cold. Courtine reckons that 'true gastronomy centres on cold dishes, which are of a more uplifting subtlety and sensibility', but in disagreement I would suggest that his criteria befit the world of haute cuisine (the book was first published in 1971) and even the tail-end of ancienne cuisine and its hero Carême, who sculpted food for the table. The glory of Potage Germiny is indeed its outrageous richness, and the role of the sorrel is surely to cut this with some acid, as the addition of lemon juice or a reduction of wine does in other foods.

'The more refined cooking becomes, the more delicate its flavours; finally, one may go from subtlety to insipid flavour, and much of the joy of eating is lost';

this from *Chinese Gastronomy* by Hsiang Ju Lin and Tsuifeng Lin. They are wise words and might explain a preference for *soupe* as opposed to *potage*. One would never find eggs and cream insipid but the 'strong beef stock' in which Courtine's sorrel is cooked must cancel out most of sorrel's inimitable presence. When sorrel is simmered rather than melted with butter or oil it loses a part of its character, lends its acid to the whole and shows none of its full and fresh identity.

Sorrel and cream sauce

This is the Berowra Waters Inn version, based on the recipe in *The Nouvelle Cuisine of Jean and Pierre Troisgros* (1980), of a sauce for salmon we all did to death in the eighties. The sorrel sauce recommended for veal in Michel Roux's *Sauces* is almost identical. (Differently, Janni Kyritsis used to make a fine sauce for rare steaks of tuna by simply melting lots of shredded sorrel in good olive oil over heat, with ground black pepper and salt added.) I made the sauce, despite my earlier vow to leave things at soup and omelette, just to check the sum of my prejudices. It is a good sauce, but the sorrel has played its part and been partly lost, unlike its taste and texture in the simple soup.

To serve six, you will need: 1 leek, finely sliced and sautéed in a little butter; 125 ml light fish stock; 125 ml dry vermouth; 125 ml white wine; 450 ml thin cream; salt and pepper; 6 handfuls of finely shredded sorrel leaves, stalks and central vein removed.

Add the fish stock, vermouth and white wine to the sautéed leek, and reduce the liquid down to about 125 ml. Add the cream and reduce the whole to the consistency of a medium-thick sauce. Season with salt and pepper. These steps may be completed ahead of use.

Just before serving, add the sorrel to the sauce. This is the best way to retain the fresh lemony tang of the leaves.

Omelette with sorrel and black olives

This makes a fine first course or a simple central dish for any meal. For four to six portions, you will need, for the omelette itself, about 8 free-range eggs plus 2 tablespoons water, and salt and pepper to taste. The filling calls for a couple of

Sour wings

very large handfuls of young sorrel leaves; the meat from about 24 large and best-quality Kalamata olives; freshly ground black pepper; sea salt; and a very large knob of butter, say 50 g.

I like to make one omelette, turning it over onto a large plate and slicing it into portions at the table. Many years ago I was given a magnificent, large green plate from Provence. It has an extremely deep rim that rises just a little, but is otherwise completely plain. Although it is round, the half-circle shape of the omelette, the yellow from the good eggs, looks marvellous on it, allowing the plate to show its deep glaze.

Proceed as for all omelettes, but use a large pan that will make a fairly thick one. Remove the stalks from all the sorrel leaves, and the vein down the centre of each leaf. Lay the leaves on top of each other, roll up and chop into fine strands. Lay this down the centre of the omelette as soon as the egg mixture is in the pan, adding the olive meat and the pepper and salt; the sorrel will wilt and turn dirty green. Slide the omelette onto the plate, turning it over on itself so that it resembles a fat half-moon. It should still be runny in the centre.

Back in the garden in order to banish thoughts of haute cuisine, the sorrel is now, late in February, slowing down. That's okay with me. I've made one more lot of soup and we'll have a rest from each other while I make hundreds of grissini and pretzels for an artist to use as part of a project we have dreamed up for the Adelaide Festival. She is making leis from edible things, the list seems limitless: native seed pods; bones (the delicacy of a bird's skull!); shellfish shells (the nacreous inside of oyster lids!); almonds, even bitter ones, from local trees; and bread. As she works I shall take her bowls of nourishment. There's sorrel soup in the freezer and it travels well.

Cloud (the sandwich)

... to say that this is a good bacon sandwich is only to say that by the criteria applied by like-minded lovers of bacon sandwiches, this one is worthy of approbation. The word good is reducible to other properties such as crisp, lean and unadulterated by tomato sauce. You will have seen at once that to a man who likes his bacon sandwiches underdone, fatty and smothered in ketchup, this would be a rather *poor* bacon sandwich ... all statements implying goodness or badness, whether in conduct or in bacon sandwiches, are not statements of *fact* but merely expressions of feeling, taste or vested interest.

George, a professor of moral philosophy, in Tom Stoppard's play *Jumpers*

We were a Vegemite family, that's Vegemite as opposed to Marmite. Were we a Marmite family it's possible that my mother might have 'cut thin slices of white or brown bread and spread each slice thinly with Marmite butter (made by mixing a little Marmite with three times as much butter). Delicious sandwiches can also be made by the addition of chopped nuts, lettuce, tomatoes, watercress, cucumber, grated cheese and other fillings.' This advice comes from 1930s issues of *Nigeria: A Quarterly Magazine of General Interest* compiled by the Education Department in Lagos. Nigeria was run by the British back then. By the forties, Marmite had ceased to advertise in my copies of *Nigeria* (rescued from someone else's recycling and sporting marvellous cover drawings by Donald Friend, who was resident there at the time); but in the thirties its campaign centred on turning snacks into meals with the magic ingredient: 'a snack is a meal – and a satisfying nutritious meal at that – if you make your sandwiches with Marmite . . . Sandwiches are a *real* meal made with Marmite.'

I was a kid in the late forties, early fifties, at primary school. It was the time of free milk and home-made lunches. Envy of much more interesting sandwiches brought by kids whose parents didn't speak English caused a fast munch through the Procera bread with its burned ceiling, sagging pale sides and the thinly spread Vegemite inside, lusting for the exotic sandwiched into the crunch of someone else's. I'd even befriended a girl who ran home to a hot lunch every day. I wanted what I didn't have: interesting food, interesting fillings. Working at the Myer department store in the late fifties, filing account-debit slips in creative ways during school holidays, earning £6 a week and rich, I ate in the store canteen and one day ordered the brain-and-bacon sandwich. Having grown up on lamb chops and mashed veg ad infinitum and too many Vegemite sandwiches, it surprises me now that I even chose to put it on the tray. If a sandwich of crumbed brains and bacon might count as a culinary epiphany, then this was mine.

Culinary epiphanies are more usually associated with haute cuisine; one climbs towards them rather than steps down. The Cambodian chef, Sottha Khunn, was interviewed by Mollie O'Neill for *The New Yorker* in 2001. She asked him what he might do after fourteen years as head chef at the famed Le Cirque in New York and a subsequent trip back to Cambodia:

> As to what he might be, the chef didn't have a clue. He thought he'd return to New York, he said, maybe open a sandwich shop: 'A good price, a good sandwich – that way I give a little piece of happiness to the maximum number of people, wash my hands, and go home and have a life.' But several minutes later he started laughing. 'Maybe there is one problem for me about the sandwich shop,' he said. 'My father always tells me the one born a swan cannot become a duck. Like that, maybe one guy who helps shape the cuisine, he cannot make a sandwich.'

Cloud (the sandwich)

I've been thinking about sandwiches a lot lately because John Resnick, my favourite fictional detective – yes, much more my cup of tea (and there's pots of it 'mashed' in John Harvey's novels, set in Nottinghamshire) than Ian Rankin's Rebus – makes a lot of them. Resnick is Polish, mostly trying to forget the fact, although he turns up at the Polish Club sometimes, and his sandwich fillings confirm his cultural roots. He shops for produce, and for the occasionally more complex food he cooks, at the delis in town:

> a pound of smoked sausage, a quarter of dried mushrooms (an extravagance that went a long way), two ounces of dill and a slice of poppy-seed cake; at the greengrocers, a January King cabbage and half a cucumber [excuse me, you can buy half a cucumber?]; at the cheese stall . . . feta, Jarlsberg and a strong cheddar; pickled herring, horseradish and sour cream from the delicatessen near the exit [of the market].

Here's a selection of his sandwiches, the first as simple as it gets: sardines in oil, onion rings and grated feta; there's dill pickle, salad and chopped liver; smoked ham, mustard, slivers of Jarlsberg. There's more: 'a thick, ridged pickled cucumber, sliced and laid across corned beef, further spiced with a liberal dash of four-grain mustard'; 'tuna and chicken livers, radicchio in a garlic sauce, dark rye bread with caraway' and 'Emmenthal and slivers of prosciutto ham, so fine they would fold back and wrap around a finger like a gold leaf'. Dining in Harry's Bar in Venice one holiday, Simon Hopkinson leant across his prosciutto and said to me, 'It should be so fine that it falls onto the plate like the finest handkerchief linen'. Harvey is right about the gold leaf.

In *Rough Treatment*, a very funny story of break, sex and enter, Harvey lays down Resnick's sandwich philosophy:

> Sandwiches, in Claire Millinder's experience, were neat slices of wholemeal bread pressed around cheese rectangles or turkey breast, augmentations of tasteless salad and a smear of low-calorie mayonnaise. For Resnick, they were more satisfying on every level: two major ingredients

whose flavours were contrasting but complementary, sharp and soft, sweet and sour, a mustard or chutney to bind them, but with the taste all its own, finally a fruit, unforced tomato, thin slices of Cox or Granny Smith.

It all sounds like an achingly good riff of jazz, doesn't it – and indeed, Lester Young, Charlie Parker, Dizzie Gillespie, Miles Davis are the sandwich-obsessed detective's heroes. But even with Resnick's creative fillings, the sandwiches show him to be alone, lonely, ill-kempt, not up to the effort of a real meal. In this he is similar to Rankin's Rebus, who never goes further than toasted cheese: 'Toasted cheese: that most solitary of meals. You never saw it on menus, never invited friends round to share a few slices. It was what you ate when you were alone. A trip to the cupboard revealing a few final slices of bread . . .' A sandwich will never quite do if one is inviting people to lunch. You don't sit down and flick open a linen napkin in order to eat a sandwich, unless alone and smearing a book (Resnick smears his ties) with some of the filling at the same time. Of course, you might set out on the table the ingredients for a great sandwich, including the bread, but I'm yet to see anyone turn the parts into a sandwich; few would take a second piece of bread and flop it over the pickings. On Radio National an eighty-something-year-old woman reflected on life in Violet Town, Victoria, after the Second World War. She remembered, with wry humour, hosting a lunch with a friend, which they'd called 'an American lunch': a table of sandwich fillings with which the guests were to make their own. Most of them mistook the fillings for salad, piled the ingredients onto their plates and looked around for forks.

Sandwiches are not quite the same in the United States. There, sandwiches comprise, for instance, so much pastrami on rye that the bread hardly matters – although it does, and nothing but rye should do. Then again, to sandwich between two John Harveys a 1974 novel by Richard Condon, *Winter Kills* (a close-to-the-grain and hilarious version of the Kennedy assassination), there was Gameboy Baker asking Joe Diamond if he wanted 'a sannawitch': 'They split three pastramis on whole wheat and two bottles of celery tonic. It was lousy pastrami.' Additional evidence for my thesis on the eating habits of single male American

Cloud (the sandwich)

mafiosi and gumshoes is best summed up by Raymond Chandler's Philip Marlowe in *The Little Sister* (1949): 'Down at the drugstore lunch counter I had time to inhale two cups of coffee and a melted cheese sandwich with two slivers of ersatz bacon embedded in it, like dead fish in the silt at the bottom of a drained pool. I was crazy. I liked it.'

What kind of thrift caused the English, and so white Australians, to be so mean with the filling? Sometimes I order a sandwich at a fast-food counter (curried egg would be a favourite if it tasted of curried egg instead of a suspicious chemical sweetness which is to do with what, exactly?) and in nostalgic mood examine the archaeology of a meat-and-salad sandwich. I want to ask for ten times the number of slices of roast beef (knowing it won't be truly rare), four times the amount of tinned beetroot (a product which, like tinned tuna, has its own legitimacy), lend the maker the pepper grinder from my bag, and advise a change to Riga extra-hot horseradish. Hold the lettuce, the tomato, the processed-cheese slice, the grated carrot, the onion ring, the alfalfa, the fluorescent sweet pickle, and sigh in memory of Jack Nicholson's finest moment on celluloid in the café in Bob Rafelson's 1970 film, *Five Easy Pieces*. When ordering all I say is 'brown bread, no salt, lots of pepper', although there's the grinder in the bag like other women carry lipstick (also fermented chilli paste, chopsticks, and a corkscrew). The 'no salt' is not for health reasons, but because the tin salt-cellar is always the size of an icing-sugar shaker and tips far too much on.

There is a certain gesture towards generosity in the Oz salad sandwich – the stuffing oozes towards and wets the edges of the wrapping paper – but it is the sum of mean parts. Interviewed on his return to Australia to lead the Sydney Symphony Orchestra in 1997, John Harding mused on his relationship with his homeland: 'I like Australians. But I like to think what made me stay was the salad sandwich . . . No mayonnaise, but it has to have the cucumber. Which I remove. People find that odd . . . And to be honest, it's very nice with white bread, or "cloud" as a friend used to call it.' The use of 'cloud', white sliced at its most poetic, reminds me of a cartoon in the now-long-defunct *Nation Review* at the time of Kenneth Clark's television series *Civilisation*. Clark, in a Leunig depiction, defines civilisation by the white-bread, corner-cut sandwich. An historian at Flinders University in South

Australia told me that one of the defining differences between South Australia and the rest of Oz in these matters is that here people cut triangles rather than squares. This was confirmed by two other women in the Barossa. (A Melbourne friend defiantly said she was a 'corner-cut' person herself but then added that her father came from South Australia.)

Of course, the corner-cut must be crustless if it is to be civilised, and its most aristocratic variation is the asparagus roll. In Melbourne, in the Royal Arcade, there probably still is a tiny café which, in my fifties childhood, served crustless white bread rolled around asparagus and 'stuck' with butter. Sometimes there were tiny double-tiered rolls with extra fillings. Except for my aunt's rock cakes and fresh white peaches, I had grown up hardly knowing what good food was, other than swapped sandwiches at school. I had also never eaten out, and to sit in this café with women who always had hats on and gloves off, and order these crustless little rolls, was to aim low and dream of a little sophistication. Some people want the opposite. Andy Dalziel, Reginald Hill's gross softie in his series of detective novels, refused to lunch at a certain café: 'No fear. They cut the crusts off your sandwiches.'

—

The solution to the ooze of salad sandwiches is to be found in the brilliant constructions at Harry's Bar's in Venice: the chicken and mayonnaise, the egg and anchovy, the prawn, all bound with freshly made mayonnaise. A place as expensive as Harry's that manages to include sandwiches on the menu has to be as confident as one gets in the restaurant business. Make the top slice of bread larger than the base, making a form-follows-function feature of it, and turn the whole into a pillow. Harry's does one sandwich which owner Arrigo Cipriani admits is 'packed so full you have to eat it with a knife and fork'. Toasted, it is called the Grilled Club Sandwich which, according to *The Oxford Companion to Food*, is usually a 'three-decker toast affair'. The 'club' allusion is thought to 'match the two-decker club cars running on US railroads from 1895'. You just have to decide whether you are counting the layers of filling or the floors and ceilings.

Cloud (the sandwich)

The first sandwich that took my blossoming, youthful, culinary fancy after the brains and bacon in the Myer canteen was the *pan bagna* in Elizabeth David's *Summer Cooking*. It literally wallows in the ooze of filling, makes it sensible and sensuous – that's the Mediterranean for you. The bread bathes in the olive oil then eats it up, and if the excess drips on your tie it's a lesson in thinking about the suitability, so to speak, of ties. The *pan bagna*, it seems to me, is a sandwiched Niçoise salad, matured by weighting. (Come to think of it, what about summer pudding as a sandwich of berries?) Now move further south and consider tapas, because although it has little to do with sandwiches in the Anglo-Saxon tradition, it is a lesson in eating on the run. The Spanish word *tapa* means 'lid' and the most generally accepted story of its transformation from word into way of eating is that Andalucian bar-owners would lay a slice of bread, *jamon* or *chorizo* over a glass of sherry to keep away the flies. The trawl of snacks that is tapas has come to speak of an attitude, a philosophy, a fabulously civilised way of life in a country where fast food on the move is a way of eating slowly. Despite the idea of the lid, tapas are not sandwiches but do sometimes come on squares of bread. I have had the good fortune to eat tapas in Logroño in the Rioja region in northern Spain, a town that does tapas proud. Some of the finest mouthfuls were differently prepared anchovies with bread to sop up the oil. And one of the finest fillings I've read about is in a Michael Dibdin novel: his Venetian detective, Aurelio Zen, 'stopped in a small grocery and ordered a roll filled with anchovies sprinkled with vinegar and a little crushed chilli'.

I've a favourite sandwich for now that depends on the local Swiss butcher having smoked some veal tongue. One tongue makes many sandwiches, even with a generous amount of filling, but smoked tongue keeps. The aroma of the tongue calls so strongly for hot mustard that you seem to be able to smell the latter before taking off the lid, a forward variation on the Proustian experience. Lightly toast two generous slices of sourdough, slice thinly lots of tongue, smear both slices of toast with English mustard, pull some of those French radishes called *cracou* from the soil, snip lots of lamb's-lettuce leaves for garnish and tumble the lot together. I'm also partial to a well-made BLT, although mine is called a BLR because I use rocket leaves for their peppery bite and, frankly, they are happier staying home in the sandwich than is iceberg lettuce. The Swiss butcher also provides the bacon, or pancetta which does just as well, and will slice it very thin if you ask. This is an American preference for an American sandwich.

So sandwiches are constructions containing whatever you choose to fill them with and deserve a higher ranking in the culinary pantheon: cold crumbed lamb's brain and bacon, stinking cheese with pickle, Vegemite with walnuts, peanut butter with jelly, salami with apple, protestant with catholic, cucumber with mint, raw sea-urchin roes and thin slices of lemon, felafel with tabbouli, Democrat with Labor; and more complex combinations with more than two ingredients.

Then there is smoked salmon with bacon and mango chutney... Now there's a sandwich! Smoked salmon, crisp warm bacon, and mango chutney between hot-buttered, thin, white, sliced and lightly toasted bread: this is 'Bacon du Bedat', my favourite sandwich of all and found in Simon Loftus's *A Pike in the Basement: Tales of a Hungry Traveller*. Loftus is a wine dealer in Suffolk and writes a good story too. Bacon du Bedat, he says, was invented by Bill du Bedat and refined by Victor Gordon; as a serious upgrade, it was suggested by Loftus to the man who won $800 000 at a card table in Las Vegas and asked for a BLT: 'Abrupt hunger after intense concentration demands a delicious snack not a meal, especially in the middle of the night. It seemed a neglected area of culinary research.' Loftus, pondering the idea of 'casino cuisine', suggests it can get no closer to heaven than Bacon du Bedat. He came to eat at Berowra Waters Inn some time in the early nineties and we made miniature versions to welcome him, placed them in front of the diners as an extra appetiser, and waited. After a bite or two, a booming cry of recognition crossed the dining-room: 'By god! It's Bacon du Bedat!'. That's the kind of moment we restaurateurs and cooks work for.

Cloud (the sandwich)

The green and the black

The teapot is glass and beautifully balanced; you would not think the handle could support the weight of water. Although it is at least thirty years old, there is not one crack or chip, even on the fine spout. It has a central funnel with which to contain and so strain the leaves from the tea, but I have put this aside. It was more a cruel, cramped trap than useful, and stole not only the fullest release of flavour but the essential aesthetic pleasure of tea, the contemplation of the unfurling leaves, the change of colour.

A tea garden climbing gently just outside Hangzhou, China, over twenty years ago. We have been allotted a guide in party uniform. No English is spoken. The rows of *Camellia sinensis* are in shining, pristine order. The 'factory' is a large airy concrete building with many windows, and the treatment of the fresh buds and leaves is the work of many men and women. Rows of wooden tubs, which resemble something between a copper, a wok or a half wine-barrel, connected to a supply of electricity, fire the tea with constant human attention. These firing tubs are really very beautiful and appear to have been in use for generations. The scene is one of industry, human industry, yet quietly rural.

Hangzhou a year ago. A tea garden quite close to the city, dormant in winter, covered in concrete dust and dirty with pollution. It is shocking. We drive higher into the hills in search of the ideal, walk a steep path to find another garden, this time unmanicured but at least green and dust-free. We have come here to escape Shanghai, for the landscape and the calm lake, for Dongpo pork, beggar's chicken, West Lake water-shield soup, West Lake vinegar fish, and fried soybean scum (*sic*) rolls.

If 'scum' were 'skin' it would make sense, taste much better, and did. We had come for shrimps cooked in Longjing tea but mostly we had come to revisit the memory of Dragon Well ('Longjing') tea, the tea for which Hangzhou is famous, a green tea which, once pan-fired directly after picking, has distinctive shiny flat pale yellow-green leaves.

The Dragon Well itself never dries up because a dragon lives in it; Australia could do with an influx of dragons. Many women were bringing buckets and containers to be filled from the well while we climbed to the source. This is one of Hangzhou's most famous tourist spots (that's Chinese tourists), and what was once a Buddhist temple has been turned into a teahouse. Dragon Well tea, they say, should always be made with water from the well. Two hundred years ago, an emperor picked tea close to the well; it was so well received by his mother that the throne demanded an annual tribute of Dragon Well tea. The bushes he picked from are still producing: tea bushes are long-lived and Dragon Well tea has been drunk here for over a thousand years. It is classified into sixteen grades: early in the year the tiny buds are picked for the very highest grade; later, the grade called 'Flag Spear' is picked. At a factory where we bought our Dragon Well tea, there is a photo of the Communist Party president who once placed his boots on their floor.

It is the late afternoon of a hot day. I bring spring water nearly to the boil and infuse the Dragon Well leaves in the glass teapot. The infusion shows the true nature of the jagged dried leaves. They have become again the twin protectors of a tiny bud, precious. The liquor is a pleasing yellow-green and has body, as if there is a slight oiliness to the infusion. I pour the tea into a small fine white cup. The aroma is intense and pleasing, definitely not one I associate with the west. I am unable to find exact words for this aroma, which is intense in a delicate way, insubstantial, perhaps like sweet roasting chestnuts and a scent of grass but also nothing like that. It is not 'green' at all. It is, almost literally, delicately intoxicating.

When Ruth Rendell's fictional Inspector Wexford, in China to solve a mystery, drinks green tea he finds it revives him 'with almost the stimulus of alcohol'; he senses hallucinations. He is, coincidentally, reading Sheridan Le Fanu's gothic tale of demonic possession, *Green Tea*, first published in 1872. Carter Dickson in *The Ten Teacups*, a 1937 mystery, also mentions Le Fanu, suggesting that the green tea was flavoured with opium, thus the hallucinations. Le Fanu was writing not long after the Opium Wars, which were not coincidental.

Alexandre Dumas (père) in his 1873 *Grand Dictionnaire de Cuisine* advised that green tea 'is lightly endowed with a property which is more or less intoxicating'. Since green tea has far less caffeine than oolong and black teas, it is mysterious that it should be the tea associated with intoxication (Dragon Well, for instance, is known to be extremely stimulating). Perhaps one simply has to follow the Chinese habit and drink it continuously. For myself, I associate the mysterious intoxication with the reverent process of making and taking green tea, which becomes meditative when observed alone, the way I like to take it. And is it simply coincidental that for the weeks over which I have been tasting many fine teas I have not wanted alcohol?

The Chinese rituals, the attention to the aesthetics of tea, had been in place for some hundreds of years before the very different connoisseurship of the Japanese tea ceremony. Old men in China still cling to and enjoy the clubbish atmosphere of their tea-rooms; tea might be an excuse for gathering, but still the rituals of its service are central to the excuse and the flavour matters. Tea is particularly good at absorbing the scent of flowers. The narrator in Daniele Vare's novel, *The Maker of Heavenly Trousers* (first published in 1935, and set in Beijing) says:

> At the end of June the gardener places pots of lotus at the doors of the pavilions . . . Sometimes I amuse myself by putting a few spoonfuls of tea into the lotus flowers, just before they close at evening. And I carefully pick the tea out again next morning all scented with the perfume of lotus.

White Paeony (Pai Mu Tan) tea from Fujian province, which some say should be classified as a green tea, is exquisite, all buds and tiny leaves covered in fine white hairs. After it is infused, I watch the buds stand tall in the now-clear yellow (there is a suggestion of orange) tea. These teas are called 'white' because of the tiny hairs on the leaf-bud, which must be picked at a certain time and so the tea is rare and expensive. White teas are said to be unique to China but in Sri Lanka, where much of the tea is strong black fannings and sent to the Middle East, I have seen tiny examples of white tea manufactured only to cause a headline in newspapers, which duly exclaim at the price it brought at the tea auctions.

White teas differ from the greens in that they are slightly fermented. Take a couple more leaves as well as the bud-leaves, and ferment a little more, and you have oolongs, which are neither green nor black. The very best oolongs are, to my taste, the most remarkable teas, their qualities pronounced by the swelling transformation, when infused, from tightly rolled 'pearls' to deep-green leaves, as though they were returning to their natural state. The release of these very large leaves is imperative. A Li San is an oolong from A Li mountain in Taiwan: the 'pearls', some still green, some darkened, stretch languidly as if in a slow expansive yawn, first making waves like seaweed dangling from the surface of a seascape and then settling to float, but submerged, the beautiful leaves horizontal. The leaves seem huge now, as though the glass from the pot has magnified the size, and there are couples attached to a tiny part of stem. The liquor is pale and has a different level of viscosity to white and green teas.

In Guangzhou, where tea is taken very seriously indeed, at a restaurant we only knew as The One with the Pigeons, the choice of tea is extensive and merits its own menu. I chose Dong Ding from Taiwan and it was worth the price. The Chin Yip Hin Tea Shop on Lamma Island in Hong Kong describes Dong Ding thus: 'Curly, well twisted strips in dark green. Fat buds and whole leaves with stems. Steeped leaves are light brown with red edges. The infusion has rich aroma which is likened to that of sugar cane.' This is true. The only tea more expensive than the Dong Ding at The Pigeon was a fifty-year-old Pu-erh, a mellow, earthy tea from Yunnan province: its infusion darkens alarmingly in the pot, but this does not affect the flavour; it grows on you. There is a saying about the people of this province, Guangdong: 'They have got the courage to have a taste of whatever is put on the table except for the table itself.' At our table the Dong Ding kept on coming. The tea bowls were the size of a large thimble or a cup in a doll's house. It is surprising how quickly one gets used to drinking from such a tiny receptacle. I think this must show that the Chinese know how to serve tea.

The green and the black

I have been sent some Supreme High Mountain oolong and also one labelled only as 'Florence's favourite oolong'. The first is a far brighter green than the second, but both have extraordinary aromas of orchid and honey. They are both teas for late afternoon and despite their being so precious they need to be used up soon. Tea must be fresh.

⟶

To have drunk all the teas in China and read all the books about tea might amount to obsession but the growing knowledge, the persistent tastings, would be hollow without the slow moment when you are overcome by the full sensation of tea. One only knows this when the ideal of tea makes fleeting, revelatory touch. It comes as something of a relief. So this is what it is! The revelation is separate to the venerable history of tea. It is dependent only on fresh clean water, the nose, the eye, and the palate. I have listened to the same kind of stories told by those who have fallen seriously under the spell of wine.

Only now does one understand why tea is essential to *cha-no-yu* ('the Way of Tea)', the Japanese tea ceremony, and also why it is, at the same time, in a sense irrelevant. A Zen paradox? Of course. Tea in that context (green and powdered) is a specifically Japanese ideal, the precious liquor around which the rituals are played out. 'A good tea-room is more costly than an ordinary mansion', writes Okakura Kakuzo, and *cha-no-yu* places the material in the service of the ephemeral, the meditative. Okakura again: 'Taoism furnished the basis for aesthetic ideals, Zenism made them practical.'

Tea has asked of the crafts an extraordinary catalogue of apparatus and even of architecture. Long before that first sight of a tea plantation in China I had bought a modern tea bowl in Tokyo. This purchase had nothing to do with the Way of Tea and all to do with an interest in pottery. It seemed to embody the ideals of wabi, *perfection in imperfection. I keep it in its box, tied as I have been shown. But it asks to be taken out, to be seen and held again, to be held in the palm of one hand and turned by the other. The stoneware body is rough; there is a vertical fold in the bowl. The glaze is in two parts, and the*

closest I might come to explaining the colours is to say that they resemble that spread made from hazelnuts and chocolate.

This tea bowl has never taken my breath away, but I felt that it was good. Recently I examined it again and saw that it would never move the stars to pity; the imperfection is forced, knowing. However, I do not regret buying the bowl. Seeing, understanding that it does not have wabi *has in itself been a moment of revelation. I showed it to Milton Moon, the great old man of Australian pottery, who had spent time in Japan. He knew immediately what it had taken me years to admit.*

Everything about the connoisseurship of tea is about the perception of subtle sensory effects. Everything about white and green teas, and even some oolongs, asks to be discovered as a scholar might interpret an ancient text on delicate paper; and yet, one realises, and this another paradox, freshness is all.

If paradox is central to Zenism, then green tea is its natural symbol. Green tea also embodies the scholarly ideal of China before foreigners; before, as travel writer Jason Goodwin puts it, 'all the strain of translation'. 'Chinese tea and Chinese writing are the same . . . You [add] to your knowledge piece by piece, stone by stone like the Great Wall.' And if green teas represent a pacific ideal, the black teas that Europe and an increasingly addicted English population began to prefer, indeed to build their own rituals around, represent dark acts of imperialism, trading profits, colonisation and war, the transformation of tea into a full-blown commodity that triggered what today we would call drug trafficking. John Le Carré, setting the scene for his novel *The Honourable Schoolboy*, dates the true beginning of his story of spying and betrayal to 1841 when 'Hong Kong became the headquarters of Britain's opium trade to China and in consequence one of the pillars of the imperial economy'. This fraught and sordid story triggered the shift of tea-growing from China to India, not only because these were the years of 'glorious' British rule there and wild tea had been identified in Assam but because opium was traded via the Bay of Bengal. Opium and tea: both pushed for our health, one insidious, one benign but its market so insatiable that it prompted all kinds of amoral and devious ploys because tea had become an article of trade. It could make people rich; its story blackened.

Tea shares the same kind of history as other commodities brought back by adventurers but which could not be grown at home – coffee, sugar, chocolate, tobacco, spices, for instance. We begin to want what we never knew existed, and when we have them they become social indicators, bolstered by the accoutrements – in the case of tea, the equipage – associated with it. Even in eighteenth-century Europe, some one hundred years after tea first came ashore, the cup and saucer were styled after the Chinese model. There is a dainty portrait from 1756 by Tischbein in which his wife drinks tea from a bowl and saucer which would be at home in China except that the decoration is the faint-pink flower of Europe. These saucers, which are more like low bowls, make me go weak at the knees. I want them revived but only by the most graceful potter. Attempting to understand why I find them so ravishingly perfect in shape, I can only reach for the repeated but widened shape of the cup, a second cup, a nest. These saucers were often used to drink from. I can count images of my grandmother on one hand; one of them is her habit of tipping tea from the cup into the saucer to sip.

But tea did not remain precious in Great Britain. It became the black tea that is brewed rather than infused; its price plummeted; the working class began to love a strong cuppa. I love the story told by an English nurse in a program about code words. Across the public address system of her hospital, mid morning and afternoon, would come the cryptic announcement 'Mrs Brown is pyrexial': Mrs Brown the Brown Betty teapot; and 'pyrexial', which is to have a fever, the brewed tea. And to bind the image of tea as hospitable comforter with its history of brutish imperialism and trafficking, what better than the cartoon headed 'Quentin Taranteatime': in it two shifty guys (dark glasses, thin ties) at a table, and on the table a tea-set; another guy, same shifty demeanour, is standing with teapot and says, 'Shall I be motherfucker?'

There is enchantment in the language of tea, its beautiful names and classifications in China ('cloud and mist', 'beautiful eyebrow' . . .), the literal and cultural translations that Goodwin hints at, the language of trade developed between the Portuguese, the British, the Cantonese. The English, embarrassed by the poetic, made it all business but cannot take the poetry out of 'flush' or 'tarry souchong'. I met a tea broker in Sri Lanka.

The green and the black

He took me to the Chamber of Commerce building in Colombo. A tea auction was in progress, no tea in sight; Aruna explained the fast-flying jargon and the shorthand of trade. Another day he set up a tasting and showed me how to noisily draw the tea from the small white bowl into the mouth. The spittoon was waste-high and stained with tannin. There were over two hundred and fifty teas; the apprentice held tiny old-fashioned scales to weigh out the portion of leaves for the water. Aruna tasted for the market but I searched for the bright, lively and pale. It is not easy to find very fine tea to purchase in Sri Lanka. The best tea was a Kandy FBOP1 (flowery, broken, orange pekoe). Compared to the usual Sri Lankan blacks, which are close to fannings, this tea has such large pieces of fermented and dried leaves that it is difficult to fill the caddy spoon.

Jason Goodwin had travelled to China, then to India and Sri Lanka, in order to follow the history of the tea trade. At the close of his journey he attended a tasting of Nilgiri high-grown tea in Ootacamund, Sri Lanka, and asked if he might add a tea he had brought from the Castleton estate in Darjeeling. 'The infusion [of the Nilgiri teas] was bright and the liquors pale. They made me think of Victorian child heroines with flaxen hair and shining blue eyes: charming, but frail, too.' The last tea in the line was the Darjeeling. 'The tea's bloom was magnificent, the muscatel aroma thoroughly pronounced, the background round and full. It all fitted and supported itself exactly. It was tea with comportment.' 'It, is, really, superb', said the planter in defeat.

Lemon posset, or not

With no apology for yet another appearance by fiction in a short essay about food, I recommend Jane Rogers' novel *Mr Wroe's Virgins* (1991). The story is set in the early nineteenth century and is based on the life of John Wroe, the leader of the Christian Israelite Church in Lancashire in the 1820s, whose flock provided him with the company of virgins.

In Rogers' novel Wroe takes, for 'comfort and succour', seven virgins (except that one, Leah, was not; she has a secret child). Another of the virgins, Sister Joanna ('She has no restraint, no distance. She is all sincerity.') advises Leah to cure the child's non-existent cough by not feeding him, but the girl disobeys. Leah says, 'Thank heavens he did not posset, for [Joanna] would undoubtedly have taken it as a miracle, the sign of food from an empty stomach.' It was in reading this that I came to wonder about the 'posset' of lemon posset, for which Simon Hopkinson had given me the recipe one year in London, and which I later saw attributed to Gary Rhodes, another English chef. In fact it is not so much a recipe as an action causing a reaction which transforms, in turn, into the best simple dessert I know.

The culinary noun must be related to the early-nineteenth-century verb. To posset is to regurgitate curdled milk and although we don't use the term much any more it is why those with babies tuck bibs and nappies over their shoulder when feeding and burping their child. According to the Oxford Dictionary, a posset is 'a drink of hot milk curdled with ale, wine or other liquor, often flavoured with sugar and spices, formerly much drunk as a delicacy or medicinally'. Like syllabub, but differently, a posset sets without eggs and so is wonderfully light compared to pots of thickened creams such as crème brûlée.

The medicinal purpose of possets reminds me of my grandmother, Ada Fealy, who kept a bottle of brandy in the kitchen for medicinal purposes only. She belonged to a sect with strict rules on alcohol, the radio (this was the fifties and before television had come to Australia), women cutting their hair, and painting one's face, from all of which she abstained. Sometimes I would plait her silky hair, as silky as lemon posset, and I wish I had asked her more questions, but adolesence made me dumb and surly. I never asked what the name of her church and faith was (they eschewed purpose-built churches and held meetings in homes), but I do know she was not a Christian Israelite.

In 1985 Alan Davidson published the first part of the seventeenth-century work *Kitchin Physick,* in which recipes are given for 'a cooling diet for hot diseases and constitutions'. The author Thom. Cocke 'swagger[ed] in print', in compliance 'with the mode and humour of [his] times', that he had spent over twenty years 'in the practice of Physick' after studying at two universities. Three of Cocke's recipes are termed possets: Tamarind Posset, Two-milk Posset and Ivory Posset. Davidson did not comment on the 'ivory' in the last of these: was it perhaps 'vegetable ivory' from an American palm? Two-milk Posset was made from milk and buttermilk; buttermilk sours milk (the American term for this is 'clabbering', a pleasing word) and in the dark ages when crème fraîche was not commercially available in Australia (it isn't exactly a supermarket item now) I used to make it by adding a certain amount of buttermilk to cream. Tamarind could be bought from an apothecary in Cocke's day and was used to curdle the milk ('two penny worth' curdled about two quarts of milk, the kind of instruction I find infuriatingly imprecise). 'Thus is made White-wine, Rhenish, Lemon, Orange, Sorrel [commonly used for its high oxalic acid content in this way in Europe], Pippin, and all Possets made of sowre things, which are excellent in Fevers, and all Diseases coming of Cholor; Vinegar Possets will do as well as any.' All this rather challenges the authenticity of the modern lemon posset. The recipe at the end of this piece, for example, is a successful dessert because the lemon juice does *not* curdle the cream, presumably because of the fat content. Better that it be called Lemon Unposset, or simply Lemon Cream.

In *Country Life* magazine in March 2000, a report on an antiques fair includes a photograph of a white tin-glazed pot with lid and two handles, twenty

centimetres tall if one includes the lid and its nipple handle. It was made in 1655 in Southwark and the indenting on the surface would, the expert said, have taken the place of coloured decoration 'for those puritan times'. The bowl has a spout that rises from the bottom of the pot: this is a posset pot, and it is thought that the spout might have come from the base so that the drinker did not have to cope with a mouthful of spices or, as possets were often drunk for medicinal purposes, so that it was easier for invalids to use.

Some time ago in *The Age*, journalist and author Andrew Masterson wrote a column in which he addressed 'the relationship between language, meaning and biscuits'. It was couched as a letter to Arnott's Biscuits Ltd and took them to task over the promise of their then-new line, the Special Edition New Maple Creme Shortbread Cream:

> Maple Creme Shortbread Cream . . . would seem to suggest that the biscuits concerned contain not one, but two types of cream. Further, it implies that the Maple Creme, which I assume to be the beige-colored stuff in the middle, is encased in Shortbread Cream, which must logically be the two solid outer layers. This surely cannot be.

Masterson quibbles amusingly over quite a lot more, and although he is poking fun at the dumb and misleading language of advertising it struck a chord with me, as the more I cook the more obsessed I become with the language of cookery – the proper nouns, the active phrases, the logic of ordering the instructions – and, further, with the words associated with the whole culture of cookery. I don't actually lose sight of the materials, but do find myself in that swampy land that exists somewhere between the practical and useless, and it is an extremely seductive country. It isn't that the food and the techniques matter less than the descriptions but that chewing over language is, in the end, to chew over more than lunch or dinner. It leads me to want to talk the lemon posset to the table, quibbling over its ambiguous name.

In Jane Grigson's *Good Things* (1971) there is a recipe for milk lemonade, which was popular in the eighteenth century and is a very good example of a posset even though it is not called one. It would seem that possets which are not and possets which are have exchanged nomenclature. Not only is milk lemonade a legitimate posset, it is a sensationally good drink and I make it for too-hot summer days, adding a fat slice of lemon and lots of ice in a tall glass; it has the appearance of barley water, but has more body. Whey, even though this would not seem to make sense, has body as well as clean flavour and so all that is left is to make something of the sweet curd that is the byproduct and reminds me of a rich, dry cheese filling for blintzes. In Davidson's entry for posset in *The Oxford Companion to Food* he mentions historic uses of the curd produced and suggests that with the addition of ingredients such as honey, sugar, eggs, even crumbled biscuit or breadcrumbs, we have the earliest forms of trifle.

I made milk lemonade out of desultory curiosity, unexpectedly found it to be marvellous and recommend its return to the kitchen syllabus. (Syllabub, by the way, is another variation on the addition of the 'sowre' to the milky.)

Milk lemonade

This is my version (a little less sweet) of Grigson's recipe. These quantities will make somewhere under two litres of milk lemonade; it keeps well for a few days.

You will need 3 lemons, 500 ml white wine, 350 g caster sugar and 1500 ml milk. Remove the peel from the lemons, pour ½ cup boiling water over the peel and leave for a few hours, even overnight.

Strain out the peel and pour the lemony water into a large bowl. Add the strained juice of the lemons (about 120 ml, on average), the wine and the sugar. Bring the milk to boiling point and pour fast into the wine mixture. Do not stir – the whole will separate into curds and whey by this action.

Leave the curds and whey to cool, then strain through a double thickness of muslin or cheesecloth (or better still, a large paper filter) into a jug (reserve the curd for some other use if you dislike waste). If you have not strained out all the curd, you will find that any particles will fall to the bottom of the whey, so simply pour it off. Chill.

Lemon posset, or not

As for lemons themselves, I can think of no more useful ingredient, except for the egg. Jane Grigson gave it a section in her *Good Things*, and in Elizabeth David's *An Omelette and a Glass of Wine* there is a fine little chapter on the lemon, which places it in historical context. (When the Queen asked Elizabeth David what she did, David replied, 'Write cookbooks, Ma'am'. 'Very useful', said the Queen.) David notes that as a condiment the lemon 'has largely replaced the vinegar, the verjuice, the pomegranate juice, the bitter orange juice, the mustard and wine compounds which were the acidifiers of 16th- and 17th-century Europe'. Having read Thom. Cocke via Alan Davidson, I would add tamarind to that list.

David enthuses over recipes which call for the use of all the fruit, meaning zest and juice, but doesn't mention Sussex Pond Pudding, which literally uses the whole lemon and so is the most useful of all. At Berowra Waters Janni Kyritsis and I developed miniature ponds using cumquats, but one of the reliefs of domestic cookery is to return to the original and to leave fiddle-me-do behind. The aroma of dark-brown sugar, butter and lemon spilling in combined and long-steamed form through the first cut into the suet crust of a Sussex Pond Pudding is one of the finest dining aromas of winter. Jane Grigson gives the recipe in her marvellous *English Food* (1974), writing that 'the genius of the pudding is the lemon'. Of course it is! It is pricked, in order for the juices to escape into the butter and sugar, and encased raw in the suet crust so that after hours of steaming it still has a 'vigorous' (Grigson) presence.

David includes a late-seventeenth-century recipe for preserving lemons 'in cloves', from the *Receipt Book of Anne Blencowe*. It begins, 'You must pare them very close. Part ye cloves . . .' and once again the dictionary proved useful: 'clove', it seems, once meant a natural segment of fruit, which makes sense once you have cleaved a lemon or any citrus, or for that matter a mangosteen, that paradisiacal fruit which looks lychee-like but is segmented. Now look at a clove (the spice) and see how it is cleaved. This is a lovely recipe, in which the lemon segments (or cloves, as I now sometimes call them with affectation of sowre knowledge) are set in apple jelly. The instructions are pitch-perfect, as someone once wrote of John Ashbery's poetry. For instance: 'So sett them by till ye next day; then heat them again as you did before, & when you think their sowrness is pretty well out, they are enough.' Talking about lemons to Marc Polese, son of Beppi whose eponymous restaurant fathered a whole tree of Italian restaurants in Sydney in the seventies, he told me that he serves a mushy digestif of prosecco, grappa and lemon sorbet at the close of a meal. It is called *Sgroppino*: In the Friulian dialect (of north-east Italy) a *gropp* is a knot in the stomach, caused from over-indulgence; adding *s* in front of *gropp* changes the meaning to a knot dissolved, all of which brings us back to apothecaries and physick and Mr Wroe's Christian Israelites. On the corner of two streets in the inner suburb of Fitzroy in Melbourne there is a small bluestone church which I have always noticed but never thought much about. After reading *Mr Wroe's Virgins* I happened to be staying near the church and at last its sign meant something, for it is a church of the Christian Israelites, with services given twice on Sundays, according to the sign. Rogers added a historical note to her novel: John Wroe, who was born in 1782, travelled widely in order to preach on the reconciliation of Jewish and Roman Catholic doctrines. He died in Melbourne in 1863.

I have mentioned syllabub, and am rather keen on it these days. For a fine syllabub and an even finer read, go to Eliza Acton, who published her first cookbook, *Modern Cookery for Private Families*, in 1845 and has a turn of phrase that delights. She gives some of her quantities not in tuppence-worths but in wine-glassfuls. A recipe for a lovely olive-oil cake, sourced from Italy in a British magazine, uses an espresso cup as a measurement. The recipe worked on the presumption that the volume of an espresso cup is 60 ml; I have guessed the Victorian wine glass to be much smaller than ours and if it is taken to hold about 50–60 ml, the syllabub is successful.

Eliza Acton's syllabub

These quantities make quite a lot of syllabub, which should not be a problem.

You will need the strained juice and finely grated peel of 2 lemons; 100 ml each brandy and dry sherry; 180 g of caster sugar; and 600 ml cream. Combine the lemon juice and peel with the brandy and the sherry, add the sugar and leave until it has dissolved. Add this mixture to the cream and whip until stiff but still soft. This last instruction is important – if the cream is too stiff it will want to separate. Eliza

Acton writes that one should skim the bubbles off the surface of the cream as one whisks. With present-day cream, which is fairly thick and has added gelatin, this is not necessary.

Divide the syllabub among small glasses (shot glasses or tiny martini glasses if you like stems, which I do not) or pour into a glass bowl. I have two beautiful Victorian 'celery' glasses that make perfect containers for the lovely off-white cream. If the syllabub has been made properly it will not separate even after days.

I am also keen on riberries (an indigenous berry related to the lillypilly), with their scent of cinnamon and clove. When poached, they shrivel like a sultana and their bright pinkness is transformed into a paler, almost translucent colour. An equally small portion of riberries in another small glass makes a wonderful accompaniment to syllabub, the spice overtones of the berries in perfect accord with the alcohols in the cream.

Lemon posset, or lemon cream

These quantities will fill about eight 100-ml pots. My measurements and instructions sit somewhere between the Rhodes (less sugar) and Hopkinson (more sugar) versions. Both Englishmen simmer the cream for three minutes, but when I have done this with Australian creams the posset separates (oh dear, this makes it a real posset).

Bring to the boil 450 ml cream (35% fat; 45% at most) and 110 g caster sugar, then *immediately* remove from the heat and stir in 65 ml strained lemon juice (about 2 lemons). Strain this mixture into a bowl, fill individual pots and allow the posset (which is not) to set in the fridge. The mixture shrinks a little as it sets and becomes more firm the longer it sits, so it is at its best on the day of making, after it sets firm, but keeps perfectly well for longer than this.

I find 100 ml to be a perfect portion; you may want more, but wanting more is surely the best way to close.

Ms Pople's potted beef

In mid-1995, Simon Hopkinson arrived in Australia from London with a clipping of one the late Fanny Cradock's recipes.

Buy the best quality raw chicken you can obtain. Smash it to a pulp, flesh, skin and bones, with a meat batter. Ram this pulp into a large bottling jar, fill it to the rim with ordinary three-star brandy – there is nothing to be gained by using fine old brandy – cover with band, lid and clip or screw-top and stand on a piece of wood in a steamer and simmer very gently for 24 hours. Strain off the liquid through a double fold of sterilized muslin and allow to set. Serve a teaspoonful at a time. It is miraculous.

The only teaspoonful that I have believed to be miraculous, and this an act of faith in literature, is the one of Tokay essence given to Johannes von Felden by his grandfather the Baron in Sybille Bedford's novel, *A Legacy*. Cadet Johannes, still a boy, had escaped the Prussian army and stumbled home starving after a couple of wretched weeks of walking and hiding. 'They really did have Tokay Essence at Landen, and they brought it up for Johannes. The cork bore the stamp of a year in the eighteenth century, and a spoonful appears to have had all the effect attributed to that fabled elixir.'

Simon and I set to and made what I shall call Battered Chicken and Brandy; the jelly was of deflating ordinariness, all cheap brandy flavour set with the gelatin from the bird. Fanny Cradock's last two sentences had raised hopes in us of an elixir comparable to the Hungarian Tokays of legend and as a result we felt duped, so duped that I have never had the urge to explore the possibilities of the recipe even with a fine brandy and a Kangaroo Island bird, and even though bashing a chicken with a hammer holds a certain transferable-to-Fanny pleasure. It is the ultimate in bad manners to talk about a recipe that doesn't work, a waste of words, but the next year Simon arrived again with a letter sent to him by a reader of his food column in *The Independent* in London, and we would both like to thank Glenys K. Pople of Poynton, Stockport, Cheshire, for sharing with Simon her potted beef and restoring our faith in the transportation of recipes from the old country to the new. The only suggestion I would make is that for the weight the family bible be replaced by the *New Shorter Oxford Dictionary* (both volumes). I have also used the two-volume edition of Edith Wharton's short stories, and Pepys' diaries. Both work well.

The ingredients for Ms Pople's potted beef are four in number: beef shin, salt, pepper and water. Shin of beef is always easily available in Chinatown – although in Cheshire the beef probably just lopes into the butcher's – and all one is instructed to do is cube the meat, cover with water, skim for as long as you are patient, then cover and simmer for ages (around three hours seems to reduce the muscle to rags, which is exactly how you want it). Season towards the end, cooking off any remaining liquid, and then mould and press under said book(s).

Ms Pople's instructions are quite lengthy, but her digressions have the warmth of generosity, the common sense and the intimate historical purposefulness that makes them invaluable as a record of a family dish that is eaten every Christmas. I've been fantasising about her age and don't want to know the truth. She writes that traditionally the pudding basin containing the shin would be placed on the 'cold flagged floor', which conjures up an image of someone who is too frail to reach for a heavy book (except, of course, for the bible which undoubtedly resides on the table). Then again, Ms Pople just might be to the manor born and have servants to dust the dictionaries in the library, or be as young and obsessed with recipes as we are in the Antipodes. As she suggests, the potted shin is admirable with a hot salad of beetroot; another time, serving a warm Kipfler potato salad with the moulded beef we were reminded of the miraculous partnership of some hot and cold foods. 'It makes the most excellent sandwiches ever', wrote Ms Pople, and she is right, especially if you smear as much as your nostrils can take of Riga's extra-hot horseradish on both sides of the bread. Hopkinson took a ridiculous number of jars of this product back to London with him and, being a generous man, will surely send one to Cheshire.

What warmed us to Ms Pople was not only the relief that her recipe worked (I don't so much mean practically as texturally and taste-wise) but also her prose and instruction. She knows what she is writing about and shows a working knowledge of her stove and of the animal she is cooking: 'Skim until the froth is no longer dirty brown or until you are tired of skimming'; 'You could vary the recipe by adding other seasonings but I have never found them to be an improvement'; 'Even Worcestershire sauce was a distraction'; 'If you want more complex flavours, do another recipe'. Bravo to that! Ms Pople's potted beef is not the food for dead palates in search of the new: it tastes of shin of beef. It keeps; it slices; and it is also pretty good with a thick paste of anchovies (once again, preferably Ortiz brand), garlic and parsley, even though I stand by the advice not to dress it up. It would certainly be a very difficult dish to dress down, and in fact one of its charms is that there are no measurements to tire the cook so the recipe is simply part of the text. I mean this text, of course, and not the one used to weight the beef.

Using parts of an animal that are usually ignored always makes one feel frugal and plain good. They have much better flavour than the parts that have worked less and been coddled for expensive soft chewing and haute cuisine. In the eighties I learned to love *onglet* on a visit to France with Simon Hopkinson: *onglet* is skirt, more specifically it is the best part of the many skirts that make up skirt, which lies between the stomach and the chest cavity. In Time Life's *Good Cook* volume on beef and veal, skirt is called the 'butcher's piece' and I've heard of it in Australia as 'slaughterman's skirt'. In both cases it is so named because its worth is supposedly known at the abattoir and it seldom gets to the butcher's shop, a fact I find hard to believe of most white Australian slaughtermen. Skirt is tender and full of flavour, and this flavour has an offal-related, liverish quality that makes it truly superb (the same goes for pigeon meat). As flesh, it is closer to the internal organs than the flank. It needs to be grilled fast and short only until very rare, then rested. I wrote about skirt in a column in the *Australian* around our potted-beef

Ms Pople's potted beef

time and a parcel arrived from a grower in western New South Wales; frozen for insurance, it was still slaughterman's skirt and made a truly great staff dinner.

———

Brisket, too, is a personal favourite. From the belly, just behind the front legs, it has a quite extraordinary muscular make-up, being a series of long strands which are difficult to describe – almost like short, deep-brown tagliatelle? – but not difficult to eat if the meat is braised for hours and hours. My local, small-town butcher, who sometimes has rabbits and will keep oxtail and saw up bones for stock instead of dog, will keep the brisket for me if I give him enough notice before the day the carcasses come in.

Cooking brisket doesn't call for measurements either, just ingredients. A piece of brisket weighing about 2 kilograms is trimmed, seasoned and browned. Following this, a big splash of red wine is reduced in the braising pan and a good beef stock is then added with some vegetable dice (onion, celery, carrot), unpeeled garlic cloves, and herbs for extra flavour. Rubbing the brisket with a mixture of the four spices the French unremarkably call *quatre épices* (usually pepper, cloves, nutmeg and cinnamon, but sometimes allspice, and easily ground at home) increases the depth of flavour of the meat and the braising liquids. The braising pan needs sealing well, the contents to be brought to a simmer on top of the stove and then the pan placed in a slow oven for at least 2–3 hours; more will hardly hurt. Towards the end of the braising time, add fresh root vegetables (parsnips are a must) and shallots and/or leeks, which are especially good as they repeat, in their long layered strands, those of the meat and are sweet.

The nicest thing about this dish is that it is portioned with two spoons rather than a knife; it is, accordingly, called Brisket à la Cuillère. We made it at Berowra Waters Inn for some time, adding star anise to the braising pan, and served it with Sauce Albert (a horseradish and mustard sauce, a version of a velouté, thickened with egg yolk and breadcrumbs). We also made a salad with brisket, the pasta-like strands making marvellous tossing pieces. A dressing thick with fresh herbs and capers, thin slices of red onion and even anchovies makes a beef salad that cannot, I think, be bettered.

Escoffier's Sauce Albert

Assemble 125 ml chicken stock (or very light beef stock); 150 g grated horseradish (Riga brand, extra-hot, if you are not up to grating the fresh root); 125 ml double cream or crème fraîche; 1 egg yolk; 1 teaspoon English mustard; about 40 g fresh breadcrumbs (amount will vary according to their quality and/or how thick you want the sauce).

Bring the stock and horseradish to the boil, remove from heat and allow to steep for a short while. Add the cream and bring to boil again. Place egg yolk and mustard in a largish bowl, then add the cream mixture gradually, so as not to cook the yolk. Check for salt. Add the breadcrumbs until the sauce is at least thick enough to be less than sloppy but not too dry.

Ms Pople's potted beef

Buried treasure

Octavio Paz, in an essay in his collection Convergences, *wrote about 'seeing and using'. He suggested that craftsmanship 'in its perpetual movement back and forth between beauty and utility, pleasure and service … teaches us lessons in sociability'. He wrote of the 'rationality' of industrial design, the impersonal uniformity. The handmade bowl is, by his definition, already sociable. So too is food prepared with discrimination and offered at the domestic table.*

The following selection has its own convergences. There is no separation between my relationship to certain foods and the particular bowls these foods are served in. The bowls ask to be touched, turned in the hands, then filled with food. I cannot handle a nest without damaging it in some small way, but despite this essential difference, I know there is a connection between the bowls and my untouchable nests: both are handmade, if we might say this about domestic arrangements made with beak and breast. The majority of the nests are bowl-like, which underlines the sense of 'holding', of protection; one thinks of cupped hands.

Nouvelle cuisine, in high profile in the seventies and eighties, brought with it to the table a self-conscious attention to the plates it was served on. Yet, used like this the plate has no organic relationship to the food, and an intelligent transformation of culinary rules became an empty aesthetic.

The transformation of green wood into charcoal seems as alchemical as the transformation of flour and water into bread celebrated by the Lyonnaise baker Luc Mano at the close of the piece on nouvelle cuisine. The stones which Phillip Searle and Cheong Liew used to store heat and so cook their remarkable banquet described in Buried Treasure hold to the same alchemical imaginings.

A pillow book for the table

(with apologies to Sei Shonagon; the headings come from the original)

Things that make one's heart beat faster

I walked through the kitchen of a Cantonese restaurant in Hong Kong once, and heard the sound that is caused when a wok is lifted from the fire it covers. One feels the tension, the release of a great passion, and now I go out of my way to pass through as many Chinese restaurant kitchens as possible. My body senses the same kind of tension in the music of Shostakovich.

Nothing annoys me so much

It annoys me to see people holding chopsticks too low. This is most often seen in American films. Using chopsticks is a great joy and seems the most delicate way to carry food to the mouth, polite and sensuous at the same time. There is a certain fast change of direction given to the chopsticks by the wrist as the morsel, having been lifted from the bowl, reaches the mouth. This action is most pleasing.

It is also annoying to see again and again the presence of grapes in films that include scenes of the close of a meal, especially scenes in grand houses. The presence of the grapes may be fitting, but one feels that often it reflects a lack of imagination rather than verisimilitude. After all, there are many more sensuous fruits to be taken from the hothouse.

I am always annoyed with myself when I eat dessert despite knowing that the sweetness will destroy the memory of the savoury.

On reaching into the fridge door to take a splendid bottle of chilled Hugel Riesling to a friend's house for dinner, I found that my daughter has opened it and taken a glassful.

It is so stifling hot

It is so stifling hot in the desert between Alexandria and Cairo that one should not travel through it after early morning. When I visited a Coptic monastery at Wadi Natrum and was invited to take tea after prayers, the incense and heat caused me to feel faint and, worse, my young daughter became sick and dehydrated. As we left, a monk who saw her distress offered salted olives and dry Egyptian flat bread and we were very grateful.

Things that give a pathetic impression

I have been at tables when others who know each other have not had the courtesy to forgo their talk of mutually known things, therefore leaving me lonely. This is not only discourteous but heartless.

Nothing can be worse

There are peaches and nectarines that look perfect but on being bitten are found to have the texture of flour.

Things that cannot be compared

The intense sugared smell of a perfect rockmelon. There are Indian songs that include lines such as 'My beloved eats cucumber, I eat melon', but I am not a fool and know that the fruits of the songs are allusions to love-making.

The intense acid sweetness of a passionfruit.

Outstandingly splendid things

Arborio rice is splendid in its size and plumpness. When it is combined with the scent of shaved white truffles it seems to be a food made in heaven, except that nothing is made in heaven.

A wine that announces itself by the sheer force of its personality, which causes a diner, halfway through a meal, to sit back and stop eating because of the realisation that the wine is extraordinary – not because they have been told so but because the wine itself speaks and cannot be ignored.

The crunch of flying fish roe infused with wasabi, and its being the colour of jade. I looked at a dish of calamari and eggplant prepared by Tim Pak Poy and thought that the tiny spoonful of these eggs was a mean portion, so I consumed it in one bite. As I continued to eat the dish, the crunch of the few remaining eggs was still there, so insistent that it seemed loud.

Things that give a clean feeling

Yoghurt.

Janni's tomato consommé.

Beancurd when it is so fresh that it is a delicate junket.

Washing up, which I enjoy after guests have left. It is to do with people having gone and one's privacy being regained, but even when I have not prepared a meal for friends I enjoy washing what has been used to cook with and eat from. This fact causes me to reflect that cooks who are truly passionate about cooking would not feel like this and that people like myself are cataloguers.

At Castle Drogo in Devon, designed by Edwin Lutyens, the large cedar sink, its wood so soft and worn, especially for the washing of glasses.

Things that give an unclean feeling

There are tastes that have the musty edge of earth in them, even of dirt: they include asafoetida and truffles, *fraises des bois*, and even tamarind and saffron. These foods must be used with wisdom and never simply, as can be the case, because one or the other has cost an enormous sum of money. At the same time there is an earthy smell to burnt toast that costs nothing and which I love as well, although I do not expect others to agree.

Pleasing things

Anders Ousback serves food from a dish at the table with such grace, which is continued as he lays back the spoons.

Sometimes the phrase of a poet or a writer exactly describes the shape or taste of a food. For instance, in the poem 'Pumpkins', Robert Gray writes of 'Pagodas of orange peel'. Aldous Huxley compares the taste of champagne to 'cutting a green apple with a steel knife'; Anders Ousback says, of the taste of a 1955 Lindemans

Porphyry, that it is hard to remember it is wet. Sybille Bedford, in her novel *A Legacy*, describing a lunch in French sunshine where pet monkeys gambol and the food is perfect, writes 'Watteau, pure Watteau, of the lightest, most sumptuous period'; but in a later chapter she describes a vegetable garden as 'Sheer Sisley' and I am cranky with her.

Embarrassing things

Tears are often a self-conscious production, and this is to be deplored. But tears should at least be welcomed when cutting onions: peel even more, slice the halves finely and play the kind of music that gives the tears greater cause; for myself, I choose Mahler's *Rückertlieder*.

Tears remind me of the salt of oysters and of the story of a goddess's tears filling a reservoir.

Michael Leunig writes, in his 'Selections from the 1992 Grand Autumn Festival of Weeping and Sobbing', of someone overcome with 'traditional percussive high saturation tablecloth weeping', but I think this is to be laughed at. And Fitz in the TV series *Cracker* says to his wife, 'How delicious grief is: a real emotion'. I suppose that drink, as much as a death in the family, caused this remark.

I once gave my friend A a plate made by the potter S. Cockatoos stand on it and written on the base are the words 'Hello sailor'. I could see that he did not like the plate and was embarrassed by it. Years later, when A was studying ceramics, S gave a lecture to his class and showed slides of her work. One was this very plate. She had made it for her lover of that time: he was a sailor and she had piled it with sausages and mash; and when he had eaten the food, he would came to the words. 'Hello sailor'. While he ate, she danced around him naked, with strings of jellybeans as her beaded costume. My friend told her that he had the plate, and as it was the only one she had ever made, she said, laughing, 'The bastard, he must have sold it!'. It took a long time, but now that the plate has a story A is not embarrassed.

Things that make one blush

Once when I was eating in a fishing village called Guetaria on Spain's Cantabrian coast we were brought *percebe*, gooseneck barnacles, a Galician shellfish that resembles a fat finger encased in a green-black shell and ending in a pointed, fingernail-like tip. On extracting the flesh I was suffused with a memory and could not help but tell the other people at the table. I was perhaps thirteen or thereabouts when in the dry Melbourne sun I climbed onto the roof of our suburban house and lay naked to sunbake. I was reading Jean Paul Sartre stories, one of which began with a description of an indolent, plump woman lying in bed and eating *rahat lokum* (Turkish delight). The icing sugar seemed to leave the page and coat my hot fingers. Our cat came onto the roof; its penis was extended. The woman in the story, the cat's penis, the heat, caused me to flush with imminent sexuality.

Having told the story I blushed. Blushing always surprises us and gives no warning.

Things that should be painted

There is a dish Tim Pak Poy has cooked which is the most painterly I have ever seen. In the first instance one looks at flavour. It comprises two plump chicken livers balancing perfectly on a roll of chopped, preserved beetroot. The livers are larger than the dark base and even recall the winged roof of Le Corbusier's chapel at Ronchamp. There is no sauce, but the livers have acquired a glaze and remind me of the surface of an oil painting; it is as if they have been burnished. The normal order of things has been upset – the roulade is a squat column, and the painted livers are raised and become eaves. The intelligence of the dish is in that inversion and in the sense of architectural weight on the plate.

Once, Phillip Searle encased quails in clay and supplied his many guests with hammers to crack the parcels open. There were no plates. When the baked clay had been smashed, the table became an open tomb of shards.

Things that should not be painted

When a friend who loves eggplants came to stay I placed in a large frond from a date tree, a natural basket, enough eggplants to fill it and set this on a wooden floor.

The purple-black of the fruits, polished by the sun, seemed to be all facet and sheen. There was a sense of plenty that would not be wasted because it was all flesh.

In another natural basket I once piled a wondrous weight of vanilla beans which, so much more black than eggplants and their shape repeating that of the container, held so many seeds of moist and powerful vanilla scent that they seemed to be alive. In one episode of *Cracker*, Fitz's wife, giving birth, cries to him in fury, 'Tell me I'm a seed pod! Tell me I'm a seed pod!'.

A woman who lives alone

A woman who lives alone will become unsettled by company in her house, but should use its unexpectedness to become hospitable again. Sometimes the guest will suggest that he or she cook a meal and this should be accepted graciously, the hostess only offering cooking utensils and condiments before absenting herself with a book or setting the table, using the loveliest plates, the finest glasses and the best linen napkins. The guest will be made to feel more welcome by this gesture of trust.

Rare things

It is rare in our society to feel real hunger, and while it would be insincere and pretentious, and insulting to those who lack enough to eat, to seek it out, there is no greater pleasure than to eat because the body needs food. A full stomach drains our palate of sensitivity, and although hunger may cause our palates to be less sensitive it may help us taste with wonder.

Although I do not believe in God, there is a point in saying grace for it makes us pause to think about the circumstances of our well-being.

Things that should be large

Rather than placing food on each plate for the guests at a table, a large plate to be spooned from is far preferable and pleases the eye with its exaggerated sense of generosity. The generosity includes the fact that this central plate or bowl allows guests to choose their own portions, so that those of small appetite may take little at first but return if the food entices, and the greedy may choose more initially and even take a second helping.

Recently I saw a film of an Italian family in Adelaide. The polenta was poured onto a table and covered with a rich tomato sauce on which grilled quails were placed. There was no room on this table for plates and settings: the family stood around it and ate from the giant plate. Afterwards a whole boned pig, roasted on a spit, was sliced and eaten in the same fashion. Food served like this is in part a result of the attitude of the Catholic Church to contraception, but that should not stop us celebrating it.

Once Phillip Searle, wanting to feed eighty people portions of his famous Chequerboard Icecream, did not simply make the larger quantity in standard moulds. He made a blown-up parody of the icecream itself, a metre square and perhaps fifteen centimetres high, a single slice to feed one hundred and mocking its own fame. It was a powerful, glorious idea and its execution the result of a sculptor's skills. The slice was so large that it needed its own cold room.

Things that should be small

The number of chairs at a table should not be more than five. Three is a thoughtful number too. The choice of odd numbers should be understood to introduce a benign irritant to the table, to promote singular voices in discussion, for it must always be remembered that tables are for conversation as much as for eating.

I have eaten lychees, both fresh and dried, in which the seed is shrivelled and so the flesh abundant.

Letters are commonplace

Letters are no longer commonplace. I have kept every letter and postcard sent to me for over thirty-five years. For more than two decades these included expressions of both criticism and praise for the food served in three restaurants. It is instructive to place those that are negative beside those that are the opposite. One kind without the other would make an unfair history, and although criticism hurts it shakes one into self-examination, and causes one to read with clearer eyes the letters of praise.

Things that are distant though near

A close friend, M, gave me a green bowl she had bought in Vietnam. It is extremely old and of such beauty that when I use it to serve food from I find that I fill it for every course, just to see it again and again. I have been told that the glaze suggests the bowl had been buried for centuries. It has also been used to cook with, being marked by fire, even though its form and glaze suggest that it would have been made for a grand table and been cared for differently. Octavio Paz has written about craft and suggests that a handmade bowl is 'already social'. This green bowl was handmade hundreds of years ago and it has held foods I will never know about.

The playwright John Simon wrote that 'However subliminally, beauty hurts. It has a strange taste, like caviar or endives or oysters; it doesn't just warm the heart, it also tears at it'. I think he is referring to beauty's uneasy pact with death. And Dorothy Porter, in a poem for the poet Gwen Harwood, who is no longer alive, contradicts the banality of the idea that it is enough that a poet lives on in her words: 'that is no substitute for feasting and flirting'.

Things that are near though distant
When I buy the ingredients to make dishes such as laksa or Chinese noodles with eggplant and minced pork, I am grateful to find the produce so fresh and accessible, but I cannot buy the collective memory of the country from which the dishes came. Particular smells – sour, sweet, bitter, salty – are at their most pungent, and only have meaning, in the landscape which created that particular menu of flavours and aromas. The earth is involved, the whole range of aromas includes a chthonic attachment to place.

There is a poem by Joseph Brodsky in which he writes about Daedalus: 'He had already invented, when he was young, the seesaw, using the strong resemblance between motion and stasis'. In Greek mythology, Daedalus threw his nephew Talos, one of his young apprentices, who had invented a saw, into the sea out of jealousy for his cleverness. Talos had also invented the potter's wheel. So-called invention in cookery is often simply a shift of ingredients, and a different way of combining them in a bowl or on a plate. Just sometimes, a cook comes along who might be named Talos and all those named Daedalus should nurture him or her.

Charcoal

For three long days and nights the smell of burning wood,
And then the fire seems to die.
The smoke is gone, but all there know
the embers still glow bright within.
And suddenly tired men regain their drive
as in each mind the thought prevails:
Has it worked, has the burn gone well?
Slowly, the cooled mound is turned back.
The tired burners smile; the prize, the charcoal,
glistens satin-black, and rings clear as a bell.

from *The Charcoal Burners* by Irvine Hunt, quoted by William Rollison in *Making Charcoal*

S tan Menz's hands are thick with calluses and charcoal dust, the kind of grime you associate with the Industrial Revolution and bleak labour in Victorian times. Indeed, to watch him making charcoal, which is in part his work, is to slip back a century or more, except for the odd and trivial anachronism like the old station-wagon he keeps on the land and the generator he keeps in the vehicle.

I got to know Stan because, knowing nothing about charcoal, I wanted to see it being made. We'd used eighty 20-kilo bags of mallee charcoal to cook for thousands of people on seashores and in paddocks (events we dubbed 'Plenty': 'fill each bowl with just enough') as part of the Adelaide Festival's regional program in 2000.

'Grills', resident in Streaky Bay on the Eyre Peninsula, an abalone fisherman and fitter and turner, had taken up the challenge of turning sixteen 44-gallon drums into artful barbecues, which we took to all four events. He'd even punched in some cute little holes to allow air-flow around the fuel level and which turned out to be a frieze of fish, scallop, octopus and crab with breaking waves a level below. Late at night, when the feeding was over and the charcoal still burning magnificently, the glow through the frieze was like a row of over-sized lanterns for kids. I met a whole truckload of admirable, warm, hard-working people during this time but the relationship that made it out of and beyond the month of Plenty was with the charcoal. It had behaved impeccably, giving off cooking heat of great intensity for hours and hours, and this from just one load in each barbecue, which at each event fed on average two thousand people. I loved to watch the burn until it outlasted me.

I'd asked around before embarking on the journeys that Plenty involved, and having found large bags of red-gum charcoal at an Adelaide wholesaler's and been impressed, was told by a young cook at Port Elliot, who made giant paellas on barbecues he'd created from rain-water tanks, that mallee charcoal was better. I switched wholesalers (there is a very large Greek community in Adelaide and they take back-yard cooking seriously) and agreed with him: more lasting heat from larger pieces of charcoal, still looking like the parts of stump they were.

The Arts Festival finished, as festivals do, and by serendipitous convergence I watched a documentary about Heligan, the magnificent Victorian garden in Cornwall which has been restored to usefulness and continues to bear produce via nineteenth-century gardening practices. You know the sort of thing: pineapples grown in straw while it snowed a path away; hothouse melons supported by nets like Gargantua's balls; walled vegetable beds. The property is about the same size as a very big modern suburb; over 40 hectares were left as a kind of Arcadian jungle and, just as the Victorians did, the gardeners now make charcoal in order to clear some of the wood and lighten the load to be carted out. Sycamore and ash, I think it was; and the logs were packed into a teepee shape with a hole in the middle. A burning piece of charcoal was dropped down the central hole, which was then shut off; it took four days for the wood to turn to charcoal.

Hell, I didn't really know what charcoal was! For the record, it's 'the residue obtained when organic matter, usually wood, is heated in the absence of air'. I learned a lot about the history of charcoal-making from little books like the one in which William Rollison explains, with the help of old photographs and diagrams, how charcoal was made in the Lake District in the latter half of the eighteenth century. The jargon of the trade adds romance to the dirty job: 'coppicing', 'coaling', 'shanklings', 'pitsteads', 'the motty peg', 'thacking' . . . Until the use of coke, charcoal, which burns hotter and cleaner than wood, was vital to the smelting of iron and other metals; the one industry needed the other. And, being the most water-absorbent material known, charcoal is also used as a filter and purifier.

However different the applications of charcoal now (Stan Menz makes charcoal for the barbecue company Weber and for 'charcoal chicken' shops), the way it is made is essentially no different from the method used centuries ago. Reading Rollison's description is to hear Stan telling me, just last month, what is happening as he tends his pits near Loxton in South Australia.

—

I kept on asking about charcoal and singing its praises. Some people go on about oysters, others wine; I'd found charcoal. I drove to the Riverlands because I'd met a woman who said she knew a man who makes charcoal. She offered a bed for the night and asked a scrubbed-up Stan and his wife over for tea the next morning. This is our first conversation:

G: When I was first testing fuels and produce I used red-gum charcoal.

S: It's rubbish.

G (triumphant but not understanding): Okay. Well, then I found mallee charcoal and it was fantastic.

S: Stumps or sticks?

G: Stumps, I guess.

S: It's rubbish.

G (shaken but showing brave front): Right, so what's yours?

Asking Stan questions made things a lot clearer, but I needed to see the process to really understand. A month or so after our first meeting, when he'd told

me that he has a permit to burn all year round, we arranged to meet on the dirt road out of Paruna into mallee scrub. I was in a frivolous little French car, and Stan and his two mates were in the right kind. We drove twenty-five kilometres, passing two magnificent clusters of mallees covering large areas that are protected under the heritage and environment rulings. Mallees are classified thus by their growth habit: they grow in response to environment, branches angled directly from a lignotuber, a large bulbous stump at the base of the tree. I find them ravishingly beautiful and my response, without wishing to be dismissed as kinky, lies somewhere between the spiritual and the sexual: their smooth, thin grey 'trunks'; their apparent disposition to seem to distance contact by angling outwards, like a family allowing space for each other without leaving home. Long threads of darker bark have been shed and then snared in the branching trunks. Mallees are never tall in this part of eastern South Australia, but the proportions are satisfying, form following function.

The land from which Stan cuts his mallee is no longer his, but he sold to a farmer who runs sheep (with five emus tagging along like poor cousins) and has retained the 'herbiage' rights. The trees regenerate within a year or two so his industry is not as destructive as it may seem to be. Still, there is a limit on how much wood Stan may cut in a year and, probably more to the point, he says that many of the 'charcoal chicken' shops he sells to are turning to heating which comes from the flick of a switch or the turn of a gas cock, and are not willing to work with charcoal. That's part of his livelihood going, and much flavour being lost to eaters.

Stan cuts only what he calls green sticks. This is dense, freshly cut, young wood (no more than fifteen centimetres in diameter and some much thinner) and clean compared to the lignotubers or stumps which, although they burn hot, tend to burn unevenly and spit sparks because of debris, including soil, collected on them. His pits are on average three metres deep and about four by five metres in area, with a piece of iron railway track laid across the top to hold up the corrugated iron sheets that act as a lid. Charcoal pits don't last for ever: of the four I saw, one had been used ten times but was near the end of its useful life; another had only been used once but was already cracking – caused by rain when the pit was still hot; another was over a year old, had been used more than twenty times and was still useful.

So what happens in these pits to produce a cooking fuel without parallel? First of all, it needs to be understood that this is not a burn. The collier's parlance is 'to cook', which is more pleasing to those dedicated to flavour than any collier might realise. Although a fire is lit using copious splashes of 'bushman's friend' and a big load of dead and dry mallee branches, leaves and sometimes spinifex, the rush of flame around a load of green sticks soon smokes and struggles to stay active. The sound this fire emits is an exciting, and almost musical, pinging crackle, anticipating the sound of first-rate charcoal hit against first-rate charcoal, a clear glassy ring, and is partly produced by the oil in the mallee leaves. Some ten minutes after its ignition, and with barely a live flame left, the corrugated-iron sheets are placed across the pit; two gaps, just four centimetres wide, are left between them to allow just enough air into the pit to keep the cooking alive. Sand and earth are shovelled around the edges of the sheets to close off any extra air. It all seems too casual to a naive observer like myself, but Stan knows what he's doing. If the wood burns (that is, too much air causes the wood to catch on fire), he's lost his load, and the pit will explode.

You might say that charcoal steams rather than cooks, as what is driven out of the wood is the moisture, and with it the chemicals. Stan will come back to the pit next day and check the progress of the changes in the wood. If this load has turned to charcoal, he will add another load of green wood and close the pit in the same way; the 'cooking' will move up to the new load, reaching for oxygen. The cooking finished, the lids are closed completely and the charcoal allowed to cool, a much longer process than the cooking itself and extremely important because if the charcoal is still hot when packed it might easily burst into flame. I touched some of the charcoal lifted and screened from another pit, and what Stan and his two helpers call hot I'd call warm, but they still closed up that pit to allow it to cool further and moved on to another.

When we came to the pit that was to be unpacked, Stan threw a handful of earth up into the air. 'Testing the wind direction', he said, and then the collection of the cooled charcoal began with what Stan called a 'front-end fork', himself in the driving seat and in charge of the machinery. The black sticks were dumped on a screen which looked as if it might be an old mattress base; the unsophisticated assembly of tools and grids looked as though they had been collected from other discarded machines and tools; everything once had another use and now the parts are again useful. Stan connected a very old fan on a stand to the very old generator in the back of the very old station-wagon, and the mist of black dust went the way he wanted it to. He was, nevertheless, wearing a hood and goggles while the two screeners chose to cop whatever flew back. Tiny shards of charcoal collected next to the pit; this has no use, Stan said, except sometimes it's added to potting mix.

When this pit was opened, your intrepid reporter gasped at the carbonised wood. The stack looked exactly the same as the cooking, except that it was black: the wood is not burned away, rather it suffers a compositional change. The best charcoal is still heavy, showing that the cooking has been perfectly judged, and the top of the pile, Stan says, is the best for Webers: larger pieces, bright and glassy black. The next layers are still good, but the charcoal breaks more easily and so makes smaller pieces: this is the bulk of the load and is sold to the take-aways that barbecue chickens. A cross-section of a piece of green-stick mallee charcoal is as shiny as glass, and if the two pieces are clicked against each other the sound is as crisp and clear as if it were glass. The best charcoal, when used for cooking, produces no flame, no sparks and no smoke.

Back at the derelict house on the land, we washed, made sandwiches and drank tea. Stan will return at the end of the day and check on the pits. He has a long iron rod which he pokes down into the load to check the cooking (if it goes right down to the bottom floor then the wood is charcoal, as it has become brittle and all debris has been cooked away), although the colour of the smoke tells him the story. It's not a clean life and it has its own demands. I reckoned he must get about a hundred and fifty 15-kilo bags from a good cooking and he concurred. Some quick arithmetic surprised me into realising that he probably makes good money, and so he should.

—

I passed through Murray Bridge recently, the largest town near Stan's patch on the road back to Adelaide, and pulled in at the local Mitre 10 hardware store to buy fuel for a barbecue the next day; no time to get to the Greek wholesaler. Surprisingly, the store did stock charcoal as well as the ubiquitous Heat Beads, but it wasn't Stan Menz's charcoal and the pieces were extremely small and dull. There's charcoal and there's charcoal.

'It's rubbish,' I can hear Stan say.

The parsley garnish

The Queen Mother came to Australia in 1953. She was offered white-bread sand-wiches in the shape of Australia, with a sprig of parsley at the south-eastern tip, thoughtfully representing Tasmania. This whimsy just might be the parsley gar-nish's most useful application, although being unattached to the continent one suspects it wasn't eaten with the mainland. Nearly two decades later the parsley gar-nish, still curly but definitely ageing, decorated the domestic dishes in the *Australian Hostess Cookbook* (1969), which I rescued from a recycling bin in 1997. The green sprig is tucked under the verandah of a lemon slice which in turn is tucked into an avocado and oyster cocktail; centres an avocado and prawn pie; adds modesty to the nether end of roasted ducks; provides the point at which tinned pineapple slices and glacé cherries decorate 'Kassler Kickshaw' (crumbed ham steaks on savoury rice); and adds colour to the béchamel-white coating of a chicken casserole.

At the Bon Goût in the seventies, the duties of maître d' and dining-room manager Alain Chagny included one that places the restaurant firmly in its dec-ade: preparing the parsley garnish. Just before service began, he would take a bunch of parsley (not the flat-leaf variety, which was definitely only for Italian res-taurants then, but the more familiar curly one, which still has its traditional place, be it plastic or real, in butchers' windows), wash it, patiently pick small 'bouquets' from the end of each stalk and leave them in a bowl of water on his side of the bench. No plate of food left that kitchen without the little parsley 'bouquet' tucked in beside the steak, duck breast, fish fillet, etc. The parsley garnish was the final touch, the ritual blessing given by the waiter.

I have hardly any memory of what the plates of food looked like at this restaurant, and even should I want to find out it would be difficult because there seem to be no photographs. This legacy of nothing again places the restaurant in its decade and explains much about our unblinking acceptance of the parsley garnish. Who decided it had to be there? Was it Alain, via an apprenticeship in formal French cuisine in a large hotel in the south of France? Was it Tony Bilson, via his youthful initiation into the mysteries of French bistro cooking under Georges Mora at the Balzac in Melbourne? Was it simply an acceptance of the ubiquitous finishing touch?

Auguste Escoffier's *Complete Guide to the Art of Modern Cookery* (*Le Guide Culinaire,* originally published 1903), Tony Bilson's bible in those days, has no photographs and so we have no visual evidence of his approach to garnishing. But the first edition of Henri-Paul Pellaprat's *L'Art Culinaire Moderne* (1935), the only other text we owned, has many. Pellaprat didn't overdo the parsley garnish, but it is there tucked under one end of dishes such as Homard ou Langouste Thermidor, Filet de Boeuf Richelieu, Poulet de Grain à la Diable, Perdreaux sur Canapés, Artichauts Entiers Cuits, Oeufs Pochés à la Reine, and many others. He was also keen on watercress as an alternative and it nestles into Jambon à la Gelée, Côtelettes d'Agneau Cyrano, Mutton Chops, Rognonnade de Veau, among others; and strewn on a table next to pizza is basil, an indicator of that dish's nationality rather than of ornamental style.

Revisiting the colour plates in Pellaprat's enormous book I am struck more by the insistence on the art of burial than by his green garnishes. By far the largest selection of dishes photographed are foods napped with chaudfroid sauces or in aspic, what we might call old-fashioned buffet food now but which took tremendous skill to assemble. With some exaggeration it might be said that the art of aspic is the cook's equivalent of the art of fresco painting: you have to know when to go with it. Escoffier said that a cook should be first of all a pastry cook, and Pellaprat lived out his advice: he wrote this book in his retirement and the decorations suspended in his chaudfroids are a testament to pastry training – the cook as jeweller – as well as to the French habit of dressing to kill. The innocuous, useless, but harmless little parsley garnish added another colour to the plate: miniature green field against browned meat or white fish, a colour that was perhaps added originally in the earlier age of haute cuisine, to suggest raw produce and so possibly a real or supposed freshness. Too generously used, the little raw bush beside the cooked flesh became a bonsai forest, the scale of the clump reminiscent of the disproportionate scenery about a model railway set.

Green sauce was the preserve of the Genovese, not the French (although Pellaprat does include a recipe for Chaudfroid Vert-pré), and coriander was not to spread its sprigs outside Chinatown for another few years. At the Bon Goût in 1973 the parsley tucked into bed beside the food was irrelevant to the dish every time. Now, if I encounter it, I eat it first and fast in order to pretend it wasn't there at all. It is not the garnish itself which is the embarrassment, but the fact that I didn't, on the grounds of form following function, fight for its removal.

La nouvelle cuisine

We went to France in 1976 and came home with a large jar of brushed and sterilised truffles. We had seen and tasted the 'new cooking' for the first time and so I made little tossed salads (served *tiède,* of course) of just-cooked green beans, matchsticks of truffle, walnut oil, and a half turn and a tap of the pepper mill. I can swear that this revolutionary and even exotic (for its time in Australia) dish was presented without a garnish of parsley. Conversion was swift and complete, and with it came self-conscious attention to the appearance of the food on the plate.

Nouvelle cuisine was, according to Henri Gault, all his fault: 'Permit the one who was its sorcerer's apprentice to be proud of his incomplete and unplanned Manifesto', he wrote in 1995 of the 1973 article that launched a cuisine, 'wishing to be without roots and open to every influence [that] honours clear sauces, sauces that blend, that exalt and sing and leave the spirit clear and the stomach light'. Gault's manifesto listed a set of rules governing the new cooking: reduced cooking time, products put to new use, a menu offering far less choice, discriminating use of modernist technology but at the same time putting it to use to produce new dishes, release from the old culinary principles, recognition of 'the pretension, the inanity, the mediocrity of those rich and heavy sauces', knowledge of nutrition and diet, understanding 'the danger of deceitful presentation' and, finally, the central place of invention. His words brings to mind that other manifesto, produced in Italy dec-ades earlier, Marinetti's 1932 *Manifesto of Futurist Cookery*, which sought to 'create a harmony between man's palate amid his life today and tomorrow' and proposed 'brand-new food combinations in which experiment, intelligence and imagination will economically take the place of quantity, banality, repetition and expense'. This book was, as Lesley Chamberlain writes in the introduction to the 1989 edition, 'designed to wrench food out of the nineteenth-century "bourgeois" past and bring it into the dynamic, technological, urban twentieth century'. As far as I know, in all the commentary about nouvelle cuisine, no one has seen these similarities of intent. Marinetti's manifesto (by the father of 'aeropoetry') was, of course, a huge joke, a 'disguised artistic game' and, according to Chamberlain, 'the only book which treats food as an artistic medium and where the recipes are also lessons in painting'. This doesn't stop a sense of crackpot silliness pervading the recipes.

Gault's manifesto was in the form of ten commandments and in the 1995 essay he admitted to having made three errors, the first the 'arbitrary number and tyrannical pretension' of these edicts. The second, he said, was not to have included the need to 'preserve the achievements of the past and to keep alive tra-ditional country cuisine'. He seems to take full credit for killing off the old order (*la cuisine ancienne*), as well as inventing the new. The third error, in his view, was that in promoting a style without roots and open to all influences, he encouraged:

> a crowd of mountebanks, antiquarians, society women, fantasists and tricksters who did not give the developing movement a good reputation. Furthermore fashions, mannerisms and trickery attached themselves to this new culinary philosophy: minuscule portions, systematic under-cooking, abuses of techniques in themselves interesting (mousses, turned vegetables, coulis), inopportune marriages of sugar, salt and exotic spices, excessive homage paid to the decoration of dishes and 'painting on the plate', ridiculous or dishonest names of dishes.

Where Marinetti owes much to the Italian reverence for anarchic attitudes, Gault seems to me to exhibit a particular French weakness for sets of written rules.

Marinetti's joke must now be seen as performance art as well as manifesto, for his dishes and menus were produced and sat down to even when they did not, and were not meant to, constitute a nutritious meal. They were a serious joker's art after all – his dictatorship of original commentary on the past, his call to arms and flight. His recipes are the illustrated manifesto, whereas Gault's prescriptions came after the fact even though he takes journalistic credit for invention by definition, something close to the heart of nouvelle cuisine. As Julia Child, co-author of *Mastering the Art of French Cooking* and most definitely pre-revolution, wrote in *New York Magazine* in 1977, 'It all made very good copy – something revolutionary, at last, to talk about'.

Digging into the *terroir*, the culinary world of nouvelle cuisine reveals just how short-lived its positive press was. In fact, if one judges the movement by the journalism it spawned, it seems only to have existed in order to be belittled. Julia Child, for instance, said that the food 'is so beautifully arranged on the plate – you know someone's fingers have been all over it'. We know what she meant (often the elements in a dish were placed so deliberately, and with such 'artistic' intention, that it didn't seem to have been made to be eaten), but did she realise what she was also saying? Cooking is one of the last legitimate hands-on professions: cooks' fingers will always touch food, albeit often in surgical gloves in these scared times, and it is that touch which is the very raison d'être of the craft, its romance as well. The cover illustration of the physically enormous 1975 menu from Louis Outhier's L'Oasis restaurant (at La Napoule on France's Mediterranean coast) is a marvellous painting of active, sweating, strong chefs, knives in their scabbards, handling immensely heavy copper pans. It seems to be a record of a past era but might just as easily be the L'Oasis kitchen. It is truthful and romantic at the same time.

But while Child wanted dishes where the touch stopped at the stove, nouvelle cuisine was encouraging the chefs – French chefs, with that particular cuisine and past – to step through the kitchen wall into the dining-room with their plates. The aspic had melted into *jus* and running with it came the chef, modern, creative, individual and noticed. These very fine cooks (supreme examples include the Troisgros brothers and, especially, Michel Guérard), who established Gault's new rules by practice, showed culinary intelligence and imagination, but the great and new dishes they produced were ultimately judged by the general public not on the basis of their composite flavours and textures but by photographs in magazines and cookbooks. Nouvelle cuisine, like all aesthetic movements, was the child of its particular age and place, and it gave its bourgeois audience a new plaything to be seen to purchase, to know about.

Barbara Santich named her collection of essays on gastronomy *Looking For Flavour*, but she was using all her senses when she chose that title. Photographs of food are as odourless as the hero in Patrick Süsskind's novel *Perfume*. Photographs of prepared dishes undo the reason, albeit transitory, for their existence; photographs have nothing to do with appetite. Yet it was by a combination of photographs of food and the chef as celebrity 'artist' that most people learned about nouvelle cuisine; few could in fact afford it. Most of the chefs lost their way and believed their artistry (not the same thing, of course, as being an artist) at the stove should be evident on the plate. One could interpret this diminution of food, its journey to a single dimension, as a loss of taste.

The nadir of nouvelle cuisine plating in my experience was at a small and much-touted restaurant in Paris, where a young chef presented a broth made from écrevisses (yabbies) in which floated a mousseline island. Rising from the island, at least fifteen centimetres high, were two chives. It seemed like an edible take on a Japanese flower arrangement, so ridiculous that I blushed for the chef and ate them as quickly as I had vowed to eat all parsley garnishes. The look of the dish was so senseless, so *nouveau*, so laughably like a cocktail Jacques Tati's Monsieur Hulot might have served in his clickety-clackety house. Marinetti would have gleefully given it an aerodynamic name.

The Two Chives Experience must have been in about 1977, which was when Gael Greene, restaurant reviewer for *New York Magazine*, was gushing over 'tiny rougets perfectly cooked and arranged in a stunning still life with string beans in tiny dice and flutter of basil'. By 1985 nouvelle cuisine had been given a semi-official adieu by Paul Levy: in an article entitled 'Has-been Cuisine', in the *Observer* newspaper, he listed Henri Gault's rules of the new cooking and suggested that 'it follow[ed] that the arrangement on the plate became the duty (and pleasure) of the cook, not the waiter – and food as art was born. Chefs everywhere made pictures on plates'. Levy had opened his obituary with the suggestion that the whole culinary movement was the creation of journalists. It was all much more complicated than that (no plate is an island), but if you think you painted the canvas then it is yours to slash: 'Once chefs started believing what they read about themselves, once they had convinced themselves that they were artists, they were bound to fall prey to Romanticism.' At least he paid some attention, if glibly, to what else was going on while French restaurant cooking went to a health farm.

It wasn't the first time that haute cuisine, as distinct from *la cuisine bourgeoise*, had mistaken the plate for a canvas. Carême had strutted upon an architectural stage with scaffoldings of sugar and there had always been a sort of serious playfulness in pushing food to pretend to be something else; to impress the diner by surprise tactics. If we take these past 'glories' into account, nouvelle cuisine must at first have made the plate look downright plain to the French.

Those two silly chives precipitated in me a loss of personal faith (the bad boys had smeared what the good boys had reformed, and it *was* all boys), but it was a great spring-cleaning for French restaurant cooking, a reformation of a kind. If it was verbose, as some have described it, the verbosity was mostly from those who made their living writing about it – the art of hyperbole about the art on the plate – while all the time the art was in the cooking.

—

Michel Guérard once told gourmet Roy Andries de Groot: 'Above all, I want my cooking to tell the truth and nothing but the truth', but *la verité* is not something to which haute cuisine ever truly aspired. Nouvelle cuisine, in bursting out of the kitchen as it did with pictures on plates, might be seen as little more than games and obfuscation, artifice and pretentious collage.

Guérard was proved innocent: that is, he was a formidably imaginative and technically gifted chef. The truth that he was referring to was something to do with the nobility of raw produce. Writing about the late chef and restaurateur Bernard Loiseau, American journalist William Echikson romanced that Loiseau 'dreamed up new recipes in the solitude of the forest', as if to make a latter-day Rousseau of the chef who invented *cuisine à l'eau*.

This conceit of noble savagery seems more to do with Adam Gopnik's assertion in a 1996 *New Yorker* article that 'All French public controversies [are] a mixture of the absurd, the profound, the inscrutable, the enviable, and, always the metaphoric'. In the shift from haute to nouvelle, French chefs were still contriving dainty dishes to put before the 'foodies' (a term said to have been invented by Paul Levy in the 1980s), and this was certainly the verdict of academic Richard Johnstone in 'Nostalgic Nosh', an article for *The Age Monthly Review* in 1987. 'Nouvelle Cuisine represents nothing so much as the individual's acquisitiveness, the desire for the pure and unattainable, for the ultimate possession . . . It represents the final, decadent transformation of food into something else entirely, into pure style.' He made a fine point in this essay, subtitled 'The Minimalism of Nouvelle Cuisine', when he wrote that it 'paradoxical[ly] appeals to the instincts for indulgence and self-denial'.

Johnstone's complaints are legitimate when directed at audiences and commentators, and at frou-frou cooks, but he is wrong to deny the reformation of French cooking its own legitimacy. Alain Dutournier, a gastronomically proud Gascon who has never used a vertical chive in his career, and one of the best chefs to arrive with the reformation, said in an interview in the *Journal of Gastronomy*, 'I don't disown Nouvelle Cuisine . . . the changes continue, but intelligently . . . we continue to evolve, but we have greater respect for flavours and products . . . for me, there are only two types of cooking: good and bad'.

There should be a rubbish bin for acoustical garbage, Stockhausen once wrote. The mouth doubles as a fine waste-disposal system for its own. In Australia, having eaten the parsley garnish and the vertical chives, we are left often with copses of arugula, mizuna and lamb's lettuce acting as futons. 'On a bed of' a menu often says (cribbing from the French), choosing this above 'in bed with', which would be more to the point if the composite ingredients of a dish all make sense.

The spotless, great white border of the plate is still the defining difference between restaurant food, which is presented, and domestic cooking, which

Pictures on plates

is served. Framing domestic food would make it less spontaneous, too thoughtful. Once, years ago and too earnestly, I put to a curator the idea of an exhibition of unframed paintings. He looked at me in astonishment and suggested that to do so would be analogous to serving food directly onto the table. We left it there, each of us knowing so much less than the other about the other's subject.

Transgressions

Photographs of food, in the magazines of material lust, now market a sense of style that advertises eating by framing perfectly-suitable-to-the-colour-of-the-month raw produce on plates available from listed dealers. Richard Johnstone saw nouvelle cuisine as the triumph of style over substance, but a photograph of raw eggplants in a white bowl on a set table (an advertisement for *Marie Claire Lifestyle*) makes nouvelle cuisine seem positively edible at first sight. Spring onions in glass vases have become chic flower arrangements (at least they might be eaten later) and expensive foods are packaged like jewellery: hands off unless you can afford it. This is the new aesthetic of seduction, a version of Arcadia without dirt and odour, without taste. The seduction for the buyers of the magazine is the flattering presumption that they know what to do with the pristine, raw ingredients, not so much to turn them into edible dishes but to artistically return them, cooked/cultured, to the same bowls at the same table. It is all about style, which is not an individual but a collective idea, the copyist making the whole notion materialise.

Michael Carter contributed a paper to his own Aesthetics of Food symposium hosted by the art-history department at the University of Sydney in 1998. He chose the theme of the meeting because 'above and beyond nourishment, food usually involves a dimension that could be called form, arrangement, appearance'. Carter, interested in 'the look of abundance' and in the gradations of 'having enough, having more than enough and having too much', returns us to Gibbon's explanation of the decline of the Roman Empire: that, in part, too much wealth was given over to the luxuries of the ruling class. Luxury as a threat to 'judicious form' is a fascinating and deeply moral concept. And Carter also uses Petronius' *Satyricon*, a description of a feast staged for the wealthy Trimalchio in ancient

Rome at which every dish served is disguised as something else, in order to show how unshared surplus 'de-natures the appetites'. He concludes that:

> A rise in the esteem in which cooks and cooking are held is not in itself fatal. It is the aestheticisation of culinary activities which opens the gates to decadence since it is the aspiration to art which subordinates the nutritional role of food to the demands to spectacle, performance and transgression.

In Vikram Chandra's novel, *Red Earth and Pouring Rain* (1995), there is a story about a cook who fooled a gourmet:

> Once (said Sunil) there was a cook named Mashooq Ali, who was famous for his mastery of food-disguise, and the tales of his prowess reached the renowned connoisseur Ajwad Raza. Ajwad Raza made a boast, in front of his friends, that no cook could fool him, and so the delighted young gentlemen set up a contest. On the proclaimed day Ajwad Raza sat down to one of Mashooq Ali's meals, took a mouthful of rice and was chagrined to discover that each grain was an artfully polished sliver of almond. Then Ajwad Raza thought to clear his palate by taking a bite of pomegranate, but the fruit was a confection of sugar, the seeds were pear juice, and the seed-kernels were almonds. And so each thing he ate was something else, until finally he accepted defeat and said the world had never seen such an artist, and Mashooq Ali said, bowing, 'Allah is generous and his ways are mysterious.'

Nouvelle cuisine's fast rise to fame and its apparently equally fast decline are instructive. In the beginning it was justly celebrated and revered: the very best chefs not only washed, dusted and polished the haute cuisine dishes of the past, they took a different approach and put the vegetable and herb garden on the plate so that the 'fresh' was still redolent in the fresh produce, and the sauces, instead of masking, made impressionistic counterpoint to the main ingredients. They did France's culinary tradition proud, and because this was the period in which Australians began to travel in earnest, nouvelle cuisine played a major part in changing the expectations of dining out in our cities. Later we began to look to Asia, the most sensible of our upstart little robberies.

Under mercenary pressure, nouvelle cuisine somehow got too big for its boots and had a great fall. The pictures on plates began to pall and the next reformatory wave began: we went to the market ourselves, and began to revere agriculture itself, the producers and the artisans without whom no restaurant chef could produce good dishes. If the nouvelle cuisine chef was once the celebrity, that title now rests with the makers of great cheeses and wines and bread, and with the growers of fine vegetables, meats and fish. Next it will be given to the earth itself, and to *Darwin's Worms* – a reverence long overdue, and much more enduring.

—

Although the best cooking seems alchemical, it is craft, not artistry, that makes it transformative. When a baker in Lyon, after hours of repetitive work when most other people are asleep, and white with flour, speaks to a camera in a 1994 documentary, *Le Menu*, I know food is simply that which keeps us alive:

> [there's] such pride in saying you're an engineer or a doctor. I was only a baker. I felt embarrassed . . . So I took a decision. Since I worked at night, I used to say I was a programmer. It was a sham . . . I was interested in alchemy, the quest for the miraculous. I used my work for that quest. I asked myself, 'What are you after?' I wanted to do something fabulous. Changing matter into gold . . . Then one day I realised I had it all here. That is, my baker's trade was my own alchemy . . . Every day you hear people say 'it smells like good bread' as if good bread were something unusual. But for me it's my daily work.

And so much more.

Nests (weaving, pressing, collecting)
for Anders Ousback

Over twenty years ago, in a house I had moved into, a friend left behind a very old, small, Japanese lacquer-and-glass cabinet. The glass is fragile, and the sides hardly hold together. The base is covered with faded, thin, green felt. On the back wall of the cabinet a pair of ginkgo leaves is incised into the wood, one still coated with tarnished silver leaf. A branch of birch stands in the centre but it does not reach the ceiling of the cabinet. Two fragile glass shelves are hinged by fitting into nicks, at different levels, in the branch. The branch has otherwise been untouched by tools, except for having had its length cut. How many hundred years ago did the maker know, in some noumenal way, that this one rustic element makes aesthetic sense, that it does not undo the elegance of the cabinet; and know too, that to please the eye it must not act as a structural element. Although it stands as a tree trunk might, the piece of birch does not pretend to represent a tree.

I live somewhere else now, a long way from that house. How carefully the lacquer cabinet had been packed. It should not, I think, house more than two or three things, small things, but in it I have placed five nests. One sits on the highest, thin glass shelf, on a slip of paper that came with it in the post, signed by the friend who left me the cabinet, a fitting way for a nest to arrive. How do I explain the size of this nest? To say it is the size of a medium-sized bowl suggests the solidity of fired clay and glaze. To give an approximate measurement would be to dismiss the haphazard nature of the collection of twigs, and the numbers misrepresent the driven intelligence of the nest-maker. An exact diameter would ignore the fragile, uneven perimeter, the thin twigs interwoven to form a near-perfect circle but none of which are entirely incorporated; nearly every one has an end that sticks out from and seems to decorate the useful whole. Inside the nest are caught one or two dry leaves and one bit of fluff, a baby's feather. The nest is light, yet unimaginably solid for all its fragility. I suppose it is plain compared to others, but its beauty lies in the slightly leaning cup shape, and the fact that this form is made by nothing else than straight or only slightly curved grey-brown twigs. In some places you can see through the nest.

Another nest ('from my family's home: N'), is the same size as the first, but its sides are higher and it is more cup-shaped. It still sits in the fork of the small branch that held it in the tree. If I tried to take the nest from the branch, it would probably fall apart. The foundation (but once again this word is wrong, suggesting concreteness and solidity) is of dried grass. A large piece of faded wrapping tape is caught on one side, along with some now-brittle bubble-wrap; the presence of this unfitting human debris in nests always makes me smile. The crowning glory is a garland of leaves, built in the space made by the point where five smaller branches grew and which still retain foliage. Because of this, the nest is prettily crowned with this garland, still green although dulled, as if some bird saw that the grass cup wanted for decoration and made play on classical Greek figures or Hedda Gabler.

The third nest is exceptional, if any nest might be seen to be more pleasing in execution and materials than another. It is held in the fork of a piece of bamboo by only a few of its grass and twig threads, so that it slides along the main branch if I move it. The inner lining is made of the finest, strong dried grass and is the shape and size of a teacup. Around this, softer, thicker, more pliable grasses take hold; at the base is a large leaf and, by accident or design, a piece of paper which, wetted like papier-mâché by the weather, might once have had writing on it. There is no card with this nest, which is remiss of me, but perhaps it came from that house where a thicket of bamboo spilled the first nest of them all and I had not yet foreseen the appeal of the collection. The piece of paper in the nest reminds me of those hand-stitched quilts that used old letters for the templates of each patch.

The fourth nest is tiny, the size of a new-born baby's knitted slipper. It is a wren's nest and was posted to me by a friend who found it some way north of Newcastle in May 2000, and so it is one of the most recent in the collection. It hangs from thin, fragile twigs extending to one side for almost a foot. How did the wren hang its nest? The outer surface is the dull grey-green of lichen. Did the bird use saliva to stick the materials to the two twigs? It is a mystery of apparent imper-manence. As in an overcoat, the lining is different to the moss-like exterior, being dry, fine grass. Although I say that it is the size of a tiny slipper, because it hangs and is oval rather than round, it is in fact more like a miniature cradle or boat, but the plant's parts which coat the outside have the texture and look of crocheting. It trembles even when I touch it delicately.

I found the fifth nest on the grass verge above Christmas Cove at Penneshaw on Kangaroo Island, in October 1999 after a wild storm. It is a grass-soft nest the size of my hand and has a flat base. The opening is a little larger than the diameter of my middle finger, hardly more than a hole, and is entirely surrounded and softened by the fluffy feathers, shiny with saliva, of just-born birds. They are like a glamorous muff for a little girl, dirty white and pale grey, and the tips of some of them flutter in my breath. A finger placed inside the nest finds it to be capacious and snug.

A friend had been on Lord Howe Island for two months. He climbed Mount Gower and found a tail feather of *Phaethon rubricauda*, the red-tailed tropicbird. It is a quill fit for Voltaire, the spine so long and black it is as if ink has been left to dry. The shaft of the feather is over a foot long, with white feathers close to the hollow, colourless base (the calamus). The white feathers each taper fast to a crimson-feathered spike; these are so short that they seem like a little daub of crimson paint on either side of the black spine. At its very tip the feather is pronged, where the black spine finishes and thin red tail feathers continue. This prong is tiny, as if the feathers forgot to stop for a moment only. Looking up a field guide, I find that except for its tail the bird is an otherwise unremarkable white sea-bird. Appar-ently its courtship display includes dazzling backward somersaults high in the air. The nest of the red-tailed tropicbird is described as 'a scrape'. I like that.

This same man once sent a nest from Coffs Harbour. It is small, tough, straw-coloured and a little prickly; there are many burrs caught in the grasses. It has a tiny hollow in the centre. I showed it to another man who loves watching birds but is not interested in the collection of nests. He laughed and told me that it was not a nest at all but a wind-driven collection of tufts and beach debris. Sometimes I think it is and sometimes I think it isn't.

When I left Sydney, the giver of the tropicbird's tail feather and the nest that might not be a nest helped to pack the collection. The larger nests were already in boxes. He opened, one after the other, the twelve drawers of the Chinese chest that holds many of the small nests. The chest is three drawers wide and four deep; in most there are four nests. I entrusted the nests to this man and he placed each one in its own container – sometimes a saved berry punnet, sometimes an old box – padding with soft paper and taping the nest in, before placing them all back in the drawers. I understood, as he did too, that his usefulness allowed him the pleasure of surprise after surprise. Unpacking them would surprise me all over again when I arrived at my new home.

—

Friends came to lunch and we talked about nests. None had been unpacked. Like German philosopher Walter Benjamin anticipating the unpacking of his book collection in his essay 'Unpacking My Library: A Talk about Book Collecting', I was waiting, making a space for the time in which I could be lost to the task, spellbound. But the talk pushed me forward: I brought one drawer, and then a second, a third, from the chest to the table. No more. A space was cleared. It is important, necessary, to keep nests in cases; they cannot be cleaned, polished, vacuumed, dusted, there can be no *vernissage*, no last-minute repairs. Because of this, the Japanese practice of keeping something beautiful and of great craftsmanship hidden from view in order to feel wonder again on lifting it out and turning it, to pay proper attention to it, makes complete sense.

Here were the bulbul's nest found abandoned in bamboo in Sydney by C, padded on the outside with what seems to be some kind of wool; a tiny nest still attached to a twig and like a delicate basket; a nest shaped like a papoose and entirely lined on the inside with feathers as soft as angora; a nest brought back by R from Cape York, again like a papoose but with a lid to provide shade and with pale shards of paperbark making up much of its structure. Here was a nest sent from New Zealand by M, a small cup lined thickly with lamb's-wool. And here too the tiny nest that fell from a tree twenty years ago, the first nest of the collection, perhaps the most exquisite and certainly the most delicate of them all, the weaving of the fine grass providing a surprisingly strong structure, even though the material – fine, dried grass – is woven like a loose net.

—

A light box arrived one day and another parcel, heavy, flat and large. When I told someone that the box contained an owl's nest from the north coast of New South Wales, he said this could not be because owls do not make nests. I was forlorn for the nest-sender. She is not acceptable to proper society, too alive with paranoia, disruptive, often too drunk, cries too easily and makes us uncomfortable. She has an incisive mind, an untarnished memory, and does not get things wrong. I rang her and found I had misunderstood. Tawny frogmouths are not owls but are owl-like. They make nests.

This nest is the least like the image that the word suggests. It is not cupped or protective, not made to nestle into, to keep eggs warm. It is an untidy, flat bed of twigs, hardly packed together, a pile of deep-grey fiddlesticks. A large feather is caught on one edge, fluffy dark grey at the base and tapering into a beautiful speckled brown, grey and white, like Florentine marbled paper. The tip of the feather is a fine thread of black. Parts of other matted feathers streak the twigs. A shard of eggshell is ensnared as well.

The flat parcel was a book, *The Nest Gatherers of Tiger Cave*. Tiger Cave is one in a line of vast sea caves on Thailand's south-west coast: four million nests were transported to China from Batavia (Jakarta) in the eighteenth century. The nests, made from the bird's saliva, were, according to this book, 'eaten for their texture and out of vanity'. Yüan Mei was an eighteenth-century poet, the Chinese counterpart of Brillat-Savarin, according to the authors of *Chinese Gastronomy*. Like Brillat-Savarin, Yüan Mei took great aesthetic interest in his food. He wrote from eastern Kwangtung (Guangdong): 'an excellent bird's nest soup made with winter melon. Two substances, clear and tender, matched to each other, cooked simply in chicken and mushroom broth. The bird's nest acquired the colour of jade – it was not pure white.'

'Phoenix Swallowing the Swallow' is a dish made by filling a chicken with birds' nests and double-boiling it in a porcelain pot to yield a clear consommé. According to Hsiang Ju Lin and Tsuifeng Lin in *Chinese Gastronomy*, 'the proper texture [of bird's nest in cooking] is a combination of *body and delicacy*'. How well this mirrors the French art of making a double consommé, which achieves exactly the same thing. In *The Oxford Companion to Food*, the entry for birds' nests shifts the nests to the Philippines and New Guinea, home to a different nest-building swiftlet, *Collocalia whiteheadi*. The entry takes on an engagingly wry tone when it addresses the question of whether, when eating bird's nest, we are consuming plant or animal food: 'Several authorities have referred apologetically to this area of doubt, but have pointed out that the high cost of a bird's nest of the right sort has tended to rule out any analytical research.'

—

Another box arrived by post, this time so light that to someone else it might seem to hold nothing, but I know that a nest is inside. The thrill of it. But inside the box is a bowl, the clay a fine porcelain, the glaze a matt creamy-white with teardrops near the base where the heat from the kiln has caused the kind of accident that makes ceramics surprising. The foot is tiny, the rim wide – a beautiful, slightly flawed bowl; not a nest. A has often sent nests by post: a blackbird's, like a flattened skein of wool, which he picked up in Hyde Park, pieces of thin rough rope entangled, cotton, plastic, feather upon feather, one piece of purple wool and pieces of bright-blue fluff; jewels. Giving me bowls, he has always done so in person. As a connoisseur of A's bowls, I am ashamed that I felt disappointment when the parcel did not reveal a nest.

Nests have no value and are not found at auctions. This is one of the great pleasures of collecting them. The stories nestled in the drawers and baskets are stories of accident and constancy. Once I met a woman at a gastronomic conference. Why do I remember that she is a vegetarian? We talked in between courses at the closing banquet, and some weeks later a large, fragile, twig-built nest

arrived unannounced in the post. I remember that she had said she was moving. There was no return address on the parcel.

Once I travelled to the north of New South Wales to visit one of my daughters and remembered an old friend nearby. We drank cold white wine on the verandah of his house and looked at the landscape beyond the pavilion he has built as a frame to view the Mullumbimby hills. For years he has sent me small stones and pieces of coral and shells, even a Port Jackson shark egg and once two enormous banksia pods from Western Australia, wood-hard. I told him that there were two feathers in the car, along with the jars of seville-orange jelly, and the conversation turned to nests. The nest J gave me that day has a different quality to the solid objects he has sent in the past. It is the size of a large saucer, quite flat, and the hollow made by the body of the bird has strands of something so fine that it might be human hair. Small flocks of dirty fleece dot the outside; also fine strands of plastic, which is common in nests made close to humans. It is the circular quality of nests like this one that amazes me.

In a letter from a different N, not long after I came back from that journey, she wrote: 'I was standing outside your door brushing through my hair just after washing it and a few strands drifted off with the wind into the grass and other unknown places. I had this strong mental image of a bird using them to build a nest. There was something comforting in that.' I used to sweep away most of the spiders' webs that surround my house, but now I leave them as building materials for birds.

An artist who lives in Boston, Rosamond Purcell, takes photographs which blur the distinctions between scientific image and art; they are often reproduced in a journal, *The Sciences*. In the month I unpacked all the nests in the chest, the shoe-boxes, the lacquer cabinet, the closed baskets, Stephen Jay Gould wrote in *The Sciences* about stability and transience. Rosamond Purcell had found, in a junkyard, a stack of two books that had been gnawed out and stuffed with straw by mice to make a nest. The essay illustrated the photograph, not the other way round. 'A readable human book' had turned into 'a nestable murine home' wrote Gould. Murine? For me this conjured up walls, out of the French word *mur*: only birds that use mud, like swallows, might be said to make nests that have walls. I looked the word up in the Oxford and it refers to mice.

Cobras, too, build nests.

—

I went to visit A, who had bequeathed the lacquer cabinet and sent me nests and the bowl that wasn't. He showed me a collection of tangles of nylon fishing line from the beach near his house. They had been made glorious by his choosing to isolate them, collect them. These are my nests, he said.

I have since found similar tangles on the beach at Second Valley on the Fleurieu Peninsula. They make a line on a window-sill and remind me of A's eye. Friends came to stay and used my bed. Open the drawers, I said, and look at the nests. He came from the bedroom and asked why I collected them. She later sent a weightless parcel from the south coast of New South Wales. It was a tangle of fishing line.

—

One morning a bold magpie rummaged with its beak in the vegetable patch where spinach, garlic, sage and oregano survive in poor soil. I yelled at the bird, selfish for my food. It flew off with a strip of the mulch I'd gathered from a beach on the Fleurieu Peninsula where the seaweed piles up in miniature hills. The magpie was collecting material for a nest.

This cottage looks over a line of strong South Australian red gums through to a vineyard. The height of the eucalypts allows rosellas and cockatoos to direct their screechings. Highest of all, in the sway of the leaves, is a great nest in a fork of branches, a thick bed of twigs at which I have never seen birds. Years ago, at Berowra Waters, while we ate a staff dinner on the terrace and slapped at invisible midges, a young man who worked in the kitchen climbed too high for comfort in a coastal *Angophora* and came down with a nest – both safe, but I hope the nest had not been in use.

I read a novel by Kiran Desai, *Hullabaloo in the Guava Orchard*, a domestic,

Nests (weaving, pressing, collecting)

amusing, modern variation on the genesis of Buddha. Sampath, the accidental hero, climbs into a guava tree and stays there:

> After about a month in the orchard, [Sampath] had come to the conclusion that collecting was only worthwhile if you lived away from what you were collecting, not if you existed amidst all the bounty of your desire, not if you lived right where all you loved grew and crawled constantly by you.

In Shanghai recently, the temperature was around 0°C. We stood in the drab, grey yard of a once-handsome 1930s house under a giant crane which swung above us day and night, building yet another fast, tall, potentially fatal building. Looking up at the crane through a bare tree we saw a nest – abandoned and, like all things in Shanghai, dirtied by pollution. I laid it tenderly on a table in the bedroom.

Next day it wasn't there. Mrs W, who cleaned for and fussed over my friend, had no English and I could not find 'nest' in the Mandarin/English dictionary, although I suspect the pictogram would include a complete square, as do 'mouth' and 'country'. Mrs W pointed to the rubbish bin and laughed a lot. Personally, I found it no laughing matter but I partly understood why she had thrown the nest away. Its dirt was part of its story for me, a Shanghai story, but for Mrs W it was something to clean or discard, shameful.

I had been collecting rose petals in the living-room, a temporary, fading archive of scents. Next day Mrs W brought me more from the vase; the day after, tulip petals that had fallen from another; and then more. I am told that when a Chinese person is deeply embarrassed and feels they have done wrong, they laugh a lot.

Gaston Bachelard, writing about nests in *The Poetics of Space*, quotes from Jules Michelet's *L'Oiseau* (1858): 'There is not one of these blades of grass that, in order to make it curve and hold the curve, has not been pressed on countless times by the bird's breast, its heart.' There is a proverb that goes like this: Men can do everything except build a bird's nest.

Although Bachelard writes about the naive wonder we feel when discovering a nest, I disagree when he suggests that a living, useful nest is valid to our set of images and metaphors associated with nests but that the empty, abandoned nest is nothing. A nest, he writes, 'is a precarious thing, and yet it sets us to daydreaming of security'. This is not what I am daydreaming about when I look with wonder at a nest. The delicate structure; the natural, dulled colour of the materials (I have never liked bright colours); the shaping; the accidental debris, the memory only, of seasonal usefulness; the architecture, the shaping of the space but not the space itself in Bachelard's philosophical terms – the beauty that literally takes my breath away sometimes – have nothing to do with images of home, warmth, security, refuge, nesting. But perhaps I cannot see for seeing, denying something buried deep inside my psyche.

~

Benjamin wrote about the 'memories which surge toward any collector as he contemplates his possessions'. 'Possessions' of books and nests are not stocks, shares, castles, yachts. The difference is that whereas Benjamin writes eloquently of the excitement of auctions and bidding for books, and of the memories of those auctions and how a particular book came into his collection, my memories are always centred on place and friendship. Each nest is the home of a loyalty, the presence of a friend. Were you, Walter Benjamin, philosopher and Arcadian, a solitary man? I think that perhaps collectors are always most at ease when alone, yet one of the greatest pleasures the nests give is showing them to others. I know a man in London who has an extraordinary collection of Lucie Rie's ceramics. When you walk into the room the bowls and the vases, beautifully displayed, are instantly seen. When I show the nests to a visitor, we must open drawers together, complicitous in surprise.

~

Nests (weaving, pressing, collecting)

I have never heard anyone explain exactly why caviar is so exquisite to the palate, or why sorrel melted inside an omelette is a perfect combination of textures and flavour. Perhaps it was the man who looked at the nests and didn't see them as miraculous, who made me want to explain their beauty, catch and limn something of this sense of wonder and admiration I feel, even though they are useless, abandoned, spent and sometimes disturbing reminders of the inexorable cycle of regeneration.

How do I describe, for instance, the difference in size and materials of this nest (taken from a shoe-box into which it just fits and in which it was brought to me from Gosford years ago) when it is also simply just another structure by a winged architect–builder. Some large nests are not delicate, too mud-caked and heavy, but this one is airy. Gourd-like, it tapers above a waist, opening at the tapered end. Caught in the base is a long feather, an arrow impossible to remove, and woven among the whole is a tendril of strong but delicate vine, dark brown among the dried grass, which is still a faded green. The entrance, now found, is so perfectly round, so smooth, even though formed with dried threads.

And if I am not to be pushed outside my home by the increase in nests, how am I to stop collecting them, when they arrive by post from faraway places like Mullumbimby and Sydney and revive friendships. In the past year I have heard from four people because they found nests. We had not spoken for years because I had moved to the country in a different state and do not like the telephone. One of these nests is small and fragile, and each layer is made of very different materials. The base is of pretty grey twigs and the nesting place is made from a kind of synthetic cottonwool with fine threads of differently coloured cottons (red, blue, black) caught up in it. The whole is like the outside and inside of a wallpapered house; by its two separate shapes and materials it also resembles a cup and saucer. There is a lot of fine nylon fishing line caught in the whole, explained by the note sent with it: 'found: Clarkes Point Reserve – a wonderful semi-bush park, adjoining Kelly's Bush, on the harbour at Woolwich . . . The nest was lying on the ground (right side up) in amongst gum trees with no sign of bird life, trauma or use, about 100 metres from the water's edge which is a favourite fishing spot. L.'

The most recent nest came from Mullumbimby in a box large enough to hold a far-too-large television. The postmistress threw it upside-down onto the back seat of the car but I knew it was safe. I have been sent nests from this person before. Home, I attended to other things first, for the perverse pleasure of making myself wait. All I could see when I pulled back the cardboard was tens of transparent pillows of air with, stamped on them, 'No pillow. No floatation device. No toy. Re-use, re-duce, re-cycle'. These instructions might well apply to nests. Around the nest was a fleecy child's blanket. Even the first lifted corner showed that the nest was magnificent. The outer circle was made from tens of sturdy branches. No other materials, no spiders' web or grasses, had been used to strengthen it and yet this strong platform was some fifty centimetres in diameter. You could see that after the framework had been put into place, the bird chose finer twigs and then still finer, building a beautiful tower as the structure for the nesting, a padded basket for the eggs. Only then did the bird seem to decide, with aristocratic taste as interior decorator, 'Gold, that's what it needs, gold!' For the lining of the bowl, the nest's shape for settling the breast in, seemed to be made from the tendrils of a delicate burnished gold vine. Looking at it again now, from all directions, I realise that it has no man-made materials caught in the structure – no fishing line because it came from a tree away from water, no dirty pieces of plastic or paper, no twine, no tape, no coloured threads as many of the nests have. This nest was built by a bird living in a clean hinterland.

In *Austerlitz*, W. G. Sebald writes about fortifications that grew after each battle yet did not increase the impregnability of the fort:

> Such complexities of fortifications, said Austerlitz . . . show us how, unlike birds, for instance, who keep building the same nest over thousands of years, we tend to forge ahead with our projects far beyond any reasonable bounds. Someone, he added, ought to draw up a catalogue of types of buildings, listed in order of size, and it would be immediately obvious that domestic buildings of less than normal size – the little cottage in the field, the hermitage, the lock-keeper's lodge, the pavilion for viewing the landscape, the children's bothy in the garden – are those that offer us at least a semblance of peace . . .

Amiable juyce (blood sausage)

'This clear, lovely and amiable juyce is the special thing that conserveth every living creature in his being . . . this treasure of life must most carefully be conserved because it is of all humours the most excellent and wholesome.' This is William Harvey writing early in the seventeenth century. It was Harvey who proposed the idea of the circulation system and the heart as pump, and we cannot read his lovely description of blood without it being tainted by modern irony. Blood has been invaded by our knowledge of what uses it to invade the body with illness, but we must never confuse the invaders with the essential, vital amiability of blood.

When, in 1992, I thought of making sausages from my own blood as one of the courses for the Body Dinner at the 1993 Symposium of Australian Gastronomy, I approached passing pathologists and lawyers in the first instance. How would I go about collecting enough blood? And keep it from coagulating? And when the guests ate the sausages? According to one lawyer, I would have to tell them what they were eating before they swallowed the first mouthful, or I might be sued over the shock of it all.

The plan was to prove my blood safe, collect about three litres, then make the sausages using the same recipe we used for the pig's blood sausages at Berowra Waters Inn. After all, human blood has similar properties to the pig's. I talked to the kitchen and only one of five cooks responded with excitement and unconditional support. Even if I made the sausages myself, I felt I needed their approval. While I was not, on one level, involving them (after all, it was to be my blood), I needed them to feel comfortable with the idea. Janni Kyritsis, who had developed the recipe for the blood sausage we served, would have no truck with it; three others laughed, but in discomfort. Except for the one cook, no one even wanted to talk about it; the taboo is too strong.

The response was so dispiriting, so overwhelmingly negative, that I shelved the idea. Now I think that I should have gone ahead in private, given that I could have found someone to test, take and store the blood. Poaching the sausages to a specific temperature would offer double indemnity. What no one seemed to understand was that this would not be a gruesome *épater la bourgeoisie* exercise, but the most generous gesture a host might make: I would be giving myself to others; no cook could do more. Mark Quinn, a British artist, had recently carved his own head from four litres (the total amount in his body) of his own frozen blood. It came to Australia as one of the exhibits in a show devoted to the body at the Art Gallery of New South Wales. Was he allowed, as an artist, to use his own blood because his sculpture was not for ingestion? Because for all of art's political and social implications it is never as participatory as the gastronomical arts *must* be? Because in his dealings with the unacceptable he knew when to stop? When the guests gathered for the symposium dinner, I was told by waiters that murmurs of my blood as ingredient were flying about the room. Let them, I thought: at least the subject has become something in the air. We did serve more conventional blood sausage as the fifth course.

Deborah Lupton, associate professor of cultural studies and policy at Charles Sturt University in New South Wales, wrote, in *Food, the Body and the Self*, about the response, not of cooks but of readers to a short piece I wrote about human blood as food in a Sydney newspaper. Human blood, she commented, 'is considered a particularly disgusting, repulsive and frightening substance. Although it is potentially nutritious, it is most definitely considered a non-food in western societies'. The word 'disgust' has alimentary links: the French word is *dégoût*; *goût* means taste and plays its part in the name of a vertical tasting menu, a *dégustation*, where it is transformed into a pleasurable idea. I have been told that when we feel disgust we are using the part of the brain that registers reactions of the stomach. Lupton continued: 'Bilson . . . made careful efforts to destigmatise the notion . . . the blood did not come from a dead person who had been murdered for the privilege, it would be given willingly and in the spirit of generosity . . . it would be rendered hygienic, it would be cooked at the level of *haute cuisine*.' Two letters of revolt were published in the paper. They used words like 'perverse', 'self-indulgent', 'stomach-turning', 'inflict', 'nauseated', 'infuriated', 'dumbfounded', 'appalling'. One reader suggested that I should give blood for medical use instead. I do, but that's not the point. The misunderstanding was about the nature of the body's circulatory system, for blood can be taken and yet not empty the arteries and veins. (This fact might indeed be seen to lessen the symbolic generosity I had deemed the strongest reason for using my blood.)

Jamaica Kinkaid wrote, in the short story 'In Roseau', about a woman who wanted to marry a man who had vowed he never would: 'Madame Labatte found a way; she fed him food she had cooked in a sauce made with her own menstrual blood, and it bound him to her, and they were married.' But this took place in a culture where voodoo and spells replace the idea that red wine be seen as a symbol of Jesus' blood. By shifts and refinement we distance ourselves and displace disgust. I recommend William Miller's *The Anatomy of Disgust* (published in 1997). He, like Joan Smith in her compilation of food writing, *Hungry for You*, is interested in St Catherine of Siena, who lived in the fourteenth century and took to disgusting practices with medieval zeal, drinking the 'corrupt matter and filth' of a fellow nun's suppurating sore. Catherine, writes her biographer, had a vision in which she slaked her thirst by 'fastening her lips upon that sacred wound' of Christ. Smith classifies Catherine's hysterical eating habits under anthropophagy, and Miller suggests that she drank pus out of love for God and as such illustrates love's ability to suspend disgust, to varying degrees at different times in history. I, too, think St Catherine went a little too far, but suspending disgust, turning it into gratitude, might have been what I wanted by offering human blood as nourishment. Then again, to simply chew on the idea and measure the reactions, may have been enough.

⟶

Bruno Paparo holds a slaughterman's as well as a butcher's licence. He collected and brought the pig's blood to Berowra Waters Inn and Bennelong for years, and rang early one morning to invite me to a property in the hills outside Bathurst where he was going to slaughter a pig for its owners. Over four hundred kilometres to see a pig become food seemed a tad too far, but it would be going against my professed interest in his trade if I begged off.

The pig's owners had set up in the paddock an old cast-iron bath near a fire, for heating water so that Bruno could scald the skin to rid it of bristles. Winter in these hills inland from the Blue Mountains was still in full sting. The pig was very big. The pig was heavy. The pig was shot and Bruno immediately 'stuck' it in order to collect the blood, stirring in one direction with his fingers as it filled the buckets and so catching the fibrous material. There was a lot of blood. The pig was then hoisted by a pulley system to hang by its back legs. Bruno slit the belly from top to bottom and a fetid stench filled the air. He looked across to the pig's owners and asked if they had castrated the animal: unless a male pig is castrated at a certain age, its testosterone contaminates the meat. He cut out the sweetbreads, as his family had always done in Italy, and we grilled them on the fire. The testosterone had done its damage, but we ate them anyway. He cut away the neck meat; this would, by curing, become pancetta.

It was so cold that we left the pig and went inside to eat. Good bread, good olives, good salad, all made or grown by the owners of the pig and served on plates and in bowls made by one of them, too. The man said, 'I wrote you a letter once'. His name was Patrick; I had not been told his surname, could think of nothing to connect him to Berowra Waters Inn and did not know what letter he meant. Once, years before, I had had a letter from a man who had driven a long way to the restaurant with his wife, made something of a pilgrimage in fact; it was to be a celebration, he had said in the letter. To use the toilets at the restaurant, diners had to cross a wide sandstone-flagged area, then climb two sandstone steps to reach them. If you stood on these steps and faced the dining-room, the long, narrow window of my bedroom (in a loft space above a small flat), showed the spines of books that were lying flat; he saw there Bernard Leach's *A Potter in Japan* and *A Potter's Book*, and wrote about this too. The letter was to say that the meal had been worth the journey. It was a beautifully written letter: the writer had made that pivotal shift which sees the worth of an experience as separate to what it costs.

Amiable juyce (blood sausage)

I had been so moved by the letter that I wrote to thank him, but the only address I could make out on the envelope was a college in Bathurst. I had driven hundreds of kilometres, despite really wanting to stay in the city and curl up in bed, to watch the pig being butchered, to grill some parts over the fire, to eat the tainted sweetbreads. As we consumed the last parts of the lunch, I learned that this was the man who had written that letter.

—

Thomas Hardy's *Return of the Native* was the first novel to make me see that I was reading literature. This was, I think, in an early year at high school. I have always remembered the name of the heroine, Eustacia Vye. The first time I went to England, a friend in Dorset took me to see his sheep and showed me what 'reddling' was, something I had only read about in Hardy's novels. Jude Fawley kills a pig in Hardy's last (1903) and great book, *Jude the Obscure*: when the man who is to slaughter the pig seems not to be coming, Arabella, Jude's wife and a Hardy-esque stone around Jude's sensitive neck (Jude is attracted to books and learning), insists that he kill the pig, for there is no barleymeal left and the pig has not eaten for the past two days. Jude is horrified and knows now why the pig has been crying. 'We always do it for the last day or two, to save bother with the innards. What ignorance, not to know that!' Arabella says. Jude wants to stick the pig deep to lessen the suffering, but Arabella is scornful of his timidity. 'Don't be such a tender-hearted fool! . . . Now whatever you do, don't stick un too deep.' The sticking knife needs to be used so that the meat bleeds well while the pig dies slowly. 'We will lose a shilling a score if the meat is red and bloody! Just touch the vein, that's all. I was brought up to it, and I know. Every good butcher keeps un bleeding long.' Jude sticks the pig deep and the blood is caught in a bucket. The pig's final convulsion causes Jude to stagger and he upsets the bucket of blood. 'There!' she cried, thoroughly in a passion. 'Now I can't make any blackpot. There's a waste all through you!'

—

It was thanks to a young cook, Laif Etournaud, who was in the kitchen at Berowra Waters Inn for a long time and who went on to have his own restaurants in Sydney, and to his friend, the butcher Bruno Paparo, that Janni Kyritsis was pushed into perfecting our recipe for blood sausages. Laif pestered us to use the blood that Bruno was so adept at collecting. Janni's starting point was the recipe in the chapter on blood puddings in Jane Grigson's *Charcuterie and French Pork Cookery*. Grigson tells the story of a neighbour who would persuade a visiting *charcutier* to cook some blood gently (blood curdles if it is boiled) over the fire, mixing in a little fat and cream; this was called a *sanguette*.

Paparo, whose Italian mother makes a sweet sausage of chocolate and blood, adding nuts and dried grapes, and which he claimed is called 'sango nutso' (too slowly, I saw the name was a joke; Bruno had spent most of his life in Australia), salts and acidulates the pig's blood as it is collected. Badgering your Australian butcher for blood might act as one small step towards releasing this peculiarly masonic-like trade from its conservative status quo.

Willunga, the small, historic and mostly unspoiled South Australian town closest to my paddock, has recently become home to a farmers' market (next to the pub, a good idea). One of the two butchers in the main street makes a blood sausage (he is Swiss and understands that every part of the pig is useful) which, if not as light as the Berowra Waters Inn version, is a fine product. The sausage is tied into a loop and my only criticism is that because of this there is one section that thins dramatically in diameter. I take off the skin and sauté thick slices in a little butter, or grill them over charcoal. Blood is sweet. In another pan, fat slices of apple caramelise. Red cabbage braised for a long time in the oven with apples and onions, a little red wine and red-wine vinegar, tastes so much of cold European countries that the meal is transporting.

Blood sausage

This recipe yields about ten 150-gram sausages, but you can of course make them any size you like. Although butchers in Chinatown often sell blood, which has been used for centuries in southern China for stir-frying and in soups (as it is in Vietnam), it is not suitable for making these sausages because it has coagulated.

Amiable juyce (blood sausage)

Pressing an Italian butcher for blood might be your best way to go. Sausage casings, thin and thick, are supplied to butchers packed in salt, and you might beg a length as a favour, asking for real casings, not synthetic. They need to be washed.

The ingredients are: 300 g finely diced onion; 300 g finely diced pork fat; 20 g unsalted butter; 200 g peeled, finely diced apple; 500 ml pig's blood; 125 ml thick cream; 20 g fine, fresh breadcrumbs; 2 teaspoons *quatre épices* (ground pepper, nutmeg, cloves and cinnamon); 1 teaspoon finely chopped fresh sage; a big pinch of brown sugar; and large sausage casing (i.e. hog casings).

Sweat the onion and 50 g of the pork fat in the butter. Add the apple and continue cooking until the apple softens. Cool this mixture, then add the remaining fat, plus the blood, cream, breadcrumbs and seasonings. Check for salt by cooking a little of the mixture in a pan: as salt is added to the blood when it is collected, there is usually no need to add any more.

Feed the sausage casing onto the end of a funnel and tie a knot in the end. Ladle the blood mixture into the casing and tie off the sausages at, say, 12-centimetre intervals, being sure to eliminate any air bubbles. If you have a sausage-making attachment for a mixer you will not need to improvise.

Bring a large pot of water to the boil. Turn off flame, place string of sausages in the water, leave for some 30 minutes (no lid) and then remove and cool. Remove string.

To serve at the restaurant, we crumbed the sausages (flour, then egg, then fine, fresh breadcrumbs), laid them on baking paper in a hot oven, turning them to make sure the whole surface was crisped and golden. Instead of filling into casings, the mixture can also be ladled into a buttered terrine mould, covered, and baked in a bain marie, later sliced and heated through in the same manner as the sausages – this is what we did at Bennelong. Now I would simply grill naked slices. When making the mixture, you are working towards a sausage which is as light and fine as a blood sausage might be. The blood sausages from my Swiss butcher are very good, but they are far, far heavier than the sausages Janni perfected at Berowra Waters Inn.

Braised red cabbage

This recipe, from *At Home with the Roux Brothers* by Michel and Albert Roux, will serve six. You will need 1 kg red cabbage (about half a large cabbage); 100 g butter (clarified butter is best); ½ onion, chopped coarsely; 1 big apple, peeled and then chopped coarsely; 2 tablespoons red-wine vinegar; 4 tablespoons red wine; salt and pepper.

Preheat the oven to 180°C. Shred the cabbage finely, discarding the tough central core. Heat the butter in an ovenproof casserole or saucepan, add the cabbage and cook over high heat for a minute or two. Add the onion and apple, and cook for a further 2 minutes. Add vinegar, wine and seasonings, cover pot and transfer to oven. Bake for about 1–1½ hours, or until the cabbage is cooked, then check for salt and pepper.

Amiable juyce (blood sausage)

Buried treasure

They're not as young as they were, these two archaeologists who buried and dug up the banquet for the Tenth Symposium of Australian Gastronomy in 1997: Phillip Searle and Cheong Liew, the artist and the sage.

After fifteen years of symposium meetings and meals in sophisticated, urban spaces, the inevitable (in retrospect) circle closed and for two days and nights this time we willingly slept on the earth, on the source of our food. A city of tents in the Grampians in north-western Victoria, coldroom temperature at night while the baker stoked his travelling oven, his unruly hair and moustache haloed in lamp-light and turning him into one of the actors in a seventeenth-century travelling theatre troupe. Mnouchkine's Molière?

Camping being what it is, preparation was public and invited help. The cooks dug a large rectangular oven in the earth and baked stones to store heat. We were to eat an alchemical feast. They stuffed and then coated young emu in sea-soned butter and flour, and wrapped them in banana leaves and paper and cloth and mesh and mud; they did variations of the same to sides of pork and to Mur-ray cod – enough, too much, for seventy people. The parcels were hugely, grandly primeval and of the earth to which they were returned, mud to mud. They were buried in a grave hours before it would be ransacked for the feeding. Above the pit, scrubbed, tight-lipped oysters were opened and tainted, by flaming eucalypt twigs and leaves, as the first course of the banquet. Blue swimmer crabs, as cold and fresh as the Grampians air, were grilled over the fire and became the unsur-passed food of the feast. Underneath, the meat and fish underwent stone-warmed changes and became food.

We watched while Searle and Liew dug for our dinner. Out of respect, no one helped; it was their privilege to unearth the food. We became audience to divine risk-taking, as the earth was shovelled out of the underworld oven, smelling of must and humidity. Symposiasts, cold-thighed in the Grampians chill, sat on this upturned earth to warm themselves, and collected the stones to warm their beds; we ate, wrapped in our bedding.

The cooks, more curious even than those to be fed, began to unwrap their gifts. Emu bones slipped away from moist flesh as easily as a beggar's chicken will fall apart; the flesh was tinged green by the wrapping leaves. When Searle opened his now-deceased restaurant in Sydney in the eighties, for abalone sandwiches he made trays of slow-baked bread dough shaped in imitation of an abalone shell. Now the wrapping from the emu was thrown aside in much the same way as the bread trays: discarded crafts, use to disuse, earth to earth. After eight hours the pork had become blubber, yet tasted wonderfully of pork. The division of texture and hue between the skin, fat and muscle had dissolved; each side had been transformed into a pork-pink sea-jelly. At the first symposium in 1984, the extraordinary banquet created by Phillip Searle, with Cheong Liew, had astounded us: a jellied seascape, an edible, wobbling sculpture in a glass tank of immense proportions was the first course. Some, like myself, never thought about food in the same way again. This slowly, slowly cooked pork reminded me of that seascape, made fifteen years earlier.

The Grampians are sandy from millennia past, reminders that time transforms on a grand, seemingly motionless scale, and eight hours of cooking with hot stones buried in the earth had given delusions of timelessness. The cooking pit had become an inverted vertical slice of evolution's inevitability, with fish the uppermost layer instead of one of its lowest. Shrouds, mummies, sleeping bags, mud-wrapped gifts of intimations of mortality, grave digging, tamed and useful fire, unkeepable experience, transforming cookery, sleep.

—

Often, when audience to live chamber-music making of the highest order, I suffer a shiver of inadequacy, a certain discomfort. Music in performance, as uncatchable as

falling stars and as unhoardable as food, doesn't seem to need me, I become irrelevant even when blessed (that conundrum of a word which means wounded as well);
but food needs me as much as I need it. Food must be eaten. It passes via the inquir-
ing tongue to the stomach and is metabolised, transformed to feed the body, to keep
one alive and thoughtful. It is necessary.

When it seems alchemical and becomes food for thought, it doesn't tran-
scend its materiality but confirms it with a confidence that is sustaining in the
face of inevitable death, plant or animal, to support life, and suggests the cruel
paradox that touches on the nature of art and the imagination. It is the work
of cookery in the hands of the alchemical few that allows us this intimation
of the sublime worth of the material, something so gloriously, so devastatingly
dependent on death. Dust to dust, ashes to ashes, flesh to transcendent moment
of consequence.

The obvious, inescapable *work* of cooking is inextricably part of the
celebration of eating. If not the hunt and fire, then the knowledge of the production, the preparation and the burying. *Experimentum Mundi*, to return to
musical comparison, is an operatic piece that celebrates artisanal work without
falsely elevating it to self-conscious art. It was performed for the forty-third time
for the 1998 Adelaide Festival of the Arts. This is opera in its most literal sense:
the performers work – they make shoes, grind knives, lay stones, chip marble,
tap wine barrels, knead pasta dough, heat and shape iron, and lathe wood. A
chorus of women chant something quite possibly mundane, pianissimo, at the
composer-conductor's cue. A paver turns his score in order to take part in the
composition but is never falsely asked to think of himself as a musician. Yet out
of the chorus of working sounds music is made. Giorgio Battistelli conducts his
score at every performance, knowing that the shift to music rests in the ordinariness of these artisan's skills. Cooks and eaters, too, experience this kind of
transformation.

We banqueters-to-be who stood close enough to Searle before the burial of
the meats and fish might have felt a certain uneasiness at the apparently experi-
mental nature of the feast, for neither Searle nor Liew had used the earth and
stones as an oven before. It wasn't that they feigned surprise at the results but that

each was wonderfully pleasured by his own work, by the kind of risk-taking that is less risky than it might appear: *experimentum mundi*.

—

Did we expect a *coup de théâtre* from Searle as a final sweet course? Given his past edible sculptures and the chill of the night, the Emperor of Icecream might have been expected to produce the rococo among the kangaroo droppings. Instead he used the travelling wood-fired oven to bake fruit and cake, containing all work to those foods and techniques that made no quarrel with the site. Fire and heat were essential and kept us alive.

For centuries, cooks with fire but without kitchens have turned flesh into aromatic, palatable food by protectively burying it with particular, suitable, hot stones. Our banquet-makers returned to the past in creating and excavating an earth-oven, and the relevance of the old shone like a new star in that heavenly, clear, cold and beautiful Grampians sky.

Upstart gruel (congee)

'A farm labourer . . . in central Sichuan province . . .
died when his intestine burst as he ate his eighth bowl
of gruel trying to win a bet.' REUTERS

In May 1995, the food writer John Newton spoke to Violet Oon, expert on the cuisines (note the plural) of Singapore, asking if she had ever considered opening one of her kitchens in Sydney. Oon was demonstrating and speaking about her home-town laksas at the time, although back there she is famous for her shepherd's pie, and Newton suggested that if she did she could 'teach us how to make a proper laksa and then our chefs [could] fiddle with it'.

Fiddling with the traditional foods of our Asian neighbours might just be the best definition of what some commentators hopefully call 'Australian cuisine', a fact brought home to me when, at the Beggars' Banquet, which was part of the Performance Space's Conference on Food and Culture in April 1996, I decided to make a version of congee, which we dubbed Upstart Gruel for we had stolen it from its original setting, in Alfred Park in Redfern. I've always loved spooning congee's soothing broth (most usually so late at night that you might think it is morning), having first eaten it in Shanghai's Jinjiang Hotel dining-room for breakfast in the early eighties when Michael Dowe (who later edited *The Good Food Guide* in Sydney for some time) and I were by confusion of booking given the suite in which Kissinger and Nixon conversed with their communist counterparts and gave John Adams a reason to write an opera. The sitting-room was long and narrow, and held an extraordinary number of antimacassared armchairs. Breakfast, in a huge dining hall separate from the hotel, was congee with pickles.

Congee may be just gruel, but it is also a lesson in the *hsien*, the natural sweetness, of rice. Part of the fiddling process is to find out as much as possible about the food that in the beginning was so foreign. In *Chinese Gastronomy* by Hsiang Ju Lin and Tsuifeng Lin (1969) we read that:

> the fine lines of gastronomy are never so clearly drawn as in the cooking of rice, and congee . . . Congee should be slightly glutinous, rice grainy . . . the *hsien* should be distributed throughout the gruel . . . Country people love to eat rice, and the rich love congee . . . Scholars in particular love to talk about it . . . Congee and pickled vegetables belong in the little hut in the mountains of landscape painting, all in keeping with the air of sophisticated withdrawal from society.

In the Song period (960–1279), certain foods were associated with Buddhist holidays and 'seven-treasure five-taste' congee was eaten on the eighth day of the twelfth moon, according to Michael Freeman in C. K. Chang's *Food in Chinese Culture* (1977). The word congee is derived from the southern Indian Dravidian word *kanji;* in Mandarin it is *cho;* and in Cantonese, *tsuk*, and commonly known as 'jook'. Rice is a food balanced in heating and cooling properties, and the Cantonese believe that congee is cooling because of the water it absorbs during cooking. Freeman also backs up the high status of congee for both the ruling class and the peasantry, commenting that 'peasants perhaps . . . and certainly the ruling house . . . were more punctilious and fervent in ritual practices'. The more we know about food, the more we explore the origins of dishes and search for authentic flavours and preparations, the more interest we show in how, in particular, the poor prepare food – indeed, paradoxically, the more we revere it, especially if the cuisine is exotic. It's the principle of topsy-turvy, the sophisticated revering the kind of dish the unsophisticated eat unselfconsciously.

But eating congee is not to go slumming. It is to understand that there is still flavour in the pot, the sweet reminder of rice, and that drinking it gives the body a rest. It is good for one's health. E. N. Anderson, in *The Food of China* (1988), refers to a 'mixture of apricot-kernel powder and congee or milk . . . used to relieve the distress of colds and sore throats' in modern China and attests to its efficacy. He is writing here about the use of nuts in Chinese food, rather than about congee. He writes of *lan fan*, rice spoiled by too much water, being used to feed the baby. By adding more water still, a gruel is made: sometimes I simply add a little minced fresh chilli and ginger to a gruel made from the rice sticking to the bottom of the saucepan after boiling it. Supposedly helpful inventions like teflon that stop food sticking to cooking pans are risks to culinary invention. The Fukienese people of south-eastern China are soup-eaters and consume a lot of congee as well as birds' nests and sharks' fins in sloppy, slippery form. The common and humble sit side by side with the rare and expensive. 'Bean curd, if good, is better than bird's nest.'

A friend who grew up in Hong Kong and who is part-Cantonese says that the key to good Cantonese congee is for it to be 'mean', which translates as a smooth amalgamation of rice and water. Her Auntie Phoebe, she says, used to achieve this by adding a few drops of oil towards the end of the cooking. The Chiuchows, she says, prefer a more watery version, where rice and liquid are more separate, and the Shanghainese eat bland congee accompanied by side dishes of peanuts, salted eggs, pickle, etc. As kids, she went on, they would have congee flavoured with dried pak choi, which you never see now; indeed, at the opposite extreme nowadays you are more likely to have the congee flavoured with chicken and abalone. The best congee for flavour, she thinks, is made with salt pork and thousand-year-old eggs (*pay darn harm sau yuk jook*). And in her view it is essential to eat congee with fried dough-sticks and salted duck eggs.

———

On that occasion in Sydney, making congee was a simple way to feed three hundred or so, and very cheaply too: we (mostly just myself at home, and later with the help of one young cook, Hugh Wennerbom, who also took part in the performance of serving) started by making somewhere over forty litres of light fish stock. Using stock instead of water was part of the fiddling process, adding body and extra flavour. We added about five kilos of short-grain rice, then fiddled on. We were giving away food to those who begged with bowl, so prawns, bamboo shoots, mushrooms, pine nuts, preserved eggs were not considered because of the expense. Wanting to add extra filling and a different texture, we prepared fish balls (one thousand were enough) and, most importantly, retained their poaching liquid to add to the stock. Beancurd (*tou-fu*), spring onions, pickled mustard greens, deep-fried shallots, fresh chillies, a dribble of sesame oil from the tips of the chopsticks, and a small dollop of that most gloriously full-bodied soybean, chilli and garlic paste from the Koon Yick Way Kee Foods Factory, Hong Kong, completed the garnishes *(sung)*.

The point of the congee at the Beggars' Banquet was to feed the hungry while they wandered among artist Anne Graham's luminous installation of tents and were entertained by performance artists using food as their medium or message. One lay naked in a bath of egg whites, whisking them to a froth and using this as shampoo and styling gel. Another wore a frightening contraption on his head: it looked like a massive dingo trap, but chopped carrots instead. The bowl of food was a free offering that centred the balmy evening's entertainment and, as if to bless the generosity, the unknown number of guests and the guessed quantity of soup we provided married perfectly, seemingly a small miracle. We worked at two burners with two huge pots of congee, with an additional container on another burner from which we replenished the serving pots. The element of performance in the serving ritual involved our naked kitchen of two trestles, the huge bins of bowls and chopsticks which the diners had to help themselves to, the ritual actions of the two servers with ladles and chopsticks, the series of additions to the bowl of hot broth, and even the queues themselves – two lines of daunting length, patiently curious and hungry for their bowl of Upstart Gruel. By performance I do not mean a false staginess but the awareness that this public serving of gruel was part of the afternoon's theatre.

The diversity of class and aspiration, expectation and palate that the queues embodied seemed to mirror the dichotomy of sophistication and rusticity inherent in congee. As the Lins say in *Chinese Gastronomy*: 'Lavish banquets satisfy the eyes, nose and palate, but starve the rest of the system. For the sake of the stomach and intestines eat congee.' But lay down the spoon and chopsticks before the eighth bowl.

Upstart gruel (congee)

Upstart gruel (a version of congee)

As at the Beggars' Banquet, these quantities will serve 250 or more. There is always room for a recipe to feed more than eight. When we celebrated the tenth anniversary of Berowra Waters Inn in 1987, the cooks, working on makeshift and public stoves, made enough risotto with fish stock, saffron, mussels and red chilli for four hundred people. I keep that recipe in its party proportions, although it would now – like the Upstart Gruel – be used to feed a community.

For the congee base, cook 5 kg short-grain rice in 40 litres very light fish or chicken stock for about an hour, or until the two are 'interlocked'. Finish with some fresh, finely sliced ginger slices.

FISH BALLS

For 1000 balls, you will need 11 kg fresh fish fillet (e.g. ling); 5 cups finely chopped spring onions; 7 tablespoons finely grated fresh ginger; 40 bird's-eye chillies, finely chopped; 4 tablespoons salt, or to taste; 22 egg whites. Mince the fish fillets and 'slap' the minced flesh on the bench to give it holding strength, then process with the spring onions, ginger, chillies, salt and egg whites, in batches. Roll into walnut-sized balls. When the pots of gruel are just simmering, add the fish balls – they cook through in no time.

FLAVOURINGS AND GARNISHES

These are as follows: 250 large pieces fresh beancurd; 15 bunches spring onions; Chinese pickles (mustard greens, ginger, etc.); 1 kg deep-fried shallots (bought); 500 g bird's-eye chillies, sliced finely; salt, to taste; sesame oil; soy sauce; chilli, soy and garlic paste (available in Chinatown). Have all these ingredients to hand at 'room' temperature and add them to the bowls of steaming-hot congee as it is plated. The heat of the gruel will warm the beancurd. The other garnishes sit on the surface.

Books and cooks

If there is a logic to the order of this book, then it might best be explained as felix culpa, a fortunate fall; a story which starts at the top of a hill and where, after tumbling down, the writer finds a version of contentment in seclusion, with far less income and the surprise of finding that the future is not a menu.

Thinking about cooks and cookbooks has meant asking questions not even thought of when younger and professionally involved. Ved Mehta has written that in the chabura, women 'learned the knack of making meals without seeming to measure the ingredients'. The crucial words here are 'without seeming to'. Recipes conserve knowledge but they also play havoc with context. The democratic generosity of written recipes means we are in danger of making meals which are incoherent. It isn't that cuisines have intellectual copyright or that they must stay intact and frozen to be authentic, but that food traditions are more than just recipes. Recipes, not generally thought of as descriptive, are clues to a cook's methodology and even to personality – Alice B. Toklas is a lively example. Afterwards, describing what one tastes is worth the stretch for accuracy. Nicolette Stasko has written in one of her poems: 'everything is hungry/ as I am hungry/ for words for the ripening/ red fruit'. It is her choice of the inclusive 'everything' that gives the line its lovely weight.

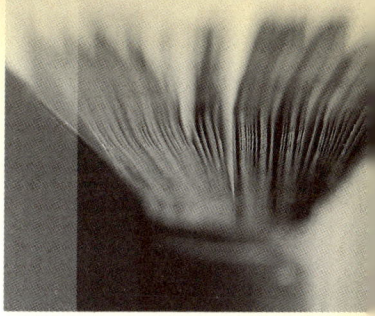

The point of Point

The inimitable Alastair Cooke, who for decades remained a comfortable constant on Radio National in Australia with his weekly 'Letter from America' (when Cooke died recently I was inclined to wish for a blank space in his time slot), once told of a survey of American students, which asked them to nominate the four greatest presidents of the United States. Not one of them named any president outside the past forty years and appeared only to think back this far because of the assassination of John F. Kennedy. Historians, asked the same question, with reason and memory on their side, and with honorable exceptions, hardly moved beyond the period of the founding fathers and their consolidators.

Although cooking is a little different from government, it does seem to me that young chefs often think they reinvented fire, that Thai food was invented by David Thompson in Sydney in the early 1990s, that the late sixties saw the first-ever revision of French cooking; and that nouvelle cuisine was a fixed and recent phenomenon. As long ago as 1742 a French chef we know only by his surname, Menon, wrote his second book and called it *La Nouvelle Cuisine*. And somewhere between Menon and Michel Guérard there lived a great French chef, Fernand Point. He was born in 1897 and died in 1955, and a very large percentage of the French chefs who practised and promoted the new cooking of the seventies were trained in his kitchen: Paul Bocuse (who dedicated his own *La Cuisine du Marché* to his father and to Point), Alain Chapel, the Troisgros brothers, Louis Outhier, and Bise *le fils*. Bise *père*, they say, shared up to six bottles of champagne with Point whenever they got together. Indeed, the one story I remembered about Point before returning to him recently was that when his doctor diagnosed a painful joint as water on the knee

Point declared that it couldn't be because he drank only champagne.

In 1969 Felix Benoit put together *Fernand Point: Ma Gastronomie.* The tone suggests something more like 'The Buddha: His Philosophy' than a cookbook, and it is in fact part Point's recipes, transcribed by Benoit from Point's personal notes, and part valediction. It includes five pages of aphorisms by the 'father of Nouvelle Cuisine', a large man with a large stomach who mistrusted thin cooks. Picking up Point sent me back to the bookshelf, this always in preference to the Internet, which I unfashionably and wilfully see as cheating. There is the distraction of different books and different subjects, which always surprise with something extra to what I went to the shelf for in the first place. This happenstance I count as one of the truly wonderful blessings of curiosity and convergence. From a dark corner, Joseph Wechsberg's 1962 *Dining at the Pavillon* fell open at the dedication: 'To the memory of Fernand Point, last of the grands seigneurs, greatest chef of our time, genius of gastronomy, "Le Roi" among his peers.' Although *Dining at the Pavillon* is in the main a book devoted to Henri Soulé and his New York restaurant Le Pavillon, it includes a piece on Point that had been published in *The New Yorker* and this, like Benoit's book, is a valediction to that wise lover of butter ('*ce mandarin amoureux du beurre frais*', according to Benoit). The menu for the last meal Wechsberg ate with Point, who died not long after, goes like this:

Terrine de Foie Gras Frais

Pâté de Chevreuil Chaud

Barquette de Moules

Saucisson de Campagne

Gratin de Queues d'Ecrevisses

Le Canard à la façon du Docteur Couchoud

Les Fromages de Reblochon et de Saint-Marcellin

Gâteau Bonne Fête

Corbeille de Fruits

Wechsberg reckons Escoffier would have judged the lunch too simple; Carême, too austere; for myself, I would have been unable to remain hungry enough to properly enjoy it, but I do see that it was a remarkable menu for the mid-fifties when haute cuisine was still in the thrall of dressage, *chaudfroid* and formally romantic description. It admirably lives up to his forty-third aphorism (see later), the invitation somehow homely and all the more inviting for that. Point, writes Wechsberg, was 'a philosopher, tolerant and wise and witty, a man of compassion . . . I've often suspected that in his later years [he] ran his restaurant mainly for the thinly veiled purpose of inviting his friends. He would have loved to invite all the customers as his guests.' Although generosity is a trait shared by all great restaurateurs, and I too, as a restaurateur and cook, have felt that wish to give rather than sell food, not all cooks are tolerant and wise.

In a scrappy journal kept from a long holiday in France in 1978, the only record of a meal at La Pyramide, Point's restaurant in Vienne, south of Lyon – which continued as a kind of chapel to Point after his death – is of the wines. The food did not sing. Point had been dead for twenty-three years, but the point is not that he needed to be there but that he had been there in a different time.

—

Le petit livre crème de Fernand Point ('Point's little cream-coloured notebook') comprises fifty rules by which Point lived to cook and which I began to translate with pleasurable curiosity and for the pleasure of shifting these rules into the twenty-first century, for even after fifty years they are all still relevant for *chefs-patrons* (owner-chefs), whatever the cuisine. I have grouped them according to subject, so they are in different order to the original, and have sometimes shifted an example so that, for instance, a chafing dish, now generally passé, becomes something more to do with cooking in television than showing off in the dining-room. And because it is the convergence of observations about quite disparate things (architecture and music, for instance, although both share numerous traits with cookery) that is one of the excitements of reading and translating and cooking, I have included the odd tangential note. I felt it legitimate to sometimes let translation shift into interpretation, still with a light heart. Louise Bourgeois, great nonagenarian French artist, replied to an interviewer that she never talked literally: 'You do not get anywhere by being literal, except to be puny. You have to use analogy and interpretation and leaps of all kinds.' Translating fifty little aphorisms has opened, if not exactly Bourgeois' box, then a whole new world of possibilities.

The only aphorism that niggles at my modern conscience is '*Du beurre! Donnez-moi du beurre! Toujours du beurre!*' While ironic currency might have been made of his butter-lust by shifting it into adoration of extra-virgin olive oil, I have too much admiration for butter as a medium for flavour to play post-modern games. If there were a typeface to represent irony, as someone once suggested there should be, this might have been possible; instead, butter it is. Waverley Root, in his *The Food of France,* makes much of the three great cooking regions of the country – those of butter, olive oil and pork/goose fats – and points out that 'a cuisine is not shaped so much by its consumers as they, again in the most literal sense, are shaped by it'. As we have seen, Point's restaurant was not far south of Lyon, which sits on the southern, buttery line of Root's culinary map.

The masculine bias in the aphorisms has been retained not only because that was Fernand Point's world but also in part because things haven't changed all that much. Women are certainly a greater part of the kitchen workforce (one cannot imagine one in Point's kitchen; his wife Mado, like many of the wives of French chefs right through to the eighties and probably still, played hostess and cashier), but hardly any choose to be 'master' of a professional kitchen.

The scholar Pierre Ryckmans, in using his pen-name (Simon Leys) when translating *The Analects of Confucius,* seems to be suggesting that in some part translation is a fictionalisation of the original text. Translation is indeed an imaginative task. It has been instructive to take on Point literally and then to try for colloquial and sensible English out of a personal understanding of his meaning. If I have any qualification for this task it is that I spent my professional culinary adolescence buried in the French way of doing things, though mostly, unlike Monselet and Point (see aphorism 47), *sans truffes*. French words such as *la cuisine* and *le cuisinier*, phrases such as *faire la cuisine*, are here specific to professional cooking, while English and the equivalent English terms for the same profession are not so narrow. The difference between 'cook' and 'chef' is sometimes blurred, especially in our less autocratic kitchens. What side of the bench one stands on over this difference makes for a separate and interesting debate.

My point is not to dredge up Point because of going to the book to check on something else (which wasn't there), but to make him useful to a generation of cooks who believe they think entirely differently about cooking and cuisine; who dismiss lineage. Even when restaurant food in the hands of Australian/American/English cooks in Australian/American/English cities have replaced onion soup with laksa and reddled the sauce for lamb with pomegranate molasses, the wave of culinary history includes vestigial tails. We are what we think we left behind as much as what we are cooking ourselves into; and however etiquettes may differ, the imperatives of good cooking and the pleasures of the table, be these banana leaves on ground mats, or linen and Lalique at the table, share the same qualities.

For myself, a select few of Point's aphorisms (19, 22, 23, 26, 38, 41, for instance) speak with shifting depth to a wider view and so make universal and wise observations; No. 26 is my favourite of all. Others address the kitchen, the restaurant and the craft specifically, with sense and sensibility (6, 7, 9, 39, 40, 41, 43, 50). I am particularly partial to his advice on the treatment of human dishwashers, and on training over goodwill.

By now, everything I read seemed relevent to the idea of translation and interpretation, which in turn seemed to have everything to do, by analogy, with making a dish from a recipe, with taking one culture's food and making sense of it at another culture's table. In a review of a new edition of George Chapman's 400-year-old translation of *The Iliad* and *The Odyssey*, Colin Burrow wrote of 'a continual argument between the translator's preoccupations and his sense of what was distinctive about Homer'; 'For Chapman translation is a dialectic between one life, one civilization, and another.' According to Burrow, in Chapman's time 'what you read and how you read it was part of who you were, and could be used to illustrate the kind of person you wished to be'. 'Tell me what you eat and I shall tell you what you are', wrote Brillat-Savarin. Burrow also suggests Chapman understood that 'if speeches do not have meanings to particular addressees they could not hope to be read or understood', which supports my approach to Point's aphorisms: as much as is legitimate, they need to speak generally rather than personally if they are to show their good sense. The culinary culture in the New World fifty-odd years after Point's death might be said to be as foreign to his ethos as Chapman's world of letters was to ancient Greece.

Royall Tyler, interviewed about his recently finished translation of the eleventh-century Japanese classic by Murasaki Shikubu, *The Tale of Genji*, depicted translation as a performance, analogous to a musician performing a composer's work, an actor giving her particular interpretive voice to a role. We might see cooking in these terms if only we knew the original composer and thought more about the idea of ownership. Or perhaps recipes are never owned? Listening to Tyler ruminating on his Herculean work makes me laugh at my task – rendering fifty aphorisms in a modern language! But it has become something else altogether, it has been deflected, by the exercise itself, from the original straightforward purpose to an amateur's reflection on translation – a journey to Ithaca taking as long as possible. I've become a tourist who doesn't have a date by which I must be home, and there are so many detours to unknown places.

Geneticist Luigi Luca Cavalli-Sforza, in the first chapter of *Genes, Peoples and Languages*, writes that 'While correcting the translation of one of my books, I was terrified to see that all my conditionals had been changed to indicatives – my safeguards had been eliminated'. In an article on *La Fura Del Baus*, the Spanish theatre troupe of the grotesque, a cast member is reported to have said 'We are right at the limit of our compromise as actors': the Spanish word *compromiso* in fact means 'commitment'. Similarly, and in ignorance, I originally presumed the French *ignorer* meant 'ignore'.

Applying the concept of translation/interpretation to cookery and recipes rather than prose (conditionals and indicatives do play very different and practical roles in recipes) raises issues of authenticity and faithfulness, and raises the worry that a text might not even be applicable in the real world of cookery. What happens when I take a recipe of Point's, for instance, and make it in Australia? Using one of his recipes here and now is surely an untrustworthy form of translation, an inevitable transformation, a shift to a different time and geography, especially because I will (in order to make a complete meal) be using different ingredients and surrounding the dish with others that would be foreign to Point's locality. Nevertheless, if cooked well and judged successful by myself and those at the table, it has its own legitimacy. Is it now mine? I think not; you may disagree. The result is not what Point would have expected of his instructions, although I suspect their recording in Benoit's book was more for immortal inscription than instruction. The change is a matter of shifting lineage.

Every one of these side steps that have thrown light on translation and interpretation, and had seemingly nothing to do with gastronomy, have been lovely little lamps of convergence and illumination. They mirror the highways, the hedgerows and the culs-de-sac of culinary wanderings too. Tyler's definition of translation as performance is particularly apt. Point's aphorisms speak universally to cookery as a professional art and it is therefore legitimate and sensible to translate them for a different culture. Yet his food, through which he most truly communicated (see aphorism 1), is not to be found in recipes – at least, only the suggestion of it and then only if one understands the produce and methods. I might follow a particular recipe, but I will make something different. This happens when cooking, just as it does in the theatre. *Exit Ariel!*

The aphorisms
ON GASTRONOMY

2.   Silence may be golden, as the proverb says, but one must talk about gastronomy.
Le 'silence est d'or', affirme-t-on, et pourtant, la cuisine, il faut bien qu'on en parle.

13.   A fine meal has the harmony of a symphony and is as finely constructed as a Romanesque church.
Un bon repas doit être aussi harmonieux qu'une symphonie, et aussi bien construit qu'une cathédrale romane.

18.   After a strong pre-dinner drink, even more after two, the palate can't distinguish between a great wine and a bottle of plonk.
Après l'absorption d'un cocktail, et à plus forte raison de deux, le palais ne peut plus distinguer un Château Mouton-Rothschild d'un grand millésime du contenu d'une bouteille d'encre à stylo!

19.   A table is convivial, and profoundly convivial when the food lifts the spirits.

A table, tous les hommes fraternisent; surtout quand on leur a enchanté l'âme.

23. To criticise a foreign cuisine or a regional speciality is to deny the legitimacy of wide-ranging tastes.

    Chaque pays, chaque région, a ses spécialités locales au sujet desquelles il est téméraire de dire 'ce n'est pas bon', car tous les goûts sont dans la nature.

26. A cook who thinks every action makes him a great chef is like a man who repaints his garden gate and thinks he is an artist.

    Il existe des quantités d'endroits où l'on affirme faire la cuisine. Tout comme il existe des quantités de gens qui, après avoir repeint la porte de leur jardin, se prennent pour des peintres.

46. Cook for your friends, not for television. (More literally: When using liqueurs and eau-de-vies in cooking one should be parsimonious, otherwise the alcohol drowns the aroma of the dish. Some waiters, completing the cooking of kidneys or crêpes in the dining-room, use too much alcohol in order to be theatrical. This is an absolute no-no.)

    Dans tous les mets comprenant un appoint d'eau-de-vie ou de liqueur, il faut être très parcimonieux, sinon l'alcool étouffe le parfum naturel qui doit se dégager d'un mets. Dans certains restaurants, certains maîtres d'hôtel qui font flamber dans la salle rognons ou crêpes, usent de l'alcool à profusion pour amuser le client et faire du spectacle. C'est une très grosse erreur.

49. Man is distinguished from other animals by taking pleasure in drinking when not thirsty. ('Man is the only animal, I believe, who pretends he is thinking of other things while he is eating.' Robert Lynd)

    Ce que distingue, entre autres, l'homme de l'animal, c'est qu'il peut éprouver du plaisir à boire sans avoir soif.

ON COOKERY

1. I speak through my craft.

   C'est avec mes fourneaux que je peuple mes silences.

3. A chef who loses his passion for cooking will lose his reputation.

   Le cuisinier perd sa réputation dès qu'il devient indifférent à son ouvrage.

6. While cookery is neither rigid nor formulaic, creativity builds on, never

ignores, the basic rules. ('All the great artists knew all the rules even if they broke them.' Robert Hale)

La cuisine n'est pas invariable comme une formule du Codex. Mais if faut se garder d'en modifier les bases essentielles.

7. Be endlessly curious in your reading and practice, if only to discover a few precious things.

En cuisine, il faut tout lire, tout voir, tout entendre, tout essayer, tout observer, pour ne retenir enfin de compte qu'assez peu de choses!

8. Just as Brillat-Savarin wrote that a master-chef is not born with his skills, so too one can train to be a cook.

On ne nait pas rôtisseur, comme l'a dit Brillat-Savarin, mais on le devient également, tout comme on devient cuisinier.

14. In general, a dish that appears simple is the most difficult to cook. ('The simpler the song, the more complex the narrative it can carry . . . When it really comes down to it, I, like the wood pigeon, may only have one song in me. But by that song, I, like the wood pigeon, can mean the sky and all the bloody stars behind it.' Paul Evans in *Guardian Weekly*, 2002).

Ce qui est le plus difficile à faire, c'est en général ce qui est apparemment le plus simple.

15. A simple dish, choucroûte for instance, is no less delectable than a complex one, but one must truly know how to prepare it. (Raymond Thuilier, born the same year as Point and the founder chef-patron of Oustaù de Baumanière at Le Baux de Provence, said 'The triumph of cooking is to be able to produce the simple things so that they taste as they were meant to'.)

Ce qu'il y a de plus simple n'est pas pour autant le moins délectable. Prenez le cas de la choucroûte, par example, mais faut-il encore savoir la faire.

20. Having been granted exquisite ingredients, it is our duty to prepare them properly and serve them with ceremony.

Si le divin créateur a pris le soin de nous laisser des choses exquises, c'est pour qu'elles soient bien préparées et servies avec cérémonie.

24. A good cook is judged by his sauces, and if the kitchen were an orchestra the 'saucier' would be a soloist. ('If we are to look at Poulenc as a musical pastry chef it should be remembered that he not only makes profiteroles.' BBC radio program)

C'est par les sauces que se distingue un bon cuisinier. D'autre part, dans l'orchestre d'une grande cuisine, le saucier est un soliste.

28. Budgeting and haute cuisine are mutually exclusive, but shopping with an eye for cheap produce is no hindrance to good cooking.

Quand on pense à la grande cuisine, on ne peut pas penser à l'argent; les deux sont inconciliables. La grande cuisine coûte très cher. Ce que n'empêche que l'on peut faire de la très bonne cuisine aves des produits bon marché.

32. Cooking demands complete dedication. Think about the sheer amount of work one must do. You may not believe me, but I have been in the kitchen since five a.m. and will not have finished cooking until eleven this evening, with only two hours' rest in the afternoon. I have worked these hours ever since my apprenticeship in 1914 at the Bristol Hotel in Paris. Crazy isn't it? But fine cooking is unsympathetic!

Répondant un jour à l'interview d'un journaliste à propos de son métier, Fernand Point ne mâcha pas les mots: 'La cuisine exige le feu sacré. Il ne faut penser qu'à son travail. Imaginez donc qu'en ce qui me concerne, mais vous n'allez pas me croire, j'étais à mes débuts en cuisine à cinq heures du matin, et je n'arrêtais pas avant onze heures du soir, avec seulement deux heures de repos dans l'après-midi! Tels étaient nos horaires, avant 1914, à l'hôtel Bristol, à Paris, où j'ai fait mon apprentissage. C'était beaucoup trop, n'est-ce pas? Mais la grande cuisine est impitoyable!'

34. All cookbooks share family traits. The best is the one you write for yourself.

Les livres de cuisine se ressemblent comme des frères. Le meilleur est celui que l'on fait soi-même.

39. ('God is in the details.' Modernist architect Mies van der Rohe, quoted in an interview in the *New York Herald Tribune* in 1958)

Le succès est une somme de petites choses mises au point.

40. All craftsmen, but especially cooks, never stop learning.

Dans toutes les professions sans doute, mais en cuisine certainement, on est à l'école toute sa vie.

44. As the right tie complements a suit, so a garnish must suit the dish.

Les garnitures doivent être assorties comme une cravate à un complet.

45.   The best cooking is dependent on seasonal produce. ('A piece of music cannot be played better than it is.' Alfred Brendl)
La meilleure cuisine est celle qui tient compte des produits de la saison.

THE PROFESSIONAL KITCHEN

16.   Never let your attention wander in the kitchen.
L'inattention ne paye jamais en cuisine.

17.   Béarnaise sauce, for instance. What does it entail? An egg yolk, some shallots, some tarragon. Believe me, it takes years of practical experience to make a perfect béarnaise! Take your eyes off it for a moment and it will be ruined! ('A Sucking Pig, like a young child, must not be left for an instant.' Thomas Love Peacock)
Prenons le cas d'une béarnaise. Qu'est-ce que c'est? Un jaune d'oeuf, de l'échalote, de l'estragon . . . Eh bien, croyez-moi, il faut des années de pratique pour que le résultat en soit parfait! Quittez-la un moment des yeux, et votre sauce sera inutilisable.

21.   Confine your work clothes to the work place. (Literally: A chef never dirties his apron outside the kitchen.)
Un bon cuisinier ne salit jamais son tablier en dehors de son travail.

22.   Instead of damning younger cooks, the older generation of chefs should try to understand their values in order to work with them. (Given that Point was a restaurateur as well as a chef, this aphorism, which could be interpreted in many ways, might relate to the role a chef plays in the dining-room and the traditional courtesy of only approaching diners in a clean apron when he appears in order to be complimented. In my opinion, the practice should be abolished as an anachronistic embarrassment. Once, after we had eaten a fine meal in the marvellously professional and friendly dining-room of Georges Blanc at Vonnas in the eighties, M. Blanc appeared at our table to say that he would be available to sign a menu after a certain hour. This was presumably because we had been spotted as tourists. We had not been going to ask him to do this, even though his apron was spotless.)
Il ne faut jamais médire de personne, car si l'on veut que le monde devienne

meilleur, il faut chercher à comprendre son prochain dans l'espoir de mieux l'aimer.

29. To avoid spoilage and waste, a chef should check what remains in the larder at the close of every service, and only then write tomorrow's menu.

   Pour la mise en place, le chef doit avoir tous les soirs le relevé complet du garde-manger, de façon à établir consciencieusement son menu du lendemain et à éviter ainsi toute perte ou gaspillage.

37. A kitchen brigade respects its chef because of the breadth of his knowledge and abilities, from purchasing to pastry, not just because he is in charge.

   Pour qu'un chef soit respecté, il ne faut pas que sa supériorité soit mise en doute. Et pour cela, il convient qu'il excelle dans toutes les parties, y compris la pâtisserie et les achats.

38. A good apprentice treats the dishwasher with as much courtesy as he does the chef.

   Un bon apprenti cuisinier doit être aussi poli avec le plongeur qu'avec le chef.

42. The best kitchen manager combines the wisdom of experience with the energy of youth.

   Lorsque'on dirige un personnel, il est nécessaire d'amalgamer l'expérience des anciens à l'enthousiasme des jeunes.

50. It is a chef's duty to pass on all he has learned through his own practice to the next generation.

   Le devoir d'un bon cuisinier est de transmettre aux générations qui le remplaceront ce qu'il aura appris, ainsi que les résultats de son expérience personelle.

FOOD AND WINE

25. Poultry should rest in the refrigerator for four or five days after it has been killed, but never freeze it.

   Les volailles doivent passer quatre ou cinq jours au réfrigérateur (et non pas au congélateur) après avoir été tuées.

33. Nutmeg is a fine spice, but use it sparingly.

   La muscade est agréable, mais il ne faut pas en mettre partout et ne jamais en abuser.

35. The taste and aroma of walnut oil pair well with red wine.

Le goût de l'huile de noix s'accorde très bien avec le vin rouge.

36.   Spinach tastes all the better for a pinch of sugar.

Les épinards sont plus savoureux si on leur ajoute un peu de sucre.

48.   Heat doesn't bring old wines back to life, so do not use them in the kitchen.

Les vins trop vieux ne conviennent pas à la cuisine. Le feu ne leur redonne pas la force qu'ils ont perdue.

27.   Having opened a bottle of champagne, leave it to settle for a good minute in the ice bucket.

Il faut toujours laisser reposer une bouteille de champagne durant une bonne minute, et la laisser ainsi dans son seau à glace, après l'avoir débouchée.

THE RESTAURANT

4.   People are not machines and a cook is sometimes tired, but the food should never let this show.

Un homme n'est pas une machine, et il arrive à un cuisinier d'être fatigué. Mais la clientèle n'en doit rien savoir.

5.   Just as trains should run on time, so should the staff meal.

L'horaire des repas du personnel d'un restaurant doit être aussi rigoureux que celui des chemins de fer.

9.   Goodwill is no substitute for training and competence in the running of a restaurant.

La bonne volonté ne peut remplacer la compétence dans l'exploitation d'un restaurant.

11.   Suffer with equanimity those who turn up their nose at your food.

Même si certains clients font la soupe à la grimace, ayez toujours le sourire.

12.   Fine cooking waits for no one; it is the eater who must be ready for it.

La grande cuisine ne doit pas attendre le client; c'est le client qui doit attendre la grande cuisine.

41.   Listen to your critics, but dismiss those who bear you a grudge.

If faut savoir admettre une réflexion désagréable. Les esprits forts ignorent la rancune.

The point of Point

43. When writing a menu, forswear pretentious descriptions and steer clear of exaggeration; simply name the dish. ('Less is more.' Mies van der Rohe on restraint, in the interview quoted after aphorism 39)

Il est indispensable d'éviter sur les menus les appellations prétentieuses, voire grotesques, tout comme il faut proscrire celles qui ne correspondent pas à la réalité.

POINT ON POINT

10. Butter is the foundation, the centre, the heart of my cooking. (Literally: Butter! Give me butter, always butter!)

Du beurre! Donnez-moi du beurre! Toujours du beurre!

30. The first time I dine at a restaurant, I always shake hands with the chef before I order. I know that if he is thin I will eat badly. If he is not only thin but unhappy, I flee.

Quand je m'arrête dans un restaurant inconnu, je demande toujours à serrer la main du cuisinier avant le repas. Car je sais que si celui-ci est maigre, je mangerai mal. Et si le cuisinier est à la fois maigre et triste, il n'y a de salut que dans la fuite.

31. Before judging a thin person, however, one must ask about his past: he may once have been fat. (A chef I worked with for many years in the seventies and early eighties, and who revered Point, was said by a French friend to be 'as thin as a *galette*'.)

Avant de mal juger un homme maigre, il faut se renseigner. C'est peut-être un ancien gros.

47. When I die I'd like to go the same way as Monselet who, on his deathbed on Christmas Eve, told his friends, with a certain wicked serenity, that he would be under the earth with truffles. (Charles Monselet was the publisher/author of the *Almanach du Gourmand*, a weekly leaflet in 1865. And by coincidence Aldo Buzzi's *A Weakness for Almost Everything* refers to the closing lines of one of Charles Baudelaire's poems: 'You old Pharaoh, Monselet!/At this unexpected sign/I thought of you: A la vue/ Du Cimetière, Estaminet!' – 'The hotel bar has a view of the cemetery!')

Monselet est mort la veille de Noël. Pressentant sa fin, il confia à des intimes: 'J'aurai un enterrement aux truffes'. Je souhaite autant de sérénité malicieuse à mon trépas.

A young man, Ben McIntyre, came to finish his cooking apprenticeship at Berowra Waters Inn and was there for the last two years before I closed the restaurant. On first, fast judgement he looked messy and ill-prepared for a life of *mise-en-place* followed by fast service, but we soon saw that he was a most ordered cook. His preparation was always impeccable, always there on time, and he moved through the mechanism of service with the same sense of operative precision. He didn't continue to climb the professional culinary ladder (which is neither here nor there), but he once said to me, years after those long days at the restaurant and in response to someone else saying that a certain cook should be put out to pasture (no one we knew): 'Cooking isn't about athleticism, it's about taste and experience.' So Ben McIntyre wasn't just a lesson for me in not being able to tell a cook by his lanky body, he was also a person with a fine sense of balance.

Young people like Ben who worked at Berowra Waters Inn filled one of four positions: as least experienced apprentice, who mainly worked at the bench rather than the stove; as first-course cook; as dessert cook; or as assistant to the main-course cook. However long they stayed, they could never rise to 'chef' because this position was taken for all of the restaurant's best years by Janni Kyritsis. This created a kind of rotation system that operated just below the peak. And being chef at Berowra Waters Inn obviously suited Janni because he stayed for over twelve years.

In 1999 Malcolm Gladwell wrote an article for *The New Yorker* that made some attempt to understand what lies behind what he called 'physical genius'. Gladwell took a neurosurgeon, a baseball player, a hockey player, a tennis professional and a cellist, and marvelled at the confidence, the fluidity and grace of their movements, movements that make them outstanding successes in their chosen fields. He described, in that most engaging *New Yorker* way, the precise movements that the brain surgeon, Charlie Wilson, makes to remove a tumour in twenty-five minutes, a tumour that another, highly competent neurosurgeon might take up to several hours to remove. He described the extraordinary co-ordination exhibited by Tony Gwynn when he hits a baseball. He talked to the cellist Yo-Yo Ma. And he talked to a Harvard University psychologist who has studied the brain's power to visualise physical acts that require practice, decision-making and imagination.

Reading Gladwell's essay, I was reminded of the years I watched and sometimes helped Janni Kyritsis. I made a list of headings that seemed to come close to covering all his attributes. There were enough felicitous explanations in Gladwell's examination of the neurosurgeon, in particular, to push me to look at what made Janni a remarkable chef. It became a complex picture and I shall only touch on parts of it. It certainly isn't a picture by which to make generalised rules about the nature of all good chefs: Janni's skills are different to Tim Pak Poy's; Tim's are different to Phillip Searle's; Phillip's are different to Damien Pignolet's; Damien's different to David Thompson's; David's different to Cheong Liew's; Cheong's different to Tetsuya Wakuda, and so on – to name only a few Australian chefs who have been justly celebrated. They might share the obvious skills, but they all differently achieve the same end: the sum of separate dishes produced in a short space of time and on the run. This is as close to a definition of 'chef' as might be made. This skill is what makes a person a chef as opposed to a cook.

Gladwell suggests that we want to believe that people like the neurosurgeon have the physical equivalent of an abnormally high IQ; that his uncanny ability to do an extraordinarily difficult operation with apparent ease, flair and confidence means he has a 'gift'. In examining the habits of the neurosurgeon, the tennis player and the cellist, Gladwell presents us with the beginnings of a different picture altogether: they all practised, and practised . . . and practise.

Commercial cookery is, notwithstanding a sometimes gullible public perception of it as an accumulation of multiple yet unique creative acts, the gestalt of its repetitions. This has some resonance with Gladwell's observation about the trait shared by his interviewees, of constant practice. Gladwell wrote that the neurosurgeon, in his first years of professorship and after long days teaching, used to practise his craft on rats: 'Wilson sees surgery as akin to a military campaign.'

Portraying great chefs as performing double somersaults on an aerial trapeze lends romance to a profession which is in fact judged, meal after meal, by single dishes arriving at the table for consumption. Most of the time a chef's skill is to produce this same fine dish over and over again. Men and women working with or under a chef in his kitchen judge him by means of more complex perceptions and interactions. The combination of craft skills and personality, of leadership, of cool under fire, of support, encouragement and the simple courtesies add up to the idea not just of a chef but of a whole person as chef.

For myself, it has never made culinary sense to work to a fast-changing menu, and this suited Janni's attitude and temperament as well. Instead of constantly coming up with the new, he found ingenious and often brilliant ways to integrate the parts of a dish into a coherent whole and then produced it over and over again. You might say he was a consummate dissector and a maker of inspired parcels. He would find a solution to a generic preparation of, say, game, bird or fish and then apply this to different produce. This is not to suggest that his was a radically different way of working but rather to explain the seemingly intuitive side-steps a chef takes in making decisions about the parts of each dish. I often watched Janni bone what must have been the ten-thousandth quail or scrape the scales from the thousandth salmon skin. He was capable of this repetition of action for such long periods that I swear his beard had grown longer by the time he stacked the last, perfectly boned bird, cleaned fish skin or scissored veal kidney. His elegant, even beautiful, hands were lovely to watch. Such was the admiration given Janni by the people who worked with him that they following his example and continued with their *mise-en-place* out of deference and well past their supposed bedtime. He asked them by example to do their best and so they did.

There is an air of military precision about a well-run service. If you control the weight and size of portions, know how long it will take to cook each variation to perfection at an exact temperature, and juggle the menu so that both the cooking equipment and the sum of the kitchen's co-operative skills are co-ordinated to maximum efficiency, then service is a hectic, repetitive breeze to those who want to excel at it. Produce doesn't come in perfect packages. One duck might be unaccountably tough, the fish might not all be the same size, ditto the vegetables; some produce might be older than the cook wants it to be, for the seasons will independently change just as a dish is mastered. Sometimes Janni, with good humour, would complain in such a way that you would think he wanted produce to share the inert properties of parts of a machine, and I'd think he was in the wrong trade, but always he found ways to cope with inconsistency. 'Obsessive preparation does two things', writes Gladwell, 'it creates consistency [and] more important, practice changes the *way* a task is perceived'.

Janni's patient repetition of the physical actions of preparation, actions that many chefs would pass on to another cook or apprentice, were a necessary part of his approach to cooking. The difference between him and many other chefs is that he never handed these tasks to the next in line. It was as though he was architect and bricklayer at the same time, and by continuing to labour became a consummate builder.

———

Gladwell writes about 'the least understood element of physical genius: imagination'. The psychologist he interviewed spoke of experts at motor tasks using their imagination in a very particular way, displaying a power to visualise that consists of four separate abilities working in combination: the ability to generate an image, to inspect and draw inferences from it, to retain it, and to transform or manipulate it. In the professional kitchen, and in Janni's hands, these might be to envisage beforehand a finished dish; to understand what it demands in preparation, to manipulate the parts and their production to make the final dish successful, and in the end zone, to produce a dish that seemed to be transformed into food which was independent, which stood alone. This is not, I think, the general method used by most good cooks, who build a dish around an impressive product with an apparent sleight of hand, knowing intuitively (seemingly, anyway, for intuition depends on practice too) what will go with what. Janni, instead, manipulated the parts to produce what it was he had decided it would be.

His most impressive talent as a cook might be called then, in a different profession, problem-solving. Solving problems, of course, involves the imagination and is creative. In this sense, Janni's work most closely approximated that of Gladwell's neurosurgeon – both thinking on their feet and through their hands – although the neurosurgeon performs his wizardry inside living people's brains while cooks work on dead flesh and only risk the ire of living customers. This is not to demean the level of spatial co-ordination which makes one chef a pleasure to watch and another nerve-wracking. You knew that Janni held control and, more, that if extraneous happenstance (a dead thermostat, a bush fire, a goanna at the back door, a returned dish from a diner who wanted less pink, a divvying up of *mise-en-place* because otherwise there wouldn't be portions enough for the number of orders taken) interrupted the flow, he coped, adjusted, amended without fuss or fury. The absolute confidence one had in his producing what the menu promised, over and over again, was his greatest gift and his greatest generosity.

A sociologist Gladwell interviewed told him of tests conducted on doctors who had not successfully completed their neurosurgery training. He concluded that 'far more than technical skills or intelligence, what was necessary for success was . . . a practical-minded obsession with the possibility and the consequence of failure'. Janni's practical single-mindedness fits in with this conclusion. Moreover, he imbued it with a kind of moral righteousness that left no one uncertain of his motives. At its most seductive (and seduction, properly exercised by a chef over his underlings should not be underestimated as a desirable trait in a kitchen) it gained him unstinting respect because there was no pretension or extraneous theatre in his work.

Janni cooked indefatigably well because he shared with the neurosurgeon the trait of 'physical genius' and all the 'chunking' moves such ability allows. Chunking, explains Gladwell, is the psychologist's term for solving problems (he uses a chess player as an example) by being able to use sequenced and multiple units of knowledge. In other words it is the sum of the four abilities. In Janni's case these might be characterised by his ability to apparently skip the conceptual nature of cooking (of thinking up dishes from the raw pieces of the jigsaw), instead going directly to the physical with the ideas included, and well they may be for this kind of cook. In fact the idea does not exist outside the physical action.

He was, I am suggesting, the irregular verb of chefs, not the noun.

⁓

In contemplating Janni's skills I wanted to come to some understanding of the mechanisms and aesthetics, as it were, of his actions, rather than simply quote what he produced. Enough has been written of what seems to be the obvious about the most successful chefs: their use of seasonal produce, their support of producers; turning Lasagne and Confit into names for different dishes altogether; using Asian ingredients, pell-mell, to spice up European food; feeding those who write and talk about food; accepting the status of high priest without any visits to the confessional. None of those practices explains why a few chefs are successful, many good enough and most left running on the spot; not one, in fact, of these practices explains what it is that makes a brilliant chef. Choosing to use seasonal produce is something even bad cooks do, because it is available and because not to do so is nothing less than foolish and undoes the whole idea of cookery. Cooking with produce which isn't fresh is just as foolish, of course, although a good cook will be able to make the most of tired produce. When chefs tell journalists what produce they like to use, who they like to feed and in what circumstances they like to feed paying diners (and, differently, friends), they say nothing about the decisions and actions that amount to what cooking is. They have not been asked to talk about their skills or the confidence with which they approach cooking.

⁓

Silk purses from sows' ears

Janni has said publicly that the dish he is most proud of and feels he 'invented' is the tomato consommé we made over and over again at Berowra Waters Inn. I know his invention to be fact; that is, he came up with the method of extracting and collecting the fresh flavour of the tomatoes without reference to any other recipe. It is interesting that many high-profile chefs, for instance Tetsuya Wakuda in Sydney and Charlie Trotter in Chicago, have also 'invented' a tomato essence or 'tea'. In *Food for the Gods* by 'Lucullus', published in 1931, there is a tomato jelly made in much the same way as these consommés; the last time I made Janni's version, I added a couple of cloves in deference to 'Lucullus' and also because the idea of a trace of cloves is not far away from the addition of Worcestershire sauce.

Janni's tomato consommé

This recipe will make approximately two litres of consommé, enough for a refined beginning, or a restful cup between courses, as part of a menu for up to fifteen people. Always serve it in a small cup, the finer porcelain the better and never more than 150 ml. Do not garnish!

In a food processor, purée together 3 kg ripe flavourful tomatoes (cores removed, but skin left on); ½ stick celery, chopped; and 100 g basil leaves. Transfer to a non-aluminium saucepan and slowly bring to simmering point, then simmer extremely gently for fifteen minutes. Strain through a double thickness of muslin or reinforced kitchen paper.

For every 2 litres of tomato essence, add 2 teaspoons salt, or to taste; 1 teaspoon Worcestershire sauce; and ¼ teaspoon Tabasco. Heat gently to serve. We sometimes made a jelly of the consommé by dissolving 20 leaves of gelatine in each 2 litres of liquid. This, sliced into cubes, makes a fine garnish for a seafood salad, or works well as an aspic in which crayfish, for instance, might be set.

The dish that became Janni's signature was rare beef fillet enclosed in a bone-marrow dumpling mixture with tapenade, and steamed. With many dishes on the river, Janni and I shared ideas but always it was Janni who worked out how to make them work. I remember suggesting that encasing the beef in the dumpling mixture would make the dish coherent and confined to a single piece of food on the plate. Wherever the dish began it became Janni's, as did everything he controlled at Berowra Waters Inn. It embodies everything that was extraordinary about his methods and everything that seemed to undo the idea of cooking in his cooking. Each portion was wrapped in plastic clingwrap and then aluminium foil before being steamed. The dumpling mixture was spread thickly on the plastic wrap, some tapenade added for gutsy flavour, the piece of beef placed on top and the whole thing rolled so that the meat was encased. Good food is hardly ever the sum of portioned weights controlled by clingwrap and foil but here the parcel was all. Sliced across the centre so that on the plate there were two rounds of fillet ringed with the off-white dumpling mixture, it was a most pleasing dish – a professional dish, which is to say that its form was as much to do with presentation on the plate as it was with the commingling of flavours.

Tapenade

This is an archetypal Provençal spread, a combination of strong flavours. The better the quality of the parts, the better the tapenade. It is a mistake to think that by combining many ingredients, the sum of the parts will disguise inferior olives, anchovies or capers. A good olive oil is also essential. Almonds are the 'secret' ingredient, as they are sweet and meaty, especially if fresh (almonds are seasonal) and blanched just before making the tapenade.

It is worth making a large amount. Tapenade keeps well in the fridge for weeks, losing none of its flavour, and is thus on hand to accompany fresh goat's curd or just-hard-boiled eggs or simply spread generously on toasted sourdough or Melba toast. It makes a good relish for a piece of beef.

These quantities will fill four 200-ml jars: 250 g pitted black olives; 100 g rinsed anchovy fillets; 100 g salted, small capers, which you will need to rinse and blanch; 4 cloves garlic, peeled; 65 ml (¼ cup) strained lemon juice; 1 teaspoon ground white pepper; a pinch of cayenne pepper; a very generous handful of fresh basil and the same of parsley; 100 g blanched almonds, chopped; and 250 ml virgin olive oil.

Place all the ingredients, except the oil, in a food processor and purée, adding the olive oil gradually. The final paste should be thick enough to hold together without the oil running out; use less olive oil if it seems too thin. Add more lemon juice if needed and adjust the salt and pepper. To bind the paste for the beef dish described above, Janni thickened it with fresh breadcrumbs.

—

When we provided dinner for two hundred and fifty guests at the S.H. Erwin Gallery in Sydney in the early nineties, a celebration of the already over-ninety-year-old painter Lloyd Rees, Rees's friends told me that he adored pot-au-feu. Janni oversaw the filling of two hundred and fifty freezer bags with individual portions of the whole dish, including its broth, which were heated through in enormous stock pots of simmering water (these sat on hired burners on the floor, for there was no commercial kitchen). Plating was simply a matter of slitting each bag and dropping the contents into a low bowl, adding blanched broad beans, fresh herbs, and the final wipe. This wrapped solution to a fast service for a large number was a brilliant production technique, a breathtakingly lateral, ergonomically sound way of sending out two hundred and fifty plates of perfectly braised and portioned food. All was under control.

When Berowra Waters Inn left the river to become Berowra Waters Out at the Adelaide Festival of the Arts in 1986, with its staff (except for the boat driver), its chairs and its cutlery, we also filled cars with specific *mise-en-place* (the most memorable were polystyrene containers of marinated hare fillet) and kitchen equipment, including oven trays and baking dishes. The ovens at the Botanic Hotel, where we set up shop and unofficial club, missed being wide enough for our equipment by less than a centimetre. Called back to the kitchen, having grabbed a purse to purchase new ones, we watched as Janni replaced the fitted oven shelves with loops made from wire coat-hangers, from which we 'hung' our trays. He saved me money, for which I was grateful, but more importantly he solved a major problem with ingenious, efficient practicality. That rock-and-roll exercise, which saw us performing a near-continuous stand-up routine for nearly a month with only two days to settle in, cost the business many thousands of dollars but gave us a working holiday Berowra Waters Inn funded and which has never been forgotten by those who came along for the ride. It was not a sensible exercise, but an adventure, which none of us regretted. With other memorable cooks and waiters Janni wrapped and tied and portioned and cooked and saved the day and night and early morning over and over again.

Janni once told me that on the Greek ship where he worked as an electrician before migrating to Australia, he made extra money by crafting macrame whatnots for the crew. I gave him my sewing machine when I saw that he was a much better tailor than me. Watching him take the food processor apart, fix the wonky wiring, meticulously clean it, and put it back together again after finishing a Sunday lunch service of usually eighty or so covers, was in many ways no different to watching him cook. In becoming chef, he didn't leave his physical genius on the back bench, he simply put it to a different set of problems.

There are others who worked at Berowra Waters Inn and who gave in inimitable and memorable ways. Of the adults, as opposed to the young apprentices, Leigh Stone-Herbert, Anders Ousback and Murray Smith stand out like beacons. Leigh, the only chef to come to the river with real training, the one who taught me most about cooking, has a catering business but is not interested in fame; Anders, the most extraordinary of them all, has taken to making pots like Lucie Rie took to the kiln; Murray, the most self-effacing, does with wood what Anders does with clay. Janni continues to cook, using his elegant hands to tell us who he is.

Silk purses from sows' ears

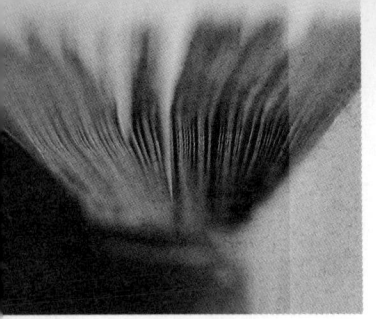

The composer John Cage once visited two friends in Milwaukee. Cage brought mushrooms as a gift. Sally said, 'But John, how should I cook them?' and Cage replied, 'Oh, Sally, when you cook them you will know.'

Four years after publicly admitting (in an essay on Elizabeth David in *The New Yorker* in 1998) that as a cook he is an anxious pedant, novelist and critic Julian Barnes (the man who turned into a cocktail at Bennelong Restaurant) admitted to having worked out why: he is 'a late-onset cook'. 'By the time I began to find out about it for myself', he explained, 'it was too late to ask my parents'. Blooming late and anxious, it seems (confessed in a food issue of *The New Yorker* in 2002), was also the result of his mother treating the kitchen as her secret place where she went about the 'transformational process'. She was not alone in doing so, if we presume Barnes to be referring to the fifties or sixties. The kitchen's separation from family life may have been a refuge for a wife and mother, a room of her own.

I've been rereading the formidable Marguerite Duras. In 1987 she published a series of interviews she had undertaken with Jérome Beaujour, entitled *La Vie materielle*:

> It's been going on for a long time. Ever since my son was a little boy *I've* brought the food from the kitchen and put it on the table. And when one course was finished and the next one was due, *I'd* go and fetch it without thinking, quite happily. Lots of women do it. Just like that, like me. They do it when the children are less than twelve years old, and

they go on doing it afterwards. With the Italians, for example, you see women of eighty serving children of sixty.

Barnes' mother knew how to do whatever she was doing to produce meals, but she didn't pass these skills on to the father and the boy. I remember reading about a traditional master boat-builder in Japan who would not take on any apprentices. He was now very, very old and had finally been persuaded to take one on; we catch our breath. The imperative of cooking, too, is practical tuition. I don't mean lessons one pays for (though I don't discount them), but the consolidation of experience passed down from one generation to the next. Cooking by its very nature is conservative, although these days cultural theorists want me to say 'traditional', which only shows that they know more about cultural theory than cooking. When the method, and even the result, are less than perfect, it is this early-onset, as opposed to 'late-onset', practical knowledge that provides comparative experience and the kind of confidence that people like the word-perfect Julian Barnes don't have. If you are used to handling food, if handling food is not a foreign activity, then the shift, through using a cookbook, from what might have been plain, nourishing food to nourishing food bursting with flavour and texture, will be a natural progression. It does, though, help to have tasted the food courtesy of someone else's hands, as a benchmark.

I understand the kind of anxiety late-onset cooks experience, because I am one myself and have never felt confident of success even when cooking professionally and mostly doing it well. By this I mean that I do not expect success and am always astonished by having produced something delicious and technically perfect. This has its own constantly renewable pleasure, but I could do without it and in doing without it would be a different kind of cook.

Cookbooks are manuals of practical instruction. They are useful. It is worth stating the obvious sometimes, in this case because there are now so many cookbooks that we would be in danger of a surfeit of instruction if that were their *raison d'être*. At their best they come a tiny part of the way to replacing generational instruction (which is a form of apprenticeship), formal apprenticeship, and as well open new doors, but they are less than one-dimensional and a poor replacement.

Cookbooks only hint at the savoury, because words don't have a taste or an aroma and you can't handle them. They also get dirty and you can't wash them. When they are not useful, they are the embodiment of seduction in the same way that window-shopping is. Because of this, those who are interested in food as voyeurs usually own rather too many of them and the books don't get grubby enough.

Jennifer Hillier has written about cookbooks. She is interested, as noted elsewhere, in the concept of *metis*. According to Hillier, for theorist James Scott 'the words that might describe *metis* are know-how, local knowledge, *savoir faire* or *arts de faire*, common sense, experience, and knack'. This concept is central to her understanding of cookbooks,

> since it gives a name to the knowledge and practices of traditional pre-recipe cuisines, typically transmitted orally and by face-to-face demonstration, across generations of women and in conditions of relatively low literacy. The opposite of *metis* is modernist 'thin simplification' – technical knowledge that is simplified, rationalised and standardised, and transmitted impersonally in written formulas – recipe knowledge in fact.

Hillier does not romanticise the concept of *metis* to the extent of ignoring the democratic distribution of knowledge that recipe books allow and encourage. Further, she points out that *metis* is not completely stamped out by the rationality of written recipes but still exists in unspoken form. My sense of this, as a solitary cook, is in the repeated making of a dish where one works towards a personal system and order of actions. The experience, the sum of repeated actions, pushes the recipe into a dish one feels comfortable with, and 'owns'.

Although I own rather a lot of cookbooks and use most of them in the circular round of cooking and reading, there is a central core that would suffice. Often it depends on whether you make a dish because of the casual seduction of a recipe, or look for a recipe because you have an ingredient. The latter is usually the more sensible way to approach cookery and is also why Stephanie Alexander's *The Cook's Companion* is a specific and personal encyclopaedia as much as it is a collection of recipes, and is all the finer for that. Fine semolina spoke up one week from the back of a cupboard (this speaks volumes for open shelves) and I decided to make semolina gnocchi, having never thought to do so until now. There are eighteen books on Italian cuisine(s) on the shelf if I don't include Marinetti's futurist cookbook; in fact, after counting I shifted him gruffly to the historical and reference section. This is not a lot, but if you think about it, just one book is surely enough. That's the thing about cuisines that have age and stability on their side – they are served by a sensible amount of instruction. Let's not even think about the introduction of the tomato: it has been there for so long that it is Italian food with tomatoes we deem to be traditional, yet also modern. The one book in this case might be Ada Boni's 1969 *Italian Regional Cooking*, or Elizabeth David's earlier and marvellous *Italian Food* (she thought it her best), or Marcella Hazan's *The Classic Italian Cookbook*.

I opened Boni and made the Gnocchi alla Romana. I swear it is the most sublime baby's food there is. Accordingly, another generic recipe was added to a private file, which always lists the source, although this recipe is so generic it does not belong to Boni but to Rome. That's the other thing about stable cuisines: the recipe doesn't belong to a cookbook writer. I checked the other books, and the recipe is almost exactly the same in them all. I'm partial to Ada Boni's book because it is not glamorous, it is inclusive, it was written a long enough time before now, and she is Italian. Just below the recipe for the gnocchi is one for Stracciatelle, the restorative broth comprising strands of egg, semolina and parmesan scrambled through a good chicken or beef stock, which I have not eaten for years. A good dictionary has the same appeal, the eye and brain are constantly distracted. Elizabeth David, who suddenly seems terribly English in this context, wrote *Italian Food* in 1954: it turned out, on this occasion, to be very useful indeed. She warns that 'if damp or stale, [semolina] tends to go lumpy.' It did. This advice is fifty years old, but it could have been written hundreds of years before. I don't need new cookbooks for practical advice or explanation; in fact, I could work my way towards a good result through trial and error, but shortcuts are sometimes sublime.

Semolina and polenta and oats and sorghum and millet all make variations on porridge and I have been making porridge recently because some biodynamic rolled oats looked so full of colour and so vital compared to the

Take one cigarette tin rice

257

usual commercial product. Finding scholarly references to porridge (apart from the fact, mentioned by Alan Bennett in his 1999 diary, that Wittgenstein, who didn't mind what he ate as long as it was always the same, didn't mind living on it) seemed somehow oxymoronic but proved worth the exercise while the oats cooked. A little trick recommended by old Scots people and recorded in the *Oxford Companion to Food* is to serve the milk separately. Eat the porridge by dipping spoonfuls into the milk so that just a little adheres; this makes you see that milk is not really necessary if the oats are good and cooked for the right amount of time, which is quite long. Even the dark-brown sugar should be added frugally, if at all, although it looks and smells good melting on the top and slipping down the side. The only imperative is salt and it feels good to say so. In Wales I have eaten oats mixed with laverbread, a seaweed treated to resemble primeval slime, as an accompaniment to eggs and bacon (it is also marvellous dolloped, with shallots and breadcrumbs, on oysters before baking to warm). This highlighted the essentially savoury nature of porridge.

When The Performance Space in Sydney held a community event, under the direction of Victoria Spence, to celebrate the winter solstice, we baked parcels of food in lotus leaves and clay in huge circles of fire in parkland opposite the theatre. Because some of the parcels had hard-boiled (the wrong word if the egg is boiled with care and you know when to stop) egg in them as part of the South-east Asian vegetarian ingredients, we needed to peel some thirty dozen eggs. They would not peel easily, the skin under the shell fighting us all the way. I was angry and puzzled. Years later, in a letter to a British gardening magazine, a woman who keeps chickens wrote to quarrel with someone who was complaining about commercial eggs being so old: 'I do warrant that fresh eggs are wonderful . . . However, if you want to boil the damn things you'll give your teeth for some that are a week old. As farm people know, truly fresh eggs can't be peeled without losing a lot of white.' We were proudly using organic, free-range, very, very fresh eggs, which had come to Sydney from Orange. Waiting eight years for an answer gave a false sense of patience, something I have learned only since growing food plants. At the opposite extreme, at the close of Plenty, the Adelaide Festival 2000 events which in total fed more than six thousand people, there were perhaps six dozen eggs left

over. Compared to the original order, six dozen was not a lot, but left alone with them it took over three months to work my way through the cartons. Not one egg was wasted and this without resorting to preserving them, which the Chinese do so well. Packaging is something nature does well.

One of the curious things about the modern craze for cookbooks in Australia, America and Britain is that over and over again the authors pay homage to cuisines that have not changed for centuries and so are steeped in the generational transmission of practical knowledge which, without actively condemning change, does not encourage it. In their attempt to persuade us of their imaginative open-mindedness, the authors make the new from corrupting what they like to be seen as acknowledging as sacred. This is, one supposes, one of the traits of the post-modern culinary world, called 'fusion' by food journalists while in fact its recipes and methods take apart what had seemed to be so fused that it would resist disassembling.

Of the Enlightenment philosopher and encyclopaedist Denis Diderot, Malcolm Bradbury wrote, admittedly in an intellectual and fictional comedy of homage, 'He knew history was the future's complaint against the present; but that past, present and future eternally interfere and interface with each other'. A good example of this – good in the sense that she is an admirable chronicler of a cuisine at the same time as shamelessly, joyously inventing another and personal one – is Barbara Tropp, the Californian author of *The Modern Art of Chinese Cooking* in 1982 and *China Moon Cookbook* in 1992. For a plain-speaking Australian her effusive West Coast prose takes a little getting used to, but it is only a gaudy lace curtain embellishing pages of intelligent and lucid instruction. The dishes in the first book celebrate traditional Chinese home cooking (she was a China scholar in Taiwan for some years); those in the next, the marriage of Chinese flavours and techniques with Californian produce, which she cooked at China Moon. In the first, the chicken dishes might be Hot and Sour Hunan or Tea and Spice-smoked, and in the second Stir-fried Hot and Sour with Black Beans and Basil or Tea-smoked Salad with Toasted Coconut, Peanuts, and Crispy Rice Sticks. One of the obvious differences is the extra number of words used to describe the food in the later and more self-conscious book, in part to do with her choice of description for the restaurant menu but also because the new 'fusion' cuisine was in need of a story: 'Once upon a time in San Francisco . . .'

If Julian Barnes were to use one of Tropp's cookbooks (sadly, she died recently), his anxious pedantry (is this a singular description or is he separately anxious and pedantic when he reads recipes?) might be calmed, because Tropp edges towards the excessive in explaining why and how. She leads you somewhere and she answers every troubled question. Her books are not in my Top Ten list, but the sheer energy and generosity of her instructions are admirable and set her apart from those cookbook writers who offer no acknowledgement to the books they have read.

Barnes chronicles his very funny but entirely justified problems when tackling a recipe for tomato soup in David's *Italian Food*. He collects the ingredients and then considers the instructions, which begin with 'Melt . . . chopped and skinned tomatoes in olive oil'. 'How could I have missed it until now? *Melt? Melt a tomato?* The implausibility of the verb froze me.' Has Barnes ever sweated over 'sweating' a leek, I wonder? To some degree my original confusion over how a paste of flour and water could ever match the consistency of a big pat of butter, as advised in Pellaprat's instructions for puff pastry, is connected to these kinds of worries. Now I know by practice, but Barnes, who writes that the soup tasted wonderful, omits to tell us if he ever got to understand the verb in relation to this particular noun. In fact, impatiently waiting for the melting moment he 'seized the potato masher and mashed the shit out of them', which is not to melt but to smash. Melt is a lovely word when used to mean what it does here, just as 'sweat' is in verbal relation to leeks, requiring the oil or butter to infuse the tomatoes or leeks by gentle heat, the one melting into the other without anything browning.

A cookbook I treasure is the 1973 second edition of Mrs K. M. Mathew's *Kerala Cookery*. It is printed on the rough, cheap, slightly brown paper characteristic of many Indian books and the dust jacket is a marvellous combination of red, yellow and blue with an outline in black of an Indian woman squatting on the author's name and eating rice with one hand. It was published by the author and distributed by National Book Stall in Kerala State, and cost 6.50 rupees. (Mrs Mathew has also published a 'profusely illustrated book on Hair Styles'.) Although

I do not use this little book to cook from because I have others that assume less, it would suffice if there were no others and if I wanted to limit myself to a southern Indian cuisine.

One of Mrs Mathew's most endearing measurements for rice and other dry ingredients, such as lentils, is the cigarette tin. For instance, for Adaprathaman, a sweetmeat soaked in a jaggery syrup, you need '1 cigarette tin raw rice'; for a chutney powder you need '¼ cigarette tin black gram dhal' and '¼ cigarette tin white gingilli seeds'. I asked Amartya Sen how big a cigarette tin was, not because he was awarded the Nobel Prize for economics in 1998 but because in an interview he had described how, as a young boy, having told his grandfather about a starving man who stumbled into his school campus, he was given 'a small cigarette tin, and [told] I could fill it with rice and give it to the starving, but only one tinful per family'. In response to my question, Sen laughed and sketched a small rectangle in the air with his hands.

Looking through *Kerala Cookery* more recently I found a recipe for gooseberry pickle that needs '2 seers (8 cigarette tins) gooseberry' and '2 cigarette tins salt dissolved in 12 cups water' and so on. A seer is roughly one kilogram, so at least I know the weight of gooseberries, but weight does not equal volume for different ingredients. I have a little picture in my head that equates this culinary measure with my father's packets of Turf and Craven A cigarettes in the fifties. A friend once suggested that, for her, cooking from a recipe was similar to having sex with a new partner: the first time it is an adventure and wildly exciting; the second time it is a disaster; and the third time it begins to make sense. In both cases, you continue or try another recipe. And that's the point really. The more you cook something the better you get at it, until the puzzle over the weight of spinach or the volume of liquid seems an embarrassing waste of time – the recipe has become part of your repertoire and you have made your own logical sentence.

What becomes important after all that culinary semantic trauma is the standard to which one cooks: the standard one sets for oneself and whether this has any relationship to the standard of others. I listened to an interview with a paramedic who had much to do with the ways in which rescue operations, say in a landslide or flood, are carried out in order to save as many lives as possible and risk as little as possible the lives of the paramedics. He said that standards are something one learns not from a book of rules but from experience. It helps to have generational and cultural references, or professional benchmarks, or both. In fact, it you have the former then anxious pedantry doesn't even come into the equation because things make sense, having been proved to make sense by participation in the warm kitchen of childhood. In this case a measurement, a weight, a consistency is not an abstract but a continuum, a tradition and a set of standards that have been shown to work and which are a foundation for confidence. Late bloomers build from scratch and books and eating out, which in the modern urban environment turns professionals into the keepers, or changers, of a cuisine. This also turns the table on the idea of 'ground-up' cuisines, those that arose from specific locations and ingredients.

'I need an exact shopping list and an avuncular cookbook', Barnes writes. Exactitude is something I am rather partial to as well, but this is probably because exactitude matters to a pastry cook and I came to savoury foods only after exclusively cooking sweet dishes and pastry. Of course, an exact shopping list asks that the products, and produce in perfect form, always be available.

At the end of each instalment of the long-lived BBC radio program *Desert Island Discs*, a well-known guest is asked to name the book, the piece of music and the food they would choose if only allowed one of each on the hypothetical island. The answer I have admired most of all was the artist Howard Hodgkin's choice of food: fresh mayonnaise. Such a practical choice – it would accompany all the fish that would thoughtfully leap from the sea onto the island, bone themselves and provide very fresh food with their last gasp.

With friends, I sometimes play a game in which we must choose no more than ten of our cookbooks to keep and give all the others to the local library. I have counted mine and there are somewhere over three hundred. This is probably a small library compared to one held by an obsessive culinary tourist, but at least it is not growing (I stopped buying cookbooks, CDs and clothes when I made the ascent to rusticity three years ago). As well, there are year upon year of magazines, which are impossibly heavy in congregation. There are the boxes of recipe cards from twenty-five years of professional involvement with cooking, a drawer of folders holding recipes on scraps of paper (a version of puff pastry sent from Finland by the mother of a young Finnish woman who worked sometimes in the dining-room at Berowra Waters Inn, a scribbled précis of something explained by a cook in a South-east Asian country). There is also a recipe file on the computer, which if printed would fill a very fat folder, even a book – one of the best uses for a computer is as pantry for files. Finally, there is a separate and even larger section of reference books of all kinds that are theoretical rather than practical, but which often help to make sense of a recipe.

You would think choosing ten cookbooks an easy game to play, but puzzling over which books to keep brings up the problem of what criteria to use. This is especially problematic, as a copy of any recipe I really like and intend to use a lot, goes into the computer so that I don't need to bother with indexes or grubbying books, or, separately with recipes that cover two pages back to back; also because often the order of instruction needs to be changed to suit my own logic and because I often change some of the measurements. Is the criterion to be practicality? The most used? The ten relevant to the cuisine I feel most comfortable with? By the evidence of meals served to friends over the past few years this would have to be somewhere on the line that separates France from Italy and Spain, though alone and hungry I choose rice, beancurd and chillies, which says something else altogether. Might it be representative of different cuisines? If so, which? Should it be those books that give intelligent background to the culture of recipes, or books that are all instruction? Half and half? Might the choice be those books to which I am emotionally attached, even though they are hardly used now? Paula Peck's *The Art of Baking*, for instance, which instructed me into a love affair with *genoise*, butter creams, choux pastry, puff pastry, brioches, croissants, Danish pastries and quite a few biscuits, yet now, over thirty years later, sits all tattered and torn and needing a rubber band and a plastic bag to hold the pages together. It is so cook-handled that the title page is missing and so the publication date on the reverse, but I remember it came out in 1961. Might the ten then be the books I know are irreplaceable and rare? Don't even bring up the worldwide web where I could, they tell me, find a recipe for everything and much more besides. I love books, the paper, the binding, the design, the way I can take them to bed (but never cookbooks, as I do novels), the way I can put them into a bag, insurance against boredom or conversations I don't want.

At the close of Elizabeth David's *French Provincial Cooking*, first published in 1960, she included a little essay on cookery books, prefaced by a quotation from Pierre de Pressac's 1931 *Considérations sur la cuisine*: 'Which is the best cookery book? The one you like best, and which gives you that confidence that cannot be called forth to order, but which is instinctively felt.' David's bibliography is sixteen pages long, which makes us all the more grateful for her book on the subject, but I have a confession to make: I hardly ever use David's recipes, although I dip into the books often; my favourite is *Spices, Salt and Aromatics in the English Kitchen*, first published in 1970 and so one of her later works. Jane Grigson's *English Food* and *Good Things* (both from the seventies) are both fine cookbooks and have been put to far more use. Grigson's 1967 *Charcuterie and French Pork Cookery* is her finest, a formidable work of research and practical advice, and would probably make it to the Top Ten because the pig, of all animals, is the greatest provider of preserved and fresh flesh, extremities and offal.

Michel Guérard's *La Cuisine Gourmande*, published in 1978, was not his first book (*La Grande Cuisine Minceur* came out two years earlier) and he was not the first celebrity nouvelle-cuisine chef to publish his opus, but this book is easily the best of them all. The recipes have nothing to do with the excesses of nouvelle cuisine, which anyway mostly took place on the plate. The dishes show the shift from classical cuisine to modern French cooking as intelligent, inspired and grounded on impeccable technique. In Guérard's hands, nouvelle cuisine had creative strength and seductive flavours. The recipes invite you to try them and do not let you down; the instructions are clear. It is, for me at least, the great French cookbook of the second half of the twentieth century. We used many of Guérard's recipes at Berowra Waters Inn, if not copying them exactly then following his techniques and ideas. We often served Guérard's *eugénies* with coffee (and the Troisgros brothers' *pamelas*). The veal kidneys in their own fat took a different turn at Berowra, but they had much in common with the original version. All the book's recipes are well within a dedicated and skilled domestic cook's abilities, although there is nothing like a little training to meet Guérard's standards with understanding.

While Elizabeth David triggered a major shift of imagination for the British after the Second World War, the next major change was generated not by the young turks of the French culinary revolution in the seventies (who refined a known cuisine and became minor celebrities in the process) but by the globalisation of palatable desires, the milkshake of methodologies and the 'Why not?' attitude of the food-lovers who were greedy for new flavours. In Australia at least, this love affair with Asian and South-east Asian foods signalled support for a more pluralist society: it was a socially inclusive act of open-mindedness, better late than never, and, as such, a political act of some significance. We also began to travel in these countries with noses and tongues participating.

In Australia in the late eighties, we began to support and celebrate the magicianship of Cheong Liew in Adelaide and he produced a book of recipes which, while not persuading us we could cook like him, showed the inclusive generosity of his attitude. David Thompson cooked Thai food in his Sydney restaurant, which seemed giddily like haute cuisine (in many ways it was). Neil Perry took Thompson's produce and technique to his own restaurant, and produced what might be the definitive version of modern Australian cooking if it were practised by real people and not just by chefs; his *Rockpool* cookbook is thus an archive of a certain time and of specific influences. But if I were to place one book produced by professional Australian cooks in the ten-to-keep pile it would be David Thompson's second book, *Thai Food*, published in 2002 and appropriately bound in gorgeous Thai silk. One of those books about which people are prone to say 'instant classic', it is a great big, impossibly heavy, precious jewel of a book, a monumental work of scholarship by a brilliant practising chef. One wants to stroke the book in homage, and then wrap it in protective paper if it is to be used in the kitchen.

But it is Indian food, over all its regions, that I spend most time joyfully cooking. When dispirited by life I make a dhal of split peas, adding the crisped leaves from the curry-leaf tree (*Murraya koenigii*) in a pot by my back door; a sweetish pilaf of basmati rice with saffron, cardamom, cinnamon and raisins; also a weak broth of mung beans, green chillies and curry leaves, finished with lemon juice. A dish of spinach with green chillies, freshly scraped coconut, yoghurt and curry leaves is marvellously better at room temperature than hot; and eggplant sautéed with apples and turmeric, a pinch of asafoetida (India's answer to the earthy pungency of truffles and an antidote to the flatulence caused by pulses) is strange and worth repeating. I roll circles of roti that have been slightly fermented through the addition of yoghurt to the dough and a rest. In Old Delhi once, the naan were so flaky and light that they superseded the status of the first perfect croissants I ate in a three-star restaurant in the south of France. When I made Scandinavian breads for a themed dinner at C's, the rye flat breads were a northern European version of chapati and I felt at home slapping them onto a hot surface. That's the key phrase, feeling at home. Whole legs of lamb braised with onion, poppy seeds and almonds, dried figs and yoghurt which is as Persian as Indian gets, a *saar* of tomato and coconut milk we used to use as a sauce for fish at Berowra Waters Inn and which now I serve as a soup or a side-dish. I'm completely besotted by Indian foods and it is the truly great vegetarian cuisine over all its regions. Yamuni Devi's *Lord Krishna's Cuisine: The Art of Indian Vegetarian Cooking* is indispensable, but one of the ten books to stay would also have to be Madhur Jaffrey's 1985 *A Taste of India*, not because it is the best but because using it has given me so much enjoyment for so many years. It is stained with turmeric and yoghurt. Mrs K. M. Mathew and her cigarette tins are more for curiosity and a smile.

A man tells an Australian woman, in Blanche D'Alpuget's novel *Turtle Beach*, that 'The Indian impulse is to fast, the Chinese to gourmandize . . . famine was the historical stimulus for both races, but the Chinese response is straightforward and optimistic, while the Indians' is subtle and pessimistic'. If I could keep only one book there is no question that it would be *Chinese Gastronomy* by Hsiang Ju Lin and Tsuifeng Lin (first published in 1969, but there has been another edition); I have quoted from it in the piece on congee. *Chinese Gastronomy* is divided into eight major sections: Ancient Cuisine, Flavour, Texture, Regional Cooking, Curiosities, Plain Cooking, Classic Cuisine, A Gastronomic Calendar. It is not an over-large book. Its scholarship is so lightly worn as to be poetic, its references made with such limpid attention to context that they build towards as profound an understanding of the principles of the cuisine as one might have without living by it. The balance of the whole is comparable to a superbly balanced meal of the finest ingredients, cooked perfectly and served with modesty. In the introduction the Lins write that they 'have tried to show by example and explanation where the artist, the peasant, the food snob and the gourmet made their contributions'. Further on they observe:

> The best team is made up of the gastronome and his cook . . . The [Chinese] cuisine did not come into its own until the critics became articulate. They found fault with the food. They developed ideas and harassed their cooks. The gastronomes contributed their sense of form to the cuisine. Their promptings made the cooks masters of flavour and texture.

It should be remembered that the Chinese began writing about food somewhere around the fourth century BC. This is when Chuangtse wrote a treatise on the use of the cleaver, in the form of a dialogue between a cook and a prince: the cook does all the work and most of the talking, and as he puts the spotless cleaver away the prince cries: 'Bravo . . . From the words of this cook I have learnt how to take care of my life.' It should not surprise you to learn that this most perfect of gastronomic texts has recipes and is useful.

When I was about eleven, despite what I remember as a complete lack of interest in cooking, I made cream puffs. Although I can still see the kitchen where I made them, there is hardly a memory of the cream puffs, but certainly they were, if not inedible, doughy and damp inside. All the aunts and uncles who were gathered for the party said how wonderful they were; I felt like a princess and have been making cakes and pastries ever since. It had not occurred to me until writing that sentence how meaningful those collapsed cushions of choux pastry were – if not the pastry, at least the praise. When the 'anxious pedant' went home and his father saw that he cooked, he looked at Barnes 'with a mild liberal suspicion that he had previously deployed when I was spotted reading *The Communist Manifesto*'. Now, when Barnes cooks for friends, he is desperate for praise even if it is undeserved and reckons this to be a trait of the late-onset cook.

Whatever the motive, making good cakes depends on craft skills, be they domestic or professional, and *The Cake Bible* by Rose Levy Beranbaum is so meticulous in its measurements and instructions that it is the West Point of cake-training academies, albeit with a maternal air. It doesn't surprise that she has an MA in 'food science and culinary arts'. If I did ever make Holiday Hallelujah Streusel Brioche or White Lilac Nostalgia, I'd leave the names in the book along with most of the decorations; they are irrelevant. Like all professional pastry cooks, she treats eggs by weight instead of number, a reassuring habit. She tells us how tall or short the cake should be, guides us on texture, gives pointers for success, her instructions are in the right order. In fact, she wants you to make a good cake and it's pretty damn hard not to from her recipes. One friend, a woman who has done lots of professional cooking, put her nose in the air when I talked about *The Cake Bible* one day: she had flicked through the book and found order but not inspiration. Another cook, one of Australia's finest, Damien Pignolet, was the person who told me that it was brilliant. Damien has a tidy and thorough mind. Someone once asked him (cocktail-party talk) what a Tarte Tatin was: he began with the exacting details of the pastry-making and progressed through the apples (with preferences as to variety) and the baking requirements, finishing with precise instructions on turning it over. The man who asked was struck dumb with instruction.

It is easy for professionals to dismiss a book like Beranbaum's. It presumes nothing, and ambitious cooks like to be presumed to know a few things. Also it is about cake-making and cakes have never quite recovered from their connection to domesticity, separate to the macho world of handling meat and fish in a professional kitchen. Beranbaum could probably write a manual to help me change the pistons in my Peugeot; like Damien, she has a tidy and thorough mind and knows how to teach, and I bet she's strong too. When you make some of the cakes, you see that she knows the way to a person's heart. She also gives credit to the people whose recipes she has no doubt perfected.

Take one cigarette tin rice

At the First Symposium of Australian Gastronomy in 1984, the guest of honour was Alan Davidson, without doubt the most erudite, witty and literate writer on food. His volume of selected essays, *A Kipper with my Tea*, would fly easily into my Top Ten list if the choice were based on thinking about food. At the symposium he led a discussion on cookbooks and suggested three criteria that might be set for all. The first is that 'the book should be founded, or largely founded, on direct experience and knowledge'. The second is that 'the recipes should be clear to the extent appropriate, and precise'. The third is that 'attributions and acknowledgements should be correctly made. This is something I feel strongly about . . . An author who appears to have dreamed up 565 recipes without any help from anybody is immediately suspect.' When Rose Levy Beranbaum introduces a cake, she tells us who inspired her version of it or who offered her the original recipe and I like her all the more for her good manners. Robert Levin, writing about the performance of piano music, proposes that the music should be played 'in such a way that it is obvious that the pianist didn't write it'. The mercurial Argentinian pianist Martha Argerich has also said something similar.

Davidson pointed out that there are cuisines that did not have printed recipes until a curious gastronome arrived with fork and pen. He told the symposiasts of 'the strange case history of a book which [his company Prospect Books] published, *Traditional Recipes of Laos*. Laos is a country which had no recipe books at all.' Davidson published the book because the author had kept a notebook when he was the chef at the royal palace in Luang Prabang and his dying wish was that the recipes live on. His widow felt strongly that she must see this through and Prospect Books did its good turn, the rationale being that as there were many Laotian refugees in America and Australia, the book, in English and Lao, would help the host countries to understand their food culture (Davidson had been the British ambassador in Vientiane in the 1970s). This hope was misplaced: the real need for the book turned out to be felt by the refugees themselves, removed from their cultural heritage.

Stories like this one, combined with Davidson's three rules, rather dull the ersatz legitimacy of current cookbooks. We have never had so many, never been told so many times that we have no time to cook, and never had so much bullying 'fast' food to choose from. These cookbooks, then, must have an entirely different motive and purpose to practical instruction, one more complex than the simple wish to 'swagger in print as well as others' as the seventeenth-century author of *Kitchin Physick*, Thom. Cocke, allowed himself. How many cookbooks do we need with a chapter called 'Things on Toast'? Actually, the idea of things on toast points to one of the many paradoxes of modern food writing – the writer wanting a large audience assumes a total lack of imagination on the part of the reader, and yet includes difficult and time-consuming recipes in proof of his expertise.

Nothing is what it is said to be any more. When Australian chef Christine Manfield's *Paramount Desserts* came out in 1997, an advertorial in an airline magazine took pains to praise the exacting architecture of Manfield's perfect slice of chocolate mocha tart, with its tall pyramid of icecream. The advertorial also told readers that the book was easy to use. Manfield learned much from working in the Sydney kitchen of chef and artist Phillip Searle, and she can cook things that most mortals can't, so why should her recipes be easy? We are invited by cookbooks to learn the secrets of the professionals, while all the while there is rather a lot of hoodwinking going on. A *New Yorker* cartoon from 1997 shows a backpacker kneeling in front of a lone monk on a hard-to-reach precipice. The caption reads: 'If I told you the secret of making light, flaky pie-crust, it wouldn't be much of a secret any more, now would it?'

The bookseller Nicholas Pounder, who graced my reading life for years in Sydney, gave and sold me many marvellous old books. (None were, in fact, too rare or secret, except perhaps for a first edition of Norman Douglas's *Venus in the Kitchen*, its dust jacket in perfect condition.) May Byron's *Jam Book*, which was given to me by Pounder, is over seventy years old and very British. On the spine it advertises 'over five hundred recipes for preserving fruit with or without sugar'. As already touched on when talking about apple jelly, I have used many of them and learned much, although I have a long way to go. The problem with jellies and jams is that one usually makes too much, always mistaking the volume of fruit for the volume of fruit and sugar. It makes itself best in small quantities. I love the list of fruits I have little chance of obtaining fresh: bilberry (also known as 'hurts' or whinberry), whortleberry, elder, medlar, damson, greengage, sloe, rowan (or mountain ash). And I love the recipes for pomegranate, quince, rhubarb, pomelo, seville orange, melon and tomato. The volume devoted to preserving in the Time Life *Good Cook* series offers the clearest instruction, but I am partial to May Byron. Hers is plain food writing of which, in a different country, Irma Rombauer's *The Joy of Cooking* is another example.

Elizabeth David is the finest exponent of plain food writing. We should never mistake the joy of revelation about sensual cuisines with the tone of her prose. She does not gush. Julian Barnes, in his piece about David, asks if she were too good a writer to be a food writer. This is definitely a 'late-onset' question, especially as it comes from one of Britain's finest. Describing breakfast in the last chapter of the novel *A History of the World in 10½ Chapters*, his character stumbles over ways of describing a sausage: 'The sausage: not a tube of lukewarm horse meat stuffed into a French letter, but dark umber and succulent . . . a . . . a sausage, that's the only word for it.' By wondering about David, even if tongue-in-cheek, he seems to be admitting to a worry that food isn't worth the prose rather than the other way around, yet his character understands that a sausage is a sausage when it is sausage as a sausage should be.

When Alice B. Toklas's publisher asked her, after Gertrude Stein's death, if she would write a book about her life with Stein, she demurred ('Gertrude did my autobiography and it's done') but said she might do a cookbook instead. When she told friends that she was soon to be published, one said 'But, Alice have you ever tried to write?' Toklas ingenuously replied (as recorded by M. F. K. Fisher in her foreword to the 1984 edition) 'As if a cook-book had anything to do with writing'. The *Alice B. Toklas Cookbook*, as well as being autobiographical despite her Steinian disclaimer, and so a companion-piece to Stein's extraordinary oeuvre, meets Alan Davidson's first rule for cookbooks admirably, in that it is founded on direct experience and knowledge. Richard Olney's 1994 *Lulu's Provençal Table*, which catalogues the dishes made by Lulu Peyraud at the family vineyard Domaine Tempier near Bandol, shares this trait and is a marvellous combination of evocative explanation and recipes, an altogether beautiful and useful book. Paul Schmidt, in an essay on the four Californian food writers placed M. F. K. Fisher and Toklas in the tradition of Brillat-Savarin and the metaphysics of cooking, and

Julia Child and Adele Davis in the rational line of Escoffier. He wrote: 'We are so taken by the charm of Alice B. Toklas's memories and menus that we forget that the major narrative concerns the way two ladies survived the two greatest wars of history in a foreign country.' This is to exaggerate to make a nice point. In the chapter on eating and cooking in the small French province of Bugey (incidentally, the homeland of Brillat-Savarin who was born in Belley, its chief town, in 1755) during the German occupation, the war is present in every bit of food that was given, scrounged and shared. When Toklas made a flummery and the guest wondered how she managed to buy the gelatin to set it, Toklas sent him away with a gift of twenty sheets for his wife. Much later, she learned that it was used by the Resistance to help make false papers. When Toklas and Stein moved to a house at nearby Culoz, it came with a fine cook who said she could not cook well in the face of rationing. 'She was old, tired and pessimistic. So it fell upon me to do most of the cooking while a great cook sat by indifferent, inert and . . . discouraged.'

So the *Alice B. Toklas Cookbook* would be among the ten to stay, even though I have taken none of her recipes to heart or personal file, not quite approving of her version of Oysters Rockefeller but feeling affection towards the Bird's-Nest Pudding of which Toklas, in plain-speaking Elizabeth David mode, writes: 'This is a pudding we should not neglect.' Another book I could not part with is Simon Hopkinson's 1994 *Roast Chicken and Other Stories*; it is subtitled 'A recipe book', to lay stress on the instruction in the face of the stories. Simon, as I have written elsewhere, is the best cook I know; we shared years of close friendship and dining, and an obsession with eggplants (which he calls aubergines). But *Roast Chicken* is more than a sentimental journey: it is a book full of good food, clear instruction and absolute confidence. 'Good cooking, in the final analysis', writes Simon, 'depends on two things: common sense and good taste.' He is unblinkingly definite on the subject of which goes with what. The book is the sum of forty main ingredients, the ones he loves. 'I have written this book, not because I am a chef, but because I like to cook and I enjoy eating good food.'

Take one cigarette tin rice

I have lost count. No matter: the exercise has brought forth the thundering past of old friends and acts of kindness, of connections and convergences, of good meals and good cooking, of little furies and strong personal views. The philosopher J. G. Collingwood held that education should, like medicine, be available when needed, but not forced on people: 'What is all this about professionalism, anyhow? Does anyone think that if a man marries he should marry no one but a whore, or that if sleeping or eating is done it should be entrusted to professional sleepers or skilled prize-winners in eating competitions?'

Cooking well is contextual and is not a matter of absolute prescription or proscription. If cooking pleases you, you will cook as well as your common sense, intelligence, good taste, experience, skills, imagination and sense of boundlessness allow. Cooking well is not something only professional chefs do. It is entirely possible to cook well without recipe books, just as it is possible to live well at no great cost. The true gastronome understands this and the good cook understands it too. It has been said of Utopians that they are constantly referring to a paradisaical past while offering a total design for the future. Our modern, late-capitalist attitude towards food tilts towards the Utopian glitch (the sacred aura of ancient traditions, the romance of agriculture) and flounders on the other hand in the possibilities of complete and irreversible commodification. Cookbooks, disconnected from usefulness, sell interpretations of dreams.

Novelist Mary McCarthy was also a critic of literature and politics, and apparently known to her friends as a good cook. When Thomas Mallon was writing his honours thesis on McCarthy in 1973, he sent it to his subject in Paris for comment and correction. She objected to Mallon's use of the term 'gourmet cooking':

> I find the phrase abhorrent and would find the thing abhorrent if I was sure what it was. It ought to mean, if anything, very rich, showy dishes, with lots of foie gras, cream, caviar, liqueurs, flambéing – the opposite of good food. I like cooking and do it well, I think. But that ought to be normal. If anybody who takes the trouble to put a decent meal together has to be classed as a 'gourmet, that is an odious situation.

McCarthy's definition of gourmet cooking sticks in its era, but she makes a nice and irrefutable point: to be a good cook is indeed to 'put a decent meal together'. Staying with Simon Hopkinson in London one year, during the period he was chef at Bibendum restaurant, I observed him one night when he arrived home after service. He dumped his ageing, shabby blue workbag in the hallway, pulled from it a package of food and a half bottle of Burgundy, turned on his domestic oven, opened the wine, slapped the pair of woodcock (for this was what was in the package) onto an oven tray, fiddled with them just a smidgen, put them in the now-very-hot oven, set a single place at the dining-room table and within thirty minutes he was eating. It was after midnight.

Watching Simon cook for himself was to watch someone who loves to eat. He never finds cooking a chore and produces again and again very fine dishes and more-than-decent meals, as if he were simply brushing his teeth. Watching him work, in a domestic situation at least, is to learn that for some people cooking comes naturally. It is what he likes to do along with eating, which is not the obvious pairing one might think.

In France in the eighties, staying with Terence and Caroline Conran in their house in Provence, which was not far from Les Baux and in another direction close enough to Arles to make its market the place to shop for food, Simon made many meals. We would go off to the market with Terence's money (a fair contract, considering Simon offered his skills and labour) and buy, say, fish from the bouillabaisse selection at the market, with which he would make a marvellous fish soup and then a *rouille* with the deep-green olive oil from trees on Conran's land. He grilled rabbits over vine cuttings, and macerated peaches. He made meals like these over and over again with such ease and always with pleasure, although he did grumble quietly once and in a different place that people always expected him to do the cooking. At the market in Arles, he asked if I knew the best combination of aromas in a hot car; we bought leeks and coffee beans to prove his point.

Staying with English and Welsh friends in a house in country not far from Cahors one year in the eighties, Simon again did most of the cooking, producing, in a rotten kitchen with a rotten stove, marvellous food for a large group of variously talented people – two singers, an artist, a designer, a dramaturge, a carpenter, etc. – who deferred to his skills. I remember making a baked orange custard with caramel for one meal (a lone gesture towards sharing the effort), taking painstaking care to measure the ingredients as accurately as possible when no measures were available and to watch it in its bain-marie in the cranky oven. It was, as it is when it is perfect, a slippery, silken, wobbly baked custard, like egg-enriched tofu, which when overturned onto a plate drips with dark caramel; but was it worth the obsessive care? My recipe had come from Paul Bocuse's cookbook and it is generic anyway, Bocuse simply taking it to a very rich conclusion. Huw Roberts, who worked at Berowra Waters Inn for some years, took the recipe with him to Bibendum, where he then worked, and Simon reproduced the recipe in a book on the best British chefs, in which he was included. I had been making this dish at Berowra Waters Inn for so long that the measurements were memorised, although the gîte near Cahors didn't seem to have cardamom pods, which we used to add with the orange peel to flavour the milk.

Simon's apparent wizardry releases cookery from this exactitude which, although it produces fine dishes, dogs me. Not that the need to be exact and careful causes shame. It is the trait of a pastry cook and stands me in good stead. I like to cook alone and there is no need to pretend to any dashing laissez-faire virtuosity for appearance's sake, as they do on television, misleading the naive viewer into believing that to be slapdash is to be confidently creative. An Australian friend J, as I have said elsewhere, once cooked in her own small restaurant in South Australia, having previously been bold enough to cook in her own restaurant in Italy. I loved her restaurant (it no longer exists) but did not give much thought to the food. Instead, the sum of the restaurant's parts gave pleasure. What I found seductive was that the garden and its produce were as visible as the plated dishes, and the sense of the amateur's joy in place and production was always palpable. There was a philosophy underpinning the commercial. The meals she cooks at home (exclusively Italian) are always impressively thoughtful yet simple, and full of flavour.

But why is she a good cook, and others like her? Good cooks are all differently good but share certain traits. About Carella, the detective who solves cases in Ed McBain's many novels, Scott Meredith wrote in *The New Yorker* (10 January 2000) that he is the best detective in the squad, 'intelligent, sceptical, proud of what he knows, modest about what he doesn't, at peace with the bad hours and the lousy pay'. These five qualities also work well to describe the good cook, at a stretch the bad hours and lousy pay applying as much to many home-based women as to professional cooks. Intelligence, scepticism and an honest, clear approach to the limits of one's knowledge and skills are high on my list of the attributes needed.

It seems to me that J exercises judgement every time she offers a meal. First, she confines herself to the cuisine she knows and by this is confident. In the face of media pressure for an 'Australian' cuisine, with mandatory nods to referential post-modernism, travel memories and pluralist shopping, there is relief to be had in confident containment. By exercising judgement, J is in fact paying attention to the appetite and pleasure of her guests; the meal as a whole makes sense. She often makes marvellous tarts for dessert (one in particular is excellent, a chocolate and pear tart with parmesan in the pastry) and her *pappa al pomodoro* is one of the most perfect dishes I have ever sat down to. If you think a thick soup of fresh tomato sauce and bread too humble to be counted as perfect, then you have underestimated the difference between a good tomato pulp and one that is exquisite, the extra and generous dribble of fine olive oil making it even more silken and slippery, the addition of saffron exaggerating the aroma and colour. J's food is the opposite of wild invention, which is most often touted as the sign of fine cooking in an age of desperate individualism. As underlined in one of Fernand Point's aphorisms, the simple is often the most difficult to get right.

It is not a sleight of hand to make going to a lot of trouble seem as though everything just fell into place. The shift from prior labour to serving a seamless meal is indeed part of the unspoken processes of hospitality. Another friend, C, is meticulous and particular about her table. She is enthralled by everything about the settings and the linen and the courtesies of the good hostess. Because she is a collector of the accoutrements of the table, to dine with her is to think about when a particular dinner set was made and where, why its compôtiers and sauce boat, soup bowls and side plates are the shape they are, and what kinds of dishes must have been common fare at the bourgeois table of the setting's original period and place. Even though it might seem to make her old-fashioned and over-formal, this increases one's expectations of her table. Unlike J, C has made an art out of going to as little trouble as possible. She has perfected the eclipse of the main course, for instance, and does just enough cooking to stake her claim on the meal. I admire her for this. Personally I am unable to invite people to eat without first making the stock and the bread even when the freezer would have supplied both. C runs a restaurant and is busy, yet invites people to dinner often, berating those who do not invite people to dine in their homes. I make no similar judgement and am content to enjoy having people eat my food because, selfishly, I need them if I am to have a reason to cook for more than one.

'A routine and a knack'

Another friend, W, who is an artist and poor, an Australian who has lived in New York City for decades, is the one domestic cook I know who has no culinary training yet produces over and over again marvellous food and seemingly out of nothing. She has a flair that most good domestic cooks cannot match; and it is not simply because she is an artist that her table is always a pleasure to observe and then taste. Years ago when she could hardly pay the rent, she instinctively laid the place for her child with care and attention to the pleasure it might add to his meal; the simple food looked inviting. Her most admirable trait is that although an emotional and strict vegetarian, she cooks meat for her partner and her friends. She is constantly playing host to people who visit from other countries and to friends who know her to be gregarious. She has mastered the art of making two tomatoes and the last of the wilting basil, or some leftover purée and a little oil, swell into a gift of abundance.

—

In *Some Buried Caesar*, one of Rex Stout's novels featuring the arrogant stay-at-home detective Nero Wolfe, there's a happy scene of feminine culinary triumph. Published in 1939, it is my favourite Stout. Because of his obsession with orchids, we find Wolfe out of his brownstone on 35th Street in Manhattan and stranded near Crowfield, upstate New York. This is most unusual: Wolfe is eccentric, very fat, employs a personal chef, is somewhat allergic to women and only ever eats at home – but as his orchids are competing at the North Atlantic exposition he's had to move his bulk beyond the front door. Archie Goodwin, Wolfe's factotum and the teller of all the tales, is at the exposition canteen run by the ladies of the First Methodist Church. Lily Rowan, Archie's quick-witted current romantic interest, orders chicken fricassee and dumplings for them both. Archie protests that they have beef pot-roast and veal on the menu. ' "No," Lily was firm. "The fricassee with dumplings is made by a Mrs Miller whose husband has left her four times on account of her disposition and returned four times on account of her cooking and is still there." ' And in a *New York Times* interview in 1998, Evelyn Cunningham, an African-American born in 1916 and a journalist on the *Pittsburgh Courier* from the 1940s to the 1960s, says about her four husbands: 'They all loved me most while I was cooking – and I am not a good cook.' My friend M and I were chatting over dinner one night and as usual M told stories about her eight brothers and sisters. One brother once said to her, 'I don't know why you can't get a husband, Mish – you're not bad-looking and you're a pretty good cook'. In a documentary about the fate of the dubha-wallahs who deliver home-cooked meals to husbands all over Mumbai in India and who have now to compete with encroaching fast-food outlets, an unhappy man says that the only dialogue he has with his wife is over cooking and that if she stops making him lunch to be delivered by the dubha-wallahs they will have nothing to talk about.

In the sixties, on Friday nights my then-husband used to play poker with other lapsed, interesting, male academics and some architects. They rotated the game among four or so homes, and when it was our turn I cooked supper and made a private game of outdoing last week's effort. Gerry played carefully and forty years later still eats from the table he won in lieu of money one night. I made stacks of crêpes, alternating savoury fillings to the exact prescription of *Mastering the Art of French Cooking*, or little pastry turnovers, or such food as the gourmet and culinary day dictated. In so doing I won the hearts of the players and unintentionally left the other female partners a tad touchy. Both our games ended after I managed, one night, to produce the food at three a.m. before announcing that the baby wouldn't stay within much longer.

Susan B. Anthony and my favourite of the two fellow suffragists, Elizabeth Cady Stanton, began campaigning for women's rights in the last half of the nineteenth century in America. In 1920 in Tennessee a young state representative cast the deciding vote in favour of the vote for women by looking at the letter from his mother, which was in his pocket and which advised that he should vote as he did. When asked why he changed his mind, for he had arrived at the meeting with a red rose for a negative vote in his buttonhole, he answered that mothers should be listened to. It is extraordinary that women, who manage the economy and health of households from the kitchen, should not have been and in many ways are still not considered worthy of a similar role in public.

Similarly, although it has always been acceptable for women to 'man' soup kitchens as a charitable and nurturing duty, it was men who made their name as great chefs. There is no female equivalent of Carême (the eighteenth century) or Escoffier (the nineteenth), even of Point (1930s–1950s) or of Bocuse, Guérard, Senderens and Ducasse (covering the recent past to the present). More tellingly, there is hardly a woman among the feted chefs in Australia today, even though we have seen a major growth of interest in professionally prepared food in the past thirty or so years, the same period that saw feminism strong and loud in supporting equal positions for women. The erudite French cuisine that Jean-François Revel posits as separate to the cuisine associated with *terroir* and produce is the domain of men; not, I think, simply because men like flexing their competitive egos and testosterone but because in general women are not interested in taking part in the competition itself.

British writer Norman Douglas, who knew a thing or two about food and cookery and made suggestive mischief of it in his collection of aphrodisiac recipes *Venus in the Kitchen* (first published in 1952, under a pseudonym), addressed the qualities of the female cook in his even more mischievous novel, *South Wind*, published in 1917. Food doesn't wait around to be eaten, but (happily) literature does: I have only recently read *South Wind*, a witty, brazenly naughty and erudite plea for the pagan over the puritan. Capri becomes Nepenthe, the Egyptian drug given by Helen to her guests Telemakhos and Pisistratos in Book IV of *The Odyssey*. Local characters and visitors are thinly fictionalised. A visiting bishop sloughs off his very English and Christian sense of morality and is swayed by the sirocco to a different and Mediterranean view. 'All culinary tasks should be performed with reverential love . . .', says Count Caloveglia, the hero, if it truly has one, of the novel:

> To say that a cook must possess the requisite outfit of culinary skill and temperament – that is hardly more than saying that a soldier must appear in uniform. You can have a bad soldier in uniform. The true cook must have not only those externals, but a large dose of general worldly experience. He is the perfect blend, the only perfect blend, of artist and philosopher. He knows his worth: he holds in his palm the

happiness of mankind, the welfare of generations yet unborn. That is why you will never obtain adequate human nourishment from a young girl or boy. Such persons may do for housework, but not in the kitchen. Never in the kitchen! No one can aspire to be a philosopher who is in an incomplete state of physical development. The true cook must be mature; she must know the world from her social point of view, however humble it be; she must have pondered concerning good and evil, in however lowly and incongruous a fashion; she must have passed through the crucible of sin and suffering or, at the very least – it is often the same thing – of married life. Best of all, she should have a lover, a fierce and brutal lover who beats and caresses her in turns; for every woman worthy of the name is subject and entitled to fluctuating psychic needs – needs which must be satisfied to the very core, if the master is to enjoy sound, healthy fare.

You will have noticed the change of sexual address halfway through this pagan cry for artistry and philosophy in the kitchen, and so too do the count's guests. Caloveglia acknowledges this, but reckons that no woman 'south of Bordeaux or east of Vienna' should be trusted in the kitchen. This pronouncement seems more about prejudice and sexual preference, although the count approves of women who drink and cook because 'It proves that she possesses the prime requisite of the artist; sensitiveness and a capacity for enthusiasm'. His own cook (male), who drinks little alcohol, makes a zabaglione in which 'You can taste his self-imposed asceticism . . . It speaks to the eye, but not to the heart'. Of this cook, Caloveglia says that he is not a born cook: 'The philosopher is represented in his nature, but not the artist. He is only a devoted Arcadian, overflowing with good intentions.'

I have been told that, in art and literature, [good intentions] will atone for deficiency of natural talent. It may be so; some persons, at least, have been able to cajole their brain into believing this. However that may be, I do not think the rule can be extended into the domain of cookery. Good intentions – no. Nobody need attempt such an imposture on his

'A routine and a knack'

stomach, an upright and uncompromising organ, which refuses to listen to nonsense. Or let them try the experiment. Gastritis will be the result of good intentions.

What to make of all this? Not too much, and not too seriously, but enough to pause at the idea of the philosopher in the kitchen, the title given by Anne Drayton to her translation of Brillat-Savarin's 1825 *La Physiologie du Goût,* a book Douglas was familiar with. Brillat-Savarin himself saw the truly great cook as someone whose skills lay somewhere 'between the chemist and the physician', that the cook, 'being charged with the maintenance of the animal machine, was superior to the pharmacist, whose usefulness is only occasional'. There is much sense in this pronouncement (eating well is to care for one's body) but questionable sensibility in his argument that the pre-eminence of French cooking was 'chiefly acquired through a vast number of cunning, light, and delicious preparations which only women could have conceived'.

The seventeenth-century Mexican nun Sor Juana Inus de la Cruz has provided the perfect riposte to the idea of unthinking women at the stove: 'What shall I tell you, my Lady, of the secrets of nature I have learned while cooking? . . . One can philosophise quite well while preparing supper. I often say, when I have these little thoughts, "Had Aristotle cooked, he would have written a great deal more".'

—

I am indebted to the poet Mark Strand for the information that Ricky Jay, who inherited New York journalist A.J. Liebling's library, reckoned that Liebling once used a piece of bacon for a bookmark. I've always sensed, by the tone of his writing in *Between Meals*, which describes his gastronomic introduction to Paris in the 1920s, that Liebling was a trencherman, a greedy eater, at home in the company of a particularly masculine conviviality. Norman Douglas's reference to 'good intentions' reminds me of something Liebling wrote about the boxer Cassius Clay in *The New Yorker* in 1962 (Liebling was as passionate about boxing as he was about food): 'Honest effort and sterling character backed by solid instruction will carry a man a good way, but unearned natural ability has a lot to be said for it.' Unearned natural ability aligns itself to notions of artistry, and even perhaps to philosophical temperament, in the context of cookery, although artistry is more properly aligned to imagination and inventiveness, which take flight, if the talent is there, only on the sound foundation of meticulous training.

As far as I'm concerned, except in the case of those very rare cooks who are professionals yet retain an aura of single-minded direction that sits outside the commercial, any sense of the philosophic is to be found exclusively in domestic situations where the table itself is so much more hospitable and the conviviality separated from payment and commercial contract. This is despite the celebration of chefs in the press, where one hears them espouse principles and passion. For the most part, I think they say what they believe the press wants to hear, their 'philosophy' is both a response and an invitation to the market; they are not asked to examine their own lives. The patter of clichés indicates nothing about the nature of cooking, which is centred on fine judgement and the movements of hands.

The philosopher in the kitchen is surely someone who doesn't live by food alone, who retains perspective, who accepts that consolation comes from something other than food. Jean-François Revel, in *Culture and Cuisine,* argues persuasively (indeed history argues persuasively) that it is the professional cook's artistry and invention that are the basis of changes in cuisine. He charts the changes in the mid-eighteenth century when those with money wanted private chefs: 'The world of finance was no more able to get along without chefs than the aristocracy.' This period saw 'a clear distinction being made between the cuisine of the female cook, transmitted by a tradition of manual skills and instructions within the family, and the cuisine of the chef, based on reflection and invention'. Although in Revel's view the chef 'thinks', I would posit that commerce nurtures competition rather than thoughtfulness in general. The untrained domestic cook lacks the skills of the professional and is therefore generally unable to be artistically inventive. Perfection might be found in the chef who turns her back on commerce and cooks for friends.

When Brillat-Savarin wrote that 'It was the meal which was responsible for

'A routine and a knack'

285

the birth, or at least the elaboration, of languages, not only because it was a continually recurring occasion for meetings, but because the leisure which accompanies and succeeds the meal is naturally conducive to confidence and loquacity', he was both describing the pleasures of the table and elevating the status of the cook to include her 'at the heart of human affairs', as Michael Symons puts it in *The Pudding that Took a Thousand Cooks*. For a cook to see this central thesis, but not let it turn her head or become anything more (or less) than the platform from which she nourishes and gives pleasure by her creative labour, is to broaden the whole idea of cookery without changing the day-to-day actions that have little to do with poetry and nothing to do with language. Revel again: 'There are regrettably more false great chefs than true good woman cooks.'

Doubling back, and paradoxically refuting all this talk of philosophy and artistry, cookery might be, as Socrates said in a discussion about the art of rhetoric in Plato's *Gorgias*, 'only a routine and a knack'. In answering Polus's question about the nature of rhetoric, Socrates said that rhetoric is a routine that 'produces gratification and pleasure', not an art. Neither, he said, is cookery, which also produces gratification and pleasure. Both rhetoric and cookery he called 'flattery'. Rhetoric, he maintained, is a form of flattery that pretends to be about legislation and justice, and cookery pretends to concern itself with the healthy body and medicine. 'Medicine, health and cookery would be indistinguishable' if the body were affected without our senses being flattered.

The argument is a scintillating piece of rhetoric as an example of rhetoric, made sublime by its use of a practical craft to illustrate the nature of intellectual persuasion. Using the *Gorgias* extract exclusively and perversely to think more about cookery, I find most seductive the idea of the cook as someone who flatters by her routine. It is the closest I might come to pinpointing why, whenever I write about cooks and cookery and find myself faltering on the precipice of making too much of it all, I need to go back to the kitchen and just do it. Where, of course, I think.

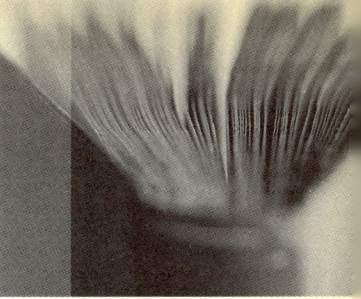

'Life as a book that has been put down'

The future is not a menu YIDDISH SAYING

Although attempting to retire far earlier than is safe, in gastronomical matters I was a late bloomer and almost thirty when catapulted into the restaurant trade by accident of partner. It was another five years before Michael Symons, who was then researching *One Continuous Picnic,* suggested that I read John Berger's partly fictional work *Pig Earth*, published in 1979. For Symons, *Pig Earth* lent weight to his thesis that white Australia lacked a peasant class and so a real cuisine. Certainly I had given no thought to an historical explanation of why we do or don't cook the way we do in Australia. Except for the American magazine *Gourmet*, I had never set out to read about food, other than having a shelf of cookbooks.

Reading *Pig Earth* caused me to think about food in a different way. In hindsight, my discomfort in the bourgeois world of commodification and competition that defines urban restaurants began at this time. I recently read again a volume of essays by Berger, *The White Bird.* One of these, 'The Eaters and the Eaten' from 1976, underlines the conviction of the historical afterword that accompanies *Pig Earth.* To reread Berger over twenty years after that first introduction was to enter once more a place of comfortable agreement; it was as if a friend who had been away for a long time had come back into the house and sat down to lunch. The romance (not always pleasant) of *Pig Earth* – the gathering of apples and pears for the distilling of *gnôle* (hooch), which is made from cakes of *marc* fermented under newspaper and walnut leaves, the 'transform[ing] of work into spirit' – is tempered by the reflection and political engagement of the afterword. There are stories of the book's main character, *La Cocadrille*, collecting kilos of dandelion leaves and rummaging for morels, which she sells for too little to a nearby restaurant. And of 'Sausages, the colour of black cherries, cooked in *gnôle*, [which] warm the heart because they are hot, arouse because they are salty, comfort because they taste of wood smoke, confer strength because they are meat, and release dreams because they are saturated with alcohol . . .' We bourgeois do not grunt, as Berger says his peasants did. In 'The Eaters and the Eaten', he writes:

> the peasant way of eating is centered on the act of eating itself and on the food eaten: it is centripetal and physical. Whereas the bourgeois way of eating is centered on fantasy, ritual and spectacle: it is centrifugal and cultural. The first can complete itself in satisfaction; the second is never complete and gives rise to an appetite which, in essence, is insatiable.

The White Bird also includes an essay on Giacomo Leopardi, deemed by Berger to be the most lucidly pessimistic of all poets. Leopardi (1798–1837) had written much about happiness without knowing it himself, which is not to deny him his own literary consolations. He wrote that 'unfathomable happiness' can only be experienced by the child and is only momentarily recoverable through 'the deceits of the imagination'. Berger ascribes Leopardi's pessimism (the reflection on happiness is not pessimism) to privileged boredom and it doesn't take much of a side-step to place this judgement beside what Berger had earlier written about the disconnection of the middle class from what they eat:

> To the peasant all food represents work accomplished. The work may or may not have been his own or that of his family, but if it isn't, the work represented is nevertheless directly exchangeable with his own work. Because food represents physical work, the eater's body already 'knows' the food it is going to eat. (The peasant's strong resistance to eating any 'foreign' food for the first time is partly because its origin in the work process is unknown.) He does not expect to be surprised by food – except, sometimes, by its quality. His food is familiar like his own body. Its action on his body is continuous with the previous action

of the body (labour) on the food. He eats in the room in which the food is prepared and cooked.

Although it is unfashionable to speak now in the way Berger did and unrepentantly still does, his description of human connection with food makes absolute sense to me, without persuading me to naively wish for a wholesale return to the land and subsistence farming, animal cunning and poverty. I enjoy Italian and Spanish cheese in Australia, although I could easily do without them. I want the fermented chilli paste from Daliang in China to which I am addicted. I want to sleep in and read essays. I cling to my small, disconnected bourgeois world from which I reflect on the essentially dystopic world of subsistence and isolation. My own isolation is considered and privileged.

The jubilant popularity of farmers' markets surely points to active, if inarticulate, agreement about connection with produce by large groups of people, although this popularity has been partly hijacked and turned into the weekend hobby of 'culinary tourism'. In the developed world we are troubled by inchoate ideas about what we risk when eating and whom and what we might trust. Farmers' markets are not inherently trustworthy, but the intimacy of the exchange creates a more trustworthy relationship, as does the useful celebration of locality, for farmers' markets make real sense only if they serve a local area and are used by those who live close to them as a basis for seasonal dishes. It is harder to look one's neighbour in the eye and lie about produce you are growing and selling and expecting her to eat when the neighbour is physically close enough to seek the truth and also to spread the word.

The autobiography of French teacher and activist Emilie Carles, as told to Robert Destanque, appeared two years before Berger completed *Pig Earth*. If any story can dispel silly Arcadian ideas about peasant life, then *Une Soupe aux herbes sauvages* (the English title is *A Life of her Own*) is it. It is in firsthand agreement with all that I had read in Berger of such an existence: a deep traditionalism and therefore conservatism; a distrust of government authority which meant that cheating the state of taxes and smuggling sheep were seen as a right; a driven dependence on alcohol to muffle the wounds of deprivation and cold;

a cruel primitivism and rapaciousness compared to our 'civilised' values; distrust of formal learning; a harsh life leavened by knowing where to find the wild herbs and how much of them to use to make a good soup, and by the *veillées*, gatherings where stories were told, songs sung.

Carles' story is one of triumphant education and humanism. She tells of the annual baking of bread in the communal oven, when the women also baked cakes and pies and made a festival of the work. Carles' father kneaded his own family's bread and also made loaves for those who were old or sick.

> To soften it ahead of time, we'd hang a few loaves in the sheep pen, just above the sheep. The heat and humidity softened it to a point, but it was a far cry from fresh bread and from one end of winter to the other, we ate it stale. We used a special knife, yet it was so hard to cut that it shattered into fragments . . . But it was good: that bread had an extraordinary smell, and what a taste! My sisters and I fought over the crusts, sucking on that bread with as much delight as if it had been cake. Dunked in café au lait, it was a feast.

Compare the modern baguette, which goes stale in a day.

Bread is mentioned again and again by Giovanni Verga, who was born in Sicily in 1840. His novels and short stories were to Italian literary realism what Zola's were to France (Visconti's *La Terra Trema* is based on his *I Malavoglia*). *Novelle Rusticane*, translated under the title *Short Sicilian Novels* in 1928, are harrowing tales of harsh Sicilian lives. There is no relief: the consolation, as Leopardi knew, is in the telling. Food is ever-present in these stories by hardly being there at all; bread is the mark of having food in the house. The cruelty of the elements is matched by the cruelty of the peasants, their cunning no match for failed crops, sick donkeys and endemic malaria. Remarkable stories ('The Story of St Joseph's Ass', for instance), which were translated by D.H. Lawrence; he also championed Grazia Deledda, the Sardinian novelist who won the Nobel Prize for Literature in 1926. I have always remembered the saying, from Deledda's novel *The Divorce*, which is not much less harrowing than Verga's tales, that thunder is God opening a bag of walnuts and tipping them down onto the earth. If you have ever tipped walnuts from one container to another, you will hear this simile's perfection.

The use of food as metaphor is as regional as food itself. In Cambodia, for instance, proverb after proverb centres on rice ('The rice seedling draws the dirt to it in clumps; the woman supports the man'; 'Don't try to hide a dead elephant with a winnowing basket'; and so on, and on) and even the verb to eat, *si bay*, means 'to eat rice'. Bread plays the same role in Carles and Verga and Deledda – indeed, in all regions where wheat is ground into flour. Food as metaphor and metonymy are strongest where connection to the land is most deeply rooted but hardly provides profit; where traditions are oral rather then recorded. The paradox is obvious. What nourished, differently to books, Giacomo Leopardi in his father's library? He needed to eat to live to read and write.

In an addendum to Simon Leys' essay (in the collection *The Angel & the Octopus*) on Luc Sante's book about his 'Belgitude', a trait that Leys shares, Leys gently takes Sante to task for not liking chicon (variously known as witlof and Belgian endive). Leys adores this slightly bitter vegetable, as do I. It is a meas-ure of his light touch that his offer to share his wife's recipe for *chicons au gratin* with Sante neither jars nor changes the tone of the essay for the worse. I smile, and determine to buy some witlof at the market next week, for it is late winter. Sometimes I simply bake them slowly with olive oil and butter, instead of doing the Franco-Belgian thing with ham and cheese and cream. Cutting through the fat bulb of wilted, softened white leaves near the base allows you to enjoy the shift from the almost crisp, almost too-brown, thin outside layer to the luxury of the now-only-slightly-bitter mouthful inside. The bitterness of witlof is comparable to *scordatura* ('out of tune'), the specific tuning of a stringed instrument away from the normal and modern; I say this to praise witlof, not to damn it. At Berowra Waters Inn we used sometimes to cook it shredded in beurre noisette, add a tiny amount of sugar and lots of cream and reduce the sauce, which then makes a good bed for a piece of salmon or slices of pink rabbit saddle.

Witlof leaves raw in salads miss their bitter point entirely. Undercooking asparagus, which cuts off the development of the best flavours, is something else that misses the point. Eating dinner one holiday in France in the mid-eighties, eating only

'Life as a book that has been put down'

to make my companion, who was hungry, feel more comfortable, I reluctantly chose warm asparagus, *asperge tiède au vinaigrette*, while he as usual chose soup, chicken and icecream. A little asparagus would hardly ask too much of appetite. The ridiculously plump white stalks (and stalk is such a thin word), still warm from a proper amount of cooking, with a small amount of lemon and oil drizzled over them, set the benchmark for all future asparagus. I am of a mind to form a society for the banishment of green asparagus, especially those stalks as thin as pencils which abound.

Digressions are one of the consuming pleasures of reading; once I put down Rohinton Mistry's novel *A Fine Balance* in order to make chapati. By digressions I do not mean reading while cooking, for they are hard to do at the same time. This is why one needs a lot of time to read, which in turn is to understand that having nothing to do is a constructive and productive use of time and mind. Leys agrees: the last essay in *The Angel & the Octopus* offers succour to readers like myself who don't have the excuse of academe, of paid legitimacy, who prefer boundless irrelevancies. Hopping, skipping, jumping from John Berger through to asparagus is to do nothing but read and think about reading. But just like the retired man who responded to Leys' congratulations upon his leisure with a defensive rebuttal that he was busier than ever, I do still need to work – I mean leisure (a new verb? I am leisuring on a book?) – on my self-esteem. Society not only takes for granted, by its tone and exhortations, that I want to work but condemns as unsuccessful those of us who don't make much money. When I last donated blood, three nurses in succession on the way to the chair asked 'Have you had a good day? How was it? Busy?' The last was rhetorical, taken for granted.

Celebrities are not only famous but famously rich. They can, as Woody Allen said, get appointments with the dentist on a Sunday. They have good teeth. It isn't enough to be able to read and cook, and to take enjoyment in both: one has to make a profit from them, to make them doubly productive. You might say that making a nice profit is what you need to do to survive, but this is only true in a competitive sense, and because of a specific system of values relating to leisure. Redefining leisure is more my cup of tea.

So how can I afford white asparagus if I make no profit nor grow it (asparagus, I mean, not money)? I can't any more, but then I don't miss it either; memory is quite filling. The local butcher makes good blood sausage that I can afford and like very much because, like all people who are bold and curious about food and have a passion for cooking well, I have an open mind about what is not only good to eat but good for my health as well. Good spinach and salad leaves grow in my vegetable plots: land cress, rocket, mizuna, curly endive. Apples to accompany the blood sausage are affordable: Golden Delicious beat Granny Smiths hands-down for tossing in butter and still tasting of apple, and the Cox's Orange Pippin tree is responding to a better diet, a little surgery and netting. The same butcher had some remarkable veal liver one week: I read a lot about liver because the kitchen sends me always to the bookshelves, even though I might have simply thrown it in a hot pan, pirouetted twice, slipped it onto a warm plate and eaten it. Marcella Hazan reckons it takes longer to read her advice on how to cook *fegato alla veneziana* ('liver and onions' here in South Australia) than it does to cook the liver. That's fine by me.

The postmistress is puzzled by the parcels that arrive. They are either as light as birds' nests or as heavy as books. One day Walter Benjamin's *The Arcades Project* turns up and turns out to have a whole section of notes on the utopian socialist Charles Fourier, in whom I am interested not only because he saw more in compotes than simply stewed fruit. I was giddy with surprise and pleasure as if, hungry, an anticipated meal turned out to include the aroma of something surprising but familiar.

Aldo Buzzi arrives in parcels too. In *Journey to the Land of the Flies*, a book of travel writings, Buzzi, finding it difficult to answer a question, compares his plight to Charles Monselet's declaration about the difficulty of 'establish[ing] precise rules for making a bouquet garni'. Aldo Buzzi is old, which makes him all the more attractive; he was born in 1910, 'just in time to see the Russia of Chekhov'. The epigraph to his piece 'Chekhov in Sondrio' (Sondrio is a town in the Italian alps, north-east of Milan) is a note to Buzzi from the artist Saul Steinberg, who had found some old Russian postcards which, he wrote, showed 'a most attractive and comprehensible time'. Slipped in behind the title page of *Journey* I found (filed there earlier and then forgotten) a photograph used by *The New Yorker*, which is where I first read Buzzi, of an old Russian postcard showing Chekhov's Russia. Buzzi wrote: 'To understand something it is necessary to have lived a long time, perhaps to die . . . and to live again.' Books resurrect.

This attraction to Buzzi (in addition to his age) is not because of his obsession with food but because he is first and foremost a formidable reader of literature and, like a happy anarchist, too old to worry about what the world thinks of his obsessions; he loves to include 'what comes out'. So confident is he of the greatness of Chekhov that listing Chekhov's endearments for his wife ('cockroach', 'mosquito', 'bug', 'turkey', 'pony', 'dog', 'bitch', 'dove') sits as comfortably as Leys' admonishment of Luc Sante for not liking witlof. In the story 'Journey to the Land of the Flies' he flits and flirts his way, like the willy wagtails in my vegetable beds, around the derivation of the name of the hotel he stays at in Sparta. In the Vucciria, the Palermo quarter where the great food market was, he finds a Street of the Land of the Flies. Peter Robb, in his *Midnight in Sicily*, writes of spending time in the Vucciria too. Robb writes brilliantly and viscerally about food in Sicily and Naples, because of which I trust him, just as I trust Simon Leys.

Buzzi writes of '*Stigghiole* . . . lamb entrails roasted on a spit with onions and parsley: azure smoke and an exquisite aroma'. In Madrid once I ate tapas under the guidance of the food writer and food performance artist, Alica Rios. One of the selection was the small intestine of lamb wound around a green grapevine stick and grilled. When I told Janni Kyritsis about this food, his national spirit rose and he showed us how the Greeks do it; and going one better, he stuffed the intestines with a mixture of herbs and breadcrumbs before winding them around the spindle and deep-frying them. Even as a garnish this preparation did not win many friends in the dining-room. At Streaky Bay on the Eyre Peninsula where a farmer donated regional fatty-tailed lambs for the Adelaide Festival 2000 community barbecue, one of the travelling cooks, an Italian friend from Sydney who came to help and who has a licence to slaughter as well as butcher, prepared the meat and brought the entrails (even the bladders, which make marvellous poaching bags) back to the little house on the bay where we were staying, and at which we had assembled a makeshift barbecue.

Another of Buzzi's journeys is to Mexico: 'We sit on tombs and take out biscotellas, marvelous toasted pieces of sponge cake, a speciality of Ticul.' I cut a slice of a pound cake made last week with left-over egg yolks and a little rum, and place it in a moderate oven for twenty minutes, turning it over once. *Bis cuit*, twice-cooked, it is better than before. Italo Calvino went to Mexico too and wrote 'Under the Jaguar Sun', a story as complex, layered and miraculous as Mexican cuisine:

> Just as colonial baroque set no limits on the profusion of ornament and display, in which God's presence was identified in a closely calculated delirium of brimming, excessive sensations, so the curing of the hundred or more native varieties of hot peppers carefully selected for each dish opened vistas of a flaming ecstasy.

The man's partner becomes greedy for more dishes, more complexity; he 'looks her in the teeth', not into her eyes. Complicity is separate but shared: this is what can happen when we eat, devouring each other, a devouring eroticism, 'the universal cannibalism that leaves its imprint on every amorous relationship'. Centuries before, the Aztecs played games in which the winner was offered to the gods through the priests' meal, flavoured with the fiery indigenous spices to enhance the taste of flesh rather than to disguise it?

In the ancient Vedic texts of India, in the Taittiriya Upanishads, it is recorded, 'They sing in wonder: I am the food of life, I am, I am; I eat the food of life, I eat, I eat.' Mexican poet and essayist Octavio Paz, himself Mexican, compares, in *In Light of India*, the cultures of India and Mexico in part through their cuisines. 'In the global gastronomic geography the two cuisines share a single place than can only be called eccentric: they are both imaginative and passionate infractions of the two great canons of taste, French and Chinese cuisine.'

Mexican pathologist F. Gonzalez-Crussi's father had such a passion for the fieriest chillies that his maid vowed she would hunt for a live rattler – 'Palates such as yours will reckon no bite in anything less malignant.' In 'Taste', one of the marvellous essays in *The Five Senses*, he writes:

> Scholars believe that the strange condiments were developed first by Aztec sacrificers, and later elaborated upon by novices of Spanish or mixed blood, who used to read accounts of transfigurations, torments, and martyrdoms in the solitude of their convents. And so I fancy that this double genealogy, with its disquieting tendencies, may have shown itself in my father as a craving for some form of sense-transcending, fire-eating ecstasy.

Sybille Bedford's *A Legacy* (her first novel and only perfection) includes a description of a meal in the south of France that is the standard by which I have judged other descriptions of meals for decades. She wrote a travel book about Mexico in 1953, *The Sudden View* (later reissued as *A Visit to Don Otavio*), but it is strangely lacking in 'sense-transcending, fire eating' flavours for a writer who loved to drink and eat and, it is reported, had a bold wine palate – perhaps that is why she left the chillies alone.

I brought dried Mexican chillies home from America one year and set about making the traditional *mole poblano*. The preparation is painstaking and includes a very long list of ingredients: *chiles mulato, chiles anchos, chiles pasilla,* lard, cloves, peppercorns, cinnamon, coriander seeds, aniseed, sesame seeds, garlic, raisins, almonds, stock, tomatoes and, yes, chocolate (but a tiny amount and as bitter as you can find, in fact unsweetened best-quality cocoa is a good substitute). What a triumphant sauce! Dark, thick, pungent, complex, the bitter chocolate serving to bind in a way that reminds me of the viscosity of blood; and so it should, given the historical and mythical provenance of Mexican cuisine. We served it at Bennelong with seared saddle of hare, a variation on the French civet, a braised dish thickened with the blood of the hare. The Italian butcher who came to the Festival barbecue at Streaky Bay community gave me his grandmother's recipe for a sweet blood and chocolate pudding.

Buzzi is rather too keen on the last mouthfuls of writers. Malcolm Bradbury, in his last novel, *To the Hermitage*, reckoned that the Enlightenment philosopher Denis Diderot died while eating an apricot. I think of three great writers who died recently, and of how their work gives me so much pleasure: Eudora Welty, R.K. Narayan, W.G. Sebald. Retreating into books with the oven on is not to retreat at all, it is to travel towards the moon. 'Held in my mouth the moon became a word', Eudora Welty wrote.

Ways to write about food: recipes, menus, anthropology, advertisement, statistical survey, the biological sciences, medical research, economics and politics (who starves, who doesn't), encyclopaedias.

Gourmet, founded in 1941, became outmoded with the advent of the new food magazines. A new editor arrived recently: perhaps she may rid it of the frustration at articles that break off, *Esquire*-mode, after two or three introductory pages, with advice to go to the back of the magazine for the rest. Among the many admirable traits *The New Yorker* (not, in my house, to be mentioned in the same breath as food magazines) has retained, though many of its editorial principles have been depraved by modernity, has been its insistence, since its first issue in 1928, that an essay begin and finish without interruption. This they deem to be simple literary good manners. Once, long ago, essays and fiction in this magazine were attributed only at their end; this left us to read unencumbered by expectation, and allowed the prose independence. I like to eat this way too, to enjoy a dish, a meal, not a meal cooked by . . .

To mark its return to competition, *Gourmet* published a collection of forty-one pieces covering sixty commissary years. Writing about food endlessly, as in *Endless Feasts*, creates myriad challenges to find words to substitute for delicious. I think it was Tarquin Winot, John Lanchester's anti-hero and murderer in *The Debt to Pleasure*, who vowed never to use 'delicious'. This led, in that virtuosic and cruel piece of fiction, to a lot of words about food and to a satire of the competitive puffery of culinary knowledge and the compilation of lists that characterises the species earlier dubbed 'the foodie'.

'Life as a book that has been put down'

The best writing about food depends on the writer's qualifications as a writer. Dismissing this as the 'bleeding obvious' is to continue to settle for the status quo of gush, advertisement and self-advertisement that dominates the 'delicious' market and depends on its readers praising the emperor's new clothes. It is why, give or take an Alan Davidson or two, the best is to be found sheltering by accident in works about other things altogether. As well, the best writing about food might be defined, as John Banville defined a different kind of writing altogether, as 'evocative exactitude'. When Hilary Mantel, reassessing Sybille Bedford with the reissue of the novels in 2001, wrote about the meal in *A Legacy*, which I find so perfect in tone and suggestion, she points to a concrete style, 'rich, detailed and particular . . . her eye is exact, and she brings to her perception of the landscape a solid concern with its utility; what grows here, how is it watered, what living does it provide?' This attention to utility is the privilege of gastronomic writing, which food historian Barbara Santich suggests is the result of the confluence of the intellect and the senses. Bedford's fictional meal evokes not only the meal as a legitimate part of the landscape but the light of that landscape captured in the olive oil; in spare strokes, the education of a young girl who had not thought any of this possible or even sensible; the social milieu, the half-cruel sophistication of the girl's suitor Julius von Felden, who seduces with culture and cuisine instead of feelings.

'Evocative exactitude' implies equal measures of craft and imagination, an increase of seduction. There is one strain of gastronomic writing that flaunts the sardonic. It is careful not to allow any saturated-table weeping to taint its brittle cleverness. On the other hand, there is the opposite extreme, which grovels before chefs and their use of produce, as demigods, and gives cooking a different kind of bad name. I have a copy of *Beethoven's Quartets*, one of two books by musicologist Joseph de Marliave. A captain in the French army during the First World War, he did not live to see his books into print. Marliave does not separate the depth of his emotional reaction to the quartets from his technical exposition, so we find such sentences as 'In the second bar the poignant cry of grief is heard in the sforzato chord on the bass and the first violin, B-sharp-D'. This is not 'evocative exactitude', but in its naked admission of emotion combined with musical knowledge

I find it liberating. The same kind of combination, without making any farcical comparison of extraordinary music with fine dishes composed by cooks, best serves gastronomy.

Like essayist and novelist Kate Jennings, I 'give [America's most famous and revered food writer] M.F.K. Fisher a wide berth'. This stance is in 'foodie' circles heretical, although I have, with relief, met a few others and formed a cadre. The very first piece in *Endless Feasts* is by Ms Fisher (1908–92) and its tone confirms the toe-curling effect of her prose. It was written in 1941, which is why, one supposes, it must be first. Elizabeth Hawes wrote a profile of Mary Frances Kennedy Fisher for *Gourmet* in 1983. She mentions Fisher's 'puzzling mystical dimension', which might be exactly what I and fellow cadre-members object to. People have accused her of coyness, by which they mean that she leaves out names, but this coyness is for me tied to an ever-present sense of self-congratulation, despite the fact that she can indeed write. It is coyness that causes her to respond with 'Ridiculous!' when told that some people designate her a 'living national treasure', and which usually stopped her accepting 'deeply felt tributes'. This wary attitude towards her and her writing is not separate from the knowledge that my own prose and that of others who travel with 'bold knife and fork' and pen, sometimes veers towards the Fisheresque and that we should not be allowed to get away with it.

To read Elizabeth David's 1970 piece on French gastronome Edouard de Pomiane is to pull oneself out of the sticky into marvellously clear prose. Pomiane wrote that 'Art demands an impeccable technique; science a little understanding'; this accords with composer Louis Andriessen's comment that the music of J.S. Bach is 'highly technical and gives comfort'. David recommends Pomiane's *Cooking with Pomiane* above his *Cooking in Ten Minutes* and writes that 'this is the best kind of cookery writing. It is courageous, courteous, adult'. Amen to that.

'Why should it take courage, as I'm told it sometimes does, to treat oneself as generously as one would a guest?' Mary Cantwell asked *Gourmet* readers in 1985. She wasn't referring to her local café but to rooms with 'tablecloths, waiters, and large, stiff menus'. I screwed up courage and dined alone at Four Seasons early in the eighties and have never looked back in terms of solitary pleasures, although I hardly dine out now even in company. Dining alone is one of the great

'Life as a book that has been put down'

pleasures of the gastronomic life, except that, if you own a restaurant and let the waiter know, he usually asks for a change of country and work. This has happened to me at Four Seasons and even at Tour d'Argent in Paris, where young Philippe Colin, the sommelier, took us to the cellar, asked for a job, and in due course arrived in Australia.

Before she sold her body to television, Nigella Lawson reviewed restaurants for *The Spectator*. In 1987 she wrote a smart column on dining alone, which started off where Fay Maschler had left off. Maschler, who reviewed restaurants too, had declared that she was rarely recognised because 'I generally take a man along with me and waiters are such misogynists they don't look at women'. Lawson reckoned it is more the way one is looked at which is objectionable, but we are inclined to disbelieve her given a subsequent career being watched by thousands as she licks chocolate and peanut butter to distract us from abysmal cooking demonstrations.

Endless Feasts is divided into five sections: travel, locality, people, produce and 'matters of taste'. Dining alone is included in the last, and Cantwell shares it with William Hamilton (*New Yorker* cartoonist for yonks), George Plimpton (late co-founder and editor of *The Paris Review*) and Joseph Wechsberg (again, the late) who saves the day with his usual easy wit and greed for good food. *Gourmet* was a mixed bag, but it did, every so often, pay for the digressions of a little treasure chest of fine writers – Anita Loos, Edna O'Brien ('In those days I did not care for bacon and cabbage, thinking it too agricultural . . .'), Robert P. Coffin, E. Annie Proulx, and so on. But where in this anthology are Anthony Burgess and Waverley Root and Richard Condon, all of whom contributed to *Gourmet* over the years? Condon was a 'big fork' and wrote marvellously about food; more to the point, he wrote marvellously about Sicilian food in the Prizzi novels. In 1982, the year he died, Waverley Root, who had been a long time in Paris as correspondent for American papers, wrote on *andouilles* and *andouillettes*, an essay I treasure and keep filed in the 'A' section in his A–Z of food, *Food*.

Feasting is not something any sensible, sensitive person would want to do endlessly. The gastronomic art is to see imaginatively the feast in the 'poor' bowl of soup made from wild herbs, in the skewer of liver grilled over charcoal in a street stall in Alexandria, and then, either wiping your fingers or not, taking out a pen. It is, at best, a republican and moderate activity. It might even be Emily Dickinson's 'Banquet of Abstemiousness'.

⁓

In the heyday of Berowra Waters Inn, I believed confidently in the à la carte menu as a sign of professionalism and skill in the kitchen; indeed, professional cooking might be defined as being able to cook as many dishes as possible at the same time. This is the kind of virtuoso juggling that can produce the frenetic and edgy celebration of cooking that New York chef Anthony Bourdain's *Kitchen Confidential* made of restaurant life. It doesn't have to be like this, only if you want it to be, and in my restaurant, for one, we found time to thank the dishwasher when handing him a pan in the middle of service and to apologise if one of us held another up. Service is a machine depending on timing, concentration and co-ordinated actions. In most ways it isn't even cooking any more, not cooking as defined by choice of produce and thoughtful decisions on what goes with which and how to cook it. It is mechanical and military and will produce perfect dishes because of the mise en place. '*Mise en place* is like a preparation for a siege in wartime', Sydney artist Adam Geczy wrote in an academic paper addressing the similarities between restaurant service and military precision for a conference on art and food. He was once a waiter at Berowra Waters Inn. If you trained someone with good hand/eye skills but no interest in cooking at all to do service, the same perfect food could be produced. But I don't want to forget the menu, because service doesn't fit the romantic view of cooking.

Offering a choice of dishes to diners is, deep down, not a courtesy to the palates and preferences, prejudices and allergies in the dining-room, but showing off the chef's abilities. When you invite friends to eat in your home you don't offer them a choice, although you might in these distrustful and allergic times ask first if they eat meat. In keeping with my defunct definition of professionalism, I used to distrust the professionalism of a restaurant like Chez Panisse in Berkeley, California, where for decades they have put the set menu up in the window and told their public what they would be cooking that day. In fact when, with Janni Kyritsis, I had been cooking in Los Angeles in 1993 and we finally got to eat there, the food was very fine and our verdict was that we had eaten very superior home cooking.

In tapas bars in the small town of Logroño in northern Spain, the shifting public move from one bar to the next when they want to eat something different. At one end of a thin street crammed with people you might choose the place that serves marinated anchovies; at the next, snails; the next, blood sausage; and, at the other end of the street, offal from lamb. Aurelio Zen, in Michael Dibdin's *And Then You Die*, having survived some life-enhancing, near-death experiences, eats at a restaurant in Rome, which is only as big as a barber's shop. Ernesto serves only one thing, 'porchetta, choice young piglets from farmers personally known to him, stuffed with fennel and herbs, slowly roasted to moist perfection on a spit and served cold with chewy fresh bread'. I ache for places where I know what I will eat because it is the only thing to eat. People who always choose the same dish at a particular restaurant, and this is common, are, without putting their finger on it, longing for lack of choice. This keeps me at home, reading and cooking.

Home, as well as legitimately denying choice (in a restaurant, choice does not usually lead to waste or excessive labour, and the chef does not expect to share your table with you; at home, choice would seem a wasteful redundancy, at the very least an eccentricity), is the place where food is not prescribed in portions as it is in western restaurants. In a recent television program in which English home cooks produced a meal superior to their normal efforts by the 'surprise' help of a well-known chef, the difference in quality was not only in the preparation and cooking but in the way food was placed on the plate. It wasn't home cooking any more; instead, it became pictures on plates. The loveliness of eating as much as you want, of a whole dish and of different parts of a dish, has been lost to what looks alarmingly like portion control.

—

Writing about the plate in *The Sociology of the Meal* (1910), the social theorist Georg Simmel suggested the circle as 'the most isolating shape'. In the perfect restaurant, which more and more I equate with eating at home, there would be no choice and all the food would be set down on the table so that diners helped themselves. In a small, busy restaurant in Paris once, in a tiny street off the Place des Victoires, we asked for the salad of ox cheek. Two large bowls came to the table, one with the thin slices of braised cheek doused with vinaigrette and tossed with herbs; another with tiny red and white oval radishes, their leaves making good handles; and butter, bread, a carafe of wine. All these things were left for us to help ourselves to, for as long as we had the appetite to want them there. This is about as courteous as a restaurant might be. Then again, in the same country in 1978, when choosing fresh fruit for dessert in a three-star restaurant – the first expensive, much-praised restaurant of my culinary education – a waiter came to the table and proceeded to peel a pear without his hands touching the fruit, which quite apart from seeming silly, meant that his presence intruded. I had chosen fruit because I had no appetite for anything more and thought cutting and peeling would take my mind off a full stomach. I wanted to do it myself and I did so, sending the waiter away to puzzle over the cost to me of my own labour. In those long-ago years when we ate too much in France in order to taste and learn (and came home so penniless that there was just enough money to buy take-away in the Cross) it became imperative to order dishes like *Ecrevisses à la nage*, which asked to be dissected and turned out to be mostly broth and shell-work.

Doing things at table is also a way to combat the isolation of plates. On 14 November 1867, Edmond and Jules de Goncourt, whose diary records the convivial lives of the literary lions of their day (Flaubert, Gauthier, Hugo, Zola, etc.) and, poignantly, the brothers' extraordinary devotion to one another, ate at Sainte-Beuve's table with their close friend the Princess Mathilde Bonaparte:

> At dinner she insisted upon serving everything and carving everything. Her father, she said, always carved. He had very pretty hands. He used to eat salad with his fingers, and when he was told that it was an unclean habit, he answered: 'In my day, if we had eaten it in any other way, we should have been scolded and told that our hands were dirty.'

Georg Simmel also wrote that 'It is the refinement of the dining-table that its beauty should still invite us to disturb it'.

It is more probably the presentation of food in restaurants, not its preparation, that causes ever-hopeful diners to mistake cooking for something artistic and elevated, and so place it in the realm of Art or at least artifice. As Barbara Santich has written in *Looking for Flavour*, we use our eyes first, and the chef has total control in those first moments. Mario Batali, talking to a journalist about his own cooking career, described working with Marco Pierre White in a tiny kitchen in a Chelsea pub in London when White was at the bottom of a ladder which, with great culinary talent and bullying, he climbed fast. He described White 'making a deep-green basil purée, and a white butter sauce, and swirling the green sauce in one direction and the white sauce in the other, and drawing a swirling line down the middle of the plate.' I have, mea culpa and a long time ago, allowed two dessert sauces to meet somewhere just left of centre, but am puzzled by the need to puddle about on the plate when two jugs might serve the same purpose. How many times have we cooks plated a dish, told the waiter to 'jump on table seven' and then, when one fish or leaf, fillet or garnish topples from its designated place in the hierarchical pile, called the waiter back and begun again, like a hairdresser making uncountable numbers of hairs pretend to be a chignon, a plait, a curl. Even a plate of gnocchi with its splash of burnt butter is defined by a clean line before the rim, and a soup must not ride the sides. '[White] was a genius on the plate', said Batali, who has left all that behind and now feeds pigs on cream, apples and walnuts, has them killed, cures them and serves them up in his New York City restaurant. The isolation of the circle becomes even more isolating when there is a 'genius on the plate'.

Portion control has been entering the modern home for as long as single-serve packets of pre-prepared food have been around. Its apotheosis is to be found in a television advertisement in which a young female chef finishes work in the professional kitchen where her training means she knows how to turn raw produce into food worth dining on faster than it takes to say à la carte, and goes home to the restricted pleasure of reconstituted long-shelf-life food. She's too tired from her job, where she is paid to cook fine food for others, to cook for herself. At least that's what we are asked to believe: that all her training has left her stumped for something to prepare easily and quickly at home. Providing a meal from the shelf for the family is always advertised as creative thinking, often combined with fuzzy maternal or paternal thoughtfulness. It deflects us from stray and querulous thoughts about cooking skills and fresh produce. A former prime minister of Australia supported retirement by praising (in Italian) a brand-name pasta sauce on television. Despite his making a fool of himself – presumably for a lot of money, for why else would he do it – we are, I suppose, supposed to be persuaded to the purchase of something that is long-lasting, bilingual, suggestive of travel and a kind of worldliness combined with intelligence, for he was an articulate, liberal and visionary head of state.

A cartoon in *The New Yorker* in 2001 showed a woman standing at the dinner table saying to her partner: 'If it says to add water, and I'm the one who adds it, I'm cooking.' Adding water doesn't in itself cancel out the possibility of making of good food – it belongs to the history of thousands of years of storage and reconstitution – but here it belongs to a frightening persuasion that divides culinary skills into, on the one hand, eccentric hobby, and on the other artisinal knowledge, which now plays little part in our culinary education. In the long run, this connects to the different and fraught area of risk and trust, where a sealed package of food with printed information about its contents is seen to be more worthy of trust than a fresh carrot, and well it might be if we don't look after our own back yard. We trust what we know.

⟓

At home there are no waiters. And at my local pizza place, which is at the same time a much-touted and sometimes misunderstood restaurant, there is no superficial delineation between the exhilaration of cooking and the pleasures of dining. There's no proscenium arch, no line the diner must not cross; the food doesn't just appear. In fact, the cooking takes place under your nose if you want it to, the pizzas being made and shovelled a metre from the back door by kids who are having the time of their lives working rather than hanging out on a street corner. And I do literally mean kids, children, kitchen babies, bursting with speedy purpose. It's all a kind of neo-Fourierist harmony – to him that state signified 'the gratification of individual desire serving to promote the common good', and work was to be pleasurable so that the division between work and leisure would not exist. As a diner at this restaurant you do a lot of the work yourself, which brings you into the kitchen emotionally as well as physically. You want to order? Find a piece of paper, a pen, and write it down yourself. This doesn't just save on staff, it involves you. You need glasses for the one of two wines the place offers, or the bottle you've brought? Grab them yourself, not because you're impatient with inattentive staff but because no one minds and it helps. Best of all, you find yourself talking to the stranger who is placing an order too, and across the room there's a friend who insists you have some of their wine. It's catching, this sense of participation. If you're not careful you'll be helping to make the pizzas, and no one would mind too much if there was room and you proved yourself as efficient as those who are already doing it. Russell Jeavons, the owner, who taught the kids to cook, comes and goes in slow motion, apparently irrelevant, avuncular.

There's something about the place – an old cottage with archetypal Aussie shed-turned-dining-room at the back, a brazier and chairs to cope with the overflow, and a good kitchen garden at the rear – that, without parody, smells like, and is, wood-fired pizza and extended family. This is not to say that Russell doesn't know exactly what he is doing. The attention paid to the cooking is not attention-seeking. The fact that the oven, and the bench on which the dough is rolled, are cheek by jowl with diners has nothing to do with the idea of an 'open' kitchen or even the back-stage kind that sends out the kind of food which reminds you it's there. The busy little bees here haven't ever considered wearing uniforms with 'Chef' embroidered on the jacket, and anyway they're probably not made in children's sizes. Can you imagine a motor mechanic wearing overalls with 'Motor mechanic' machined on the bib? The two are equal trades in many ways, except that one practitioner fixes something that doesn't answer back.

Peter Sellars, the American opera director who came to Australia to mount a visionary Adelaide Festival of the Arts in 2002, dined at my local and favourite before being run out of town (in part for suggesting that the arts might be shared with indigenous peoples, communities in disenfranchised suburbs, and hospitals, instead of the box office). When Russell Jeavons said to Peter that his aim is to take the attention away from the plate, Peter understood, and he reckons that Russell is striving for coherence. Another friend suggests that the balance of power makes harmonic sense at this restaurant, which is to say, I think, that principles are not only kept to but the audience gets to like the principles; they are willingly changed by eating there. Taking the attention away from the plate allows this restaurant to fulfil an engaged and three-dimensional role in a community without double-speak; it also takes attention away from the 'chef', if a bevy of hard-working kids might be called 'the chef'. The atmosphere is so pervasively friendly that you turn to speak to the stranger at the next table instead of ogling the cooks. It's pizza they're making, good pizza; it's only pizza, but it's much more than pizza.

Late at night at Russell's, the tin shed becomes a dance floor and the regional eccentricity is let loose: Argentinian tango. The first time I ate there (did I say it is only open one night a week?), a couple of the teenage girls who'd been cooking and serving danced, one with angels' wings pinned to her flimsy frock. This one was to be found later digging up and bucketing rocks and soil from the excavation of an old cellar at the restaurant. She'd exchanged her tango shoes for Doc Martens, but kept her wings on for balance: a chrysalis, wings still a little wet, bursting towards flight.

In truth Russell's pizza place is not quite without waiters, but it feels like it has none. When a restaurant diner thanks a waiter for food that has been enjoyed, she is thanking the cook via a courier; the gratitude is deflected. No wonder chefs make awkward forays into the dining-room in order to feel a little more wanted. Their enclosure exalts them, of course; rumours abound, things need clarifying. Exaltation in part devalues. It's all frighteningly like telling a mother that her child is smart or pretty or charming and forgetting to tell the child.

There is an old Yiddish saying: 'The future is not a menu.' For nearly thirty years I wrote an à la carte menu, directed and took part in service that prescribed portions on plates, handed the food over to waiters to carry to diners, paid dish-washers to pass all the accoutrements of the table through big steaming machines, and sent the tablecloths and napkins to the laundry. It had its moments.

'Life as a book that has been put down'

Acknowledgements

Conversations at the table, about food, cooking and culture, have influenced the way I approach gastronomy. As well as through his books, the most influential have always been with Michael Symons. I also want to acknowledge Jennifer Hillier, Barbara Santich and Catherine Kerry.

A central group of chefs have taught me about cooking by their practice: Phillip Searle, Tim Pak Poy, Damien Pignolet, Simon Hopkinson, Tony Bilson and Janni Kyritsis.

There are those who have thrown light on life's little disturbances as well as on the culinary life and whose friendship I count as a blessing: Anders Ousback (1951–2004), Michelle Garnaut, Kevin (Gerry) Morris, Mandy Press, Don Anderson, Johnny Apple, Peter Sellars, Ihab Hassan, Sally Hassan, Keith Lewis, Kit Grover, Wendy Frost, Terry Clarke, Nicholas Pounder, Lynne Clarke, Jonathan Mills, Damon Moon and Leo Schofield.

My gratitude to Julie Gibbs, who commissioned *Plenty*; to the designer, Sandy Cull; and especially to Sarah Dawson, the book's editor, who became part teacher, part confidante.

Some of the pieces were originally published elsewhere and have been substantially revised. 'Nothings' (issue 33, 2003), 'Apple to rabbit' (issue 32, 2003), 'Sour wings' (issue 29, 2002), 'Cloud' (issue 27, 2001), 'Charcoal' (issue 24, 2000), 'Silk purses from sows' ears' (issue 21, 1999) were all first published in *Divine*. 'Lemon posset, or not' (1997), 'Ms Pople's potted beef' (as 'Pressing matters', 13 Apr. 1996), 'A pillow book for the table' (1996), 'Amiable juyce' (as 'The blood of others', 14 May 1994) and 'Upstart gruel [congee]' (8 Jan. 1997) were all first published in the *Sydney Morning Herald*. 'Buried treasure' was first published in the Proceedings of the Tenth Symposium of Australian Gastronomy, 1998. 'Pictures on plates' (4 Dec.1999) was first published in *Artlink*. 'Nests' (2001) was first published in *Southerly*. 'The green and the black' was first published in the exhibition catalogue 'Rituals of Tea', JamFactory Galleries, Adelaide, Jan. 2002.

Sources for quoted material not identified in the text are as follows: p. 46, Rayner Banham in *Design Book Review*, MIT Press, 1988; p. 47, Philip Drew, *Touch this Earth Lightly: Glenn Murcutt in his own Words*, Duffy & Snellgrove, 2000; p. 77, Alan Davidson, *The Oxford Companion to Food,* 1999, by permission of Oxford University Press; p. 78, Richard Condon, *Winter Kills,* Dial Press, 1974; p. 79, Peter Fuller, *Marches Past* (pp.22–3), Chatto & Windus, 1986, copyright © Peter Fuller 1986; p. 81, Evelyn Waugh, *Brideshead Revisited* (p. 198), Penguin Classics, 1999, copyright © Evelyn Waugh 1945, reproduced by permission of Penguin Books Ltd; p. 174, extract from William Rollison, *Making Charcoal*, Dalesman Publishing Co., p. 98; p. 132, Tom Stoppard, *Jumpers*, Grove Press, 1989; p. 133, interview with Sottha Khumm, *The New Yorker*, 2001; p. 134–5, John Harvey, *Rough Treatment,* Henry Holt, 1990; p. 412, extract from *The Maker of Heavenly Trousers* by Daniele Vare, published by Black Swan. Used by permission of The Random House Group Limited; p. 185, Henri Gault, 'Nouvelle Cuisine' in Harlan Walker (ed.), *Cooks and Other People: Proceedings of the Oxford Symposium on Food and Cookery 1995,* Prospect Books, 1996; p. 191, Michael Carter, paper delivered at Aesthetics of Food symposium, University of Sydney, 1998; Vikram Chandra, *Red Earth and Pouring Rain*, Little Brown, 1995; p. 202: Kiran Desai, *Hullabaloo in the Guava Orchard*, Faber & Faber, 1999; p. 205, from *Austerlitz* by W.G. Sebald (tr. Anthea Bell), copyright © 2001 by Anthea Bell. Used by permission of Random House, Inc.; pp. 221, 268, Hsiang Ju Lin & Tsuifeng Lin, *Chinese Gastronomy*, Thomas Nelson & Sons, 1969; pp. 288–9, from *The White Bird* by John Berger, Chatto & Windus, 1985; p.290, Emilie Carles & Robert Destanque (tr. Avriel H. Goldberger), *A Life of her Own: A Countrywoman in Twentieth-Century France,* © 1991 by Rutgers, the State University; p. 293, from *Journey to the Land of the Flies* by Aldo Buzzi, copyright © 1996 by Aldo Buzzi. Used by permission of Random House, Inc.; p.295, Italo Calvino, 'Under the Jaguar Sun' in *Under the Jaguar Sun*, Harcourt Brace & Co., 1988; p. 296, excerpt from *The Five Senses*, © 1989 by Frank Gonzalez-Crussi, reprinted by permission of Harcourt, Inc; pp. 254–5, Marguerite Duras, *La Vie Materielle*, Flammarion, 1998; p. 276, Mary McCarthy quoted by Thomas Mallon in 'Our Saint, Our Umpire', *Atlantic Monthly,* 29 October 2002; pp. 282–3, Norman Douglas, *South Wind*, Martin Secker, 1917. Every attempt has been made to contact and acknowledge copyright holders: the author and publishers would be grateful to be notified of any unintentional omissions.

Index